For Richard and Zora, who raised me to be a communicator with an educator's touch.

And especially for Sarah, who inspires me to be better at everything I do.

Contents

Communicating Design

Developing Web Site Documentation for Design and Planning

DANIEL M. BROWN

 PEACHPIT PRESS

Communicating Design

Developing Web Site Documentation for Design and Planning

Daniel M. Brown

New Riders

1249 Eighth Street ∘ Berkeley, CA 94710
510/524-2178 ∘ 800/283-9444 ∘ 510/524-2221 (fax)

Find us on the World Wide Web at: www.newriders.com
To report errors, please send a note to errata@peachpit.com

New Riders is an imprint of Peachpit, a division of Pearson Education

Acquisitions Editor ∘ Michael J. Nolan
Development Editor ∘ Amy Standen
Production Editor ∘ Andrei Pasternak
Proofreader ∘ Liz Welch
Compositor ∘ Maureen Forys, Happenstance Type-O-Rama
Indexer ∘ James Minkin
Book designer ∘ Mimi Heft with Happenstance Type-O-Rama and Andrei Pasternak
Cover designer ∘ Gee + Chung Design

ISBN 0-321-39235-3

9 8 7 6 5

Printed and bound in the United States of America

Preface

This book, in a word, is about documentation. Sounds boring, doesn't it? Documentation—the collection of documents prepared over the course of a project—is, in many ways, the underbelly of web design. After all, documents usually appear on paper and end up sitting on a shelf where no one reads them. How cool could that be?

But anyone who has worked to design a web site knows that documentation can make or break the project, that it moves the process along by capturing the design concept and helps project team members communicate with each other. Web design documents—or "deliverables," as they're sometimes called—also serve as milestones, marking progress in an otherwise seemingly interminable process. They're historical, allowing people who come to a project later to get up to speed on the decisions made by earlier project teams.

In short, a document captures an idea. Perhaps this is a little existential for the web design business but, getting down to brass tacks, if we can't communicate an idea effectively, how can we hope to create a web site around it?

The value of good documentation is indisputable, but there's very little discussion about it in the web design canon. This isn't to say that deliverables have never been addressed. Stumble onto the blog of any designer or information architect and you're bound to see at least one article on effective wireframing, or a set of shapes to use in a flow chart. But on a larger scale, there has never been a careful look at what makes design documentation effective.

On the surface, this book will help you improve your documentation, providing advice on how to plan your deliverables and use them effectively in meetings and on projects. In the course of doing so, it will also attempt to uncover what makes a document good, and help you recognize the difference between a bad document and a bad idea.

What You Should Know about This Book

- **It doesn't cover every deliverable.** This book discusses ten of the most common web design deliverables—the ones you won't be able to avoid if you spend any time at all in this business. These are user experience deliverables, so if you're looking for advice on creating entity relationship diagrams or unified modeling language diagrams, you might want to go elsewhere. There are countless documents for user experience work that this book could have addressed, but many are not common, or they're proprietary, or they've been discussed in elsewhere. Check out the book's companion web site, www.communicatingdesign.com, for more information about all kinds of web design documents.

- **It doesn't care what methodology you use.** Methods come and go, but documents appear to remain more or less consistent. One of the central assumptions of this book is that anyone should be able to use it, regardless of the methodology they use. That being said, it's difficult to write about documentation without any sense of timing or dependency, so I will make a *few* methodological assumptions; they're detailed below. These assumptions provide structure for the book, but they won't render it useless if you're using a different method.

- **It's a how-to book, but not a software book.** This book will help you make better deliverables. It will help you present those deliverables better to your clients and team members. It will even help you anticipate risks in creating and sharing deliverables. But it will not tell you how to use software applications to make those deliverables. Different people prefer different tools, but the choice of tool should have little impact on the message and purpose of your documentation.

- **It's a cookbook.** Each chapter in this book is a recipe for working with a different kind of document, and you'll have your own ideas about what makes a dish work and what doesn't. Feel free to add notes in the margin. You may even find that a technique described for one kind of document works well for a different kind of document. Although the book tries to make each chapter self-contained, you may find inspiration for one kind of deliverable in other chapters.

Three Kinds of People

This book is written for people who make deliverables, use deliverables, and approve deliverables.

- **Making deliverables:** Whether you're new to web design or have been doing it for years, if you're making deliverables, this book will help keep your efforts on track. It will either introduce you to new techniques for planning or presenting deliverables, or provide a refresher if it's been awhile since the last time you had to crank out a deck of wireframes, for example.

- **Using deliverables:** It may not be your responsibility to create the site map, but you're the one who has to consult it for the next several days or weeks or months as you migrate content from the existing site to this new structure. Or perhaps you're a developer who needs to write code for making the web site behave as documented in the wireframes. Or maybe you're the client, and you face an uphill battle in your organization in selling the idea of this redesign—those personas will sure come in handy, but you want to make sure they're airtight. This book will help you make sure you know what you're getting and prepare you for conversations with the user experience designers on your team.

- **Approving deliverables:** If the buck stops with you, you'll want to make sure all the i's are dotted and t's are crossed. As the client or main stakeholder—let's face it, the money person—you have a lot riding on these documents. They're essential for moving the project along, judging whether you're getting your money's worth, and keeping the design team honest. This book can help you make sure you know what to expect from your team's deliverables.

Continuing the Conversation

Deliverables have changed a lot since I started writing about them for Boxes and Arrows in 2002. They've undergone major transformations since the web started in the early '90s. This book is a place to start talking about documentation. The conversation will continue at www.communicatingdesign.com, where you'll find

- Downloadable samples, both from the book and contributed by readers

- Tutorials for creating all kinds of documents

- Templates and other tools for creating deliverables

- Advice for user experience professionals on presenting your documents and collaborating with team members

- More of the same for deliverables not mentioned in this book

Acknowledgments

Without Marjorie Baer, Michael Nolan, and my whole project team at New Riders, this book would still just be a bunch of ideas floating around the back of my head.

Stephen Anderson, Ashley Cook, Jesse James Garrett, Bryce Glass, Paul Gould of MAYA Design, James Melzer, Sarah Rice, and Todd Warfel are brilliant user experience professionals who know that communicating an idea is just as important as having an idea. They lent their work to this book, and I'm grateful for the excellent examples they contributed.

Thomas Vander Wal, who put me in touch with New Riders, and Geoff Shott, who said "I would totally buy that book," when I pitched the idea to him.

Steve Swasey and Gary McMath at Netflix graciously gave me permission to copy the screen design of the movie page for the illustrations in Chapter 10.

I'm grateful to Kateryna Andryushchenko and everyone at Computer Systems Odessa, who provided a complimentary copy of ConceptDraw 5 after I burned through my demo version.

My thanks also go to Erin Malone and Christina Wodtke, who thought a regular column on deliverables was actually a good idea. Thanks also to the various editors at Boxes and Arrows who have turned my bizarre ideas for articles into useful tutorials.

Lou Rosenfeld, Peter Morville, and Jesse James Garrett all know what it takes to write a book and still thought I could do it. I'm grateful for their encouragement.

There are two online communities every experience design professional should join. Both the Information Architecture Institute's members' mailing list and AIGA's Experience Design mailing list were consistently reliable and thoughtful resources for soliciting document samples and vetting ideas.

Everyone who visits D.C. and interacts with our information architecture community says the same thing: "You've got a great group of people there." DCIA is our local information architecture organization, consisting of over 300 people in the greater Washington metro area. Our events are always well attended, and the community's contributions are consistently thoughtful and enthusiastic. This group, especially co-founders Marcy Jacobs and Stacy Surla, provides a constant source of inspiration and encouragement. I can't imagine a better place to be in the user experience business.

Every donkey needs a carrot on a stick to keep going. This author is no different, and I promised myself a new mandolin upon finishing the book. That mandolin is the Collings MT. Thanks to the Collings Guitar and Mandolin Company for crafting such a beautiful piece of work, and to the Music Emporium in Boston and especially its superlative fretted instrument sales guy, Adam Dardeck.

The Collings MT Mandolin, a fine instrument.

Whenever I was in a pinch, whether it be about a particular point or an entire chapter or even the table of contents, I would solicit James Melzer for advice. James and I met at the IA Summit 2002 in Baltimore and found that we had a lot more in common than IA. We've been close friends ever since. Whenever I consulted James, he provided succinct and well-conceived advice. If it weren't for him, this book wouldn't have a chapter on competitive analysis. (I can't acknowledge James without mentioning his wife, Becky, who put up with a lot of shoptalk.)

My parents, sister, and friends who asked me, "So how's that book coming?" fed my ego regardless of my response.

Amy Standen, my editor, put up with missed deadlines and enthusiastically long run-on sentences, all while living seven time zones away. I could not have picked a better editor, and I'm grateful for her pragmatic wisdom and patience with my fragile ego.

Sarah Holden, my wife, unquestioningly accommodated my unusual writing schedule and habits. While I spent the last nine months thinking about wireframes and personas, Sarah spent them pregnant with our first child. Her support throughout this process has been unwavering and confident, just what a new author (and new dad) needs.

Colophon

The text was composed on a Macintosh iBook G4 running NeoOffice, a version of OpenOffice for OS X. See www.openoffice.org for details.

The original illustrations were created in ConceptDraw, a powerful diagramming program for OS X. See www.conceptdraw.com for details.

The author was fueled by clean, natural lattes, various forms of mandolin music, the undying devotion and support of his amazing wife, and the impending arrival of his son.

This book was typeset in Bembo and MetaPlus. It was printed at Malloy Inc. in Ann Arbor, Michigan on 50# Lynx Opaque paper.

CHAPTER ONE

Introduction

dee-liv'-er-a-bul (n.)

A document created during the course of a web design project to facilitate communications, capture decisions, and stimulate innovation.

Deliverables do many things, but at the end of the day, there are three reasons to produce them:

- **Consistency of vision:** Web designers who work on small teams and know their team members intimately have the luxury of working in an environment that's not unlike a marriage. It's not as feasible to anticipate each other's moves and reactions on a large team, where the players might change from project to project. As the conception of a web site evolves, different people will be involved at different stages. With large teams and large projects, the risk is that everyone ends up with a slightly different understanding of the concept. Documentation can make sure everyone gets on the ride together and stays together—that everyone can make worthwhile contributions to the project because they understand where the project is and where it's going.

- **Accountability:** Whether you're a web designer consulting for an organization or one working inside an organization, you need a way to make sure everyone understands the decisions that have been made and the implications of those decisions.

- **Traceability:** Documentation is a paper trail, even if you never print out a single deliverable. By capturing the decisions as the project progresses, you have a record of the entire project and can easily look back to see where the team made crucial decisions. Reaching the end of a project, you may realize that you don't remember why you did certain things—was there a reason for this button's placement or that page's unusual layout? Having a collective history in its documentation allows you to uncover the rationale behind these decisions.

Even if you don't work on a large team, you may find these reasons relevant to your situation. Small web development shops may also need to provide some legal accountability when working on a contract. Teams may find that their client is easily distracted by internal politics, and need a document to help preserve the direction of the project.

Every once in a while, the user experience community flares up against documentation. A new methodology comes along that discourages extensive (or any!) documentation, or people just get collectively frustrated at the difficulty of pleasing clients. These discussions are useful because they help refine and focus our understanding of the purpose of documents. Like any tool, documents can be misused. The greatest misuse of a document is to create it for its own sake, and not to ensure its contribution and value to your project, your team, or the end product.

The Ten Deliverables (Stone Tablets Not Included)

This book follows a (mostly) strict organization. Each chapter is dedicated to a different deliverable, ten in all. Each chapter is divided into three sections—creating the document, presenting the document, and putting the document in context. The book follows this structure so it can give you the same kind of advice for every document. This book describes three kinds of documents:

- User Needs Documentation: One crucial component of designing a web site is coming to an understanding of the people using it. User needs documents support this process. Part of this process is documenting what you know about the users, usually as a result of some research, in the form of **personas**. Another part of this process is conducting testing, and the **usability test plan** and **usability test results** are the two documents that come from this activity.

- Strategy Documentation: Some ideas must be put in place before you can do any design work. **Concept models** capture underlying conceptual structures, **content inventories** illustrate the scope of content on the site, and **competitive analyses** benchmark competitive web sites.

- Design Documentation: Finally, you need to define the user experience itself. These design documents are like different lenses that highlight specific aspects of the experience. **Wireframes** show the structure of each page, **flowcharts** detail the interaction between user and system, **site maps** address the structure of the overall site, and **screen designs** communicate its look and feel.

Layered, Like a Cake

For each deliverable in this book, the chapter describes three layers, three different kinds of information you can include. This doesn't mean that the deliverable should be actually divided into layers that you can peel away. It's a metaphor to describe how important certain information is to each document.

- **Layer 1:** This layer captures the most important elements of the document. Without any of this information, it may be difficult to call the deliverable what it is. For example, one of the layer 1 elements of a site map—the structure of a web site—is content areas. Without content areas, it would be difficult to create a document that counts as a site map. (We're getting existential again, but if you're going to think hard about deliverables, you might as well go all the way.)

- **Layer 2:** Some elements enhance the message, providing more background information or fleshing out some of the relationships you're trying to show. These second layer elements are not required, like those in the first layer, but adding them can provide information to people reading the document to help them understand it. You don't have to use every element described on the second layer.

- **Layer 3:** The third layer of information on a document really varies by document, but usually includes stuff that puts the document into a larger context, outside the immediate need for it. References to other documents, for example, if they're not essential to understanding the deliverable, are counted as third-layer elements.

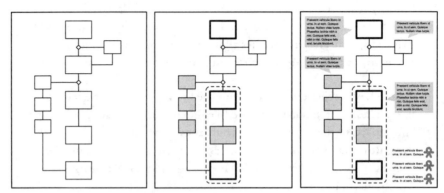

FIGURE 1.1 This sample representation of the layers in a document is, in some ways, metaphorical. Actual layers of information may not be so distinct. As you add more information to a document, it becomes easier to obscure the main message of the document.

If you haven't produced much documentation before, you might be tempted to put as much information into your deliverables as possible. This is not a good idea, and that's one of the reasons this book uses the layered approach. If you're unsure about creating a document, focus on the first-layer elements. This will get all the essential information. If you feel comfortable evolving the document, try adding one or two elements from the second layer. As you develop your own style of documentation, you'll cultivate a sense of judgment about what kinds of information you should include. You'll also get candid feedback from clients and team members.

Some Assumptions

Although this book tries to remain agnostic about process, it does make some assumptions about how you operate and what your working environment is like. You may find yourself in a different situation, but it should not affect the content of your documentation. If you have any questions about how to adapt the advice in this book to your situation, check out *Communicating Design*'s companion site, www.communicatingdesign.com.

The project team

You will frequently see references throughout this book to "the project team." This group of people includes anyone directly related to the project—decision-makers, designers, project managers, developers, and so on. Your company may have a finance person, for example, but his role doesn't necessarily make him part of the "project team."

This book paints the project team in broad strokes. Clients, designers, and developers—regardless of their particular expertise—are seen as single groups. A developer, for example, may focus on database design or system architecture or programming, but for the purposes of this book, he or she is a technologist whose focus is on building the guts of the system.

The client, too, is portrayed as a single group, but the nuances among that group's members create one of the fundamental challenges of our work. The main thing driving a particular client's agenda may be money or ego or doing the right thing. In this book, "client" and "stakeholder" can refer to any one of these kinds of people. As much as the book tries to help you cater to these different needs, it's up to you to figure out how your clients roll.

When the book refers to "the design team," it's referring to anyone involved in the design process. Your team may consist of you and you alone, or you may be a graphic designer on a team with four or five other specialized roles.

The book also assumes that there's a central member of the project team, the project manager, who runs the show. Different organizations use project managers differently, but for the most part, they have daily contact with the client and facilitate activities between the team members.

The methodology

The advent of the web brought about a sea of change, not only in business, but also in software development. The speed of "Internet time," the demand of customers, and evolving technologies rendered "traditional" software engineering methods—which depended on longer cycles, more stable releases, and less involvement from end users—useless. The extinction of such methods, however, is gradual, and several younger methodologies are competing to take their place.

The relationship between methodology and documentation is all but intractable. A methodology is frequently defined by its outputs as much as by its activities and process. Yet many methodologies still count on the same kinds of documents and many project teams still find value in certain kinds of documents, regardless of the methodology they're using.

That said, this book makes reference to three different kinds of activities. Most methodologies include some variation on these concepts, if not the specific activities themselves.

- **Requirements:** Most methodologies are based on the premise that you can't create a web site unless you know what it needs to do. To capture this need, web site designers and developers define "requirements." Requirements usually appear as a collection of statements describing different things the system should do. Different methodologies do this differently: Some methods put little emphasis on requirements-gathering, while others make it the central activity. The process of documenting requirements also varies dramatically, from voluminous spreadsheets to drawings of stick figures to three-sentence "stories." Ultimately, the purpose is to define the problem you're trying to solve. Your methodology may insist that you have a complete definition of the problem before attempting to solve it, or it may recognize that you can never truly understand a problem until you try to solve it. Regardless of your approach, this book assumes you will spend at least a little time listening to the client and doing some research into the target audience to figure out what it needs.

- **Design:** Once members of the project team have an understanding of the problem at hand, they design a solution. In this case, the solution is a web site that will meet the needs of the business and the target audience. Like requirements-gathering, this activity varies from methodology to methodology. Some call for quick bursts of design followed by testing, while others call for extended design cycles punctuated by occasional testing, and still others call for building a prototype and refining it over time. This book assumes that your design activities are preceded by some type of requirements-gathering, and that you use design documents (like wireframes and flowcharts) to establish a direction for how the final product will look and behave.

- **Test:** The final major activity in most methodologies is testing. Typically, this is some form of quality control, evaluating whether the web site performs and behaves as documented. For user experience professionals, testing almost always implies some kind of usability testing—putting the web site (or some reasonable approximation of the site) in front of users to make sure they understand it.

Testing may precede requirements as a way to see what works (or doesn't work) with the current site, or with related sites. Testing may also occur throughout the design process, a way to constantly evaluate and refine your work.

There's no direct relationship between these activities and the kinds of documents described in this book. The design documents, for example, do not necessarily correspond to the design activity. As you'll see in the chapters themselves, these deliverables—though mostly used for design—can also be used as tools for gathering requirements and testing.

The culture

Beyond methodology, project teams maintain an unwritten set of rules for working together. This is the project culture—an understanding of the value each team member brings to the table, of how communications happen between team members, and the role of documentation in the organization.

This book assumes, perhaps naively, that a good project team should be built on collaboration and consensus. Most projects fare better when they operate under the assumption that everyone wants to make a worthwhile and meaningful contribution and that people should feel some ownership for their work. Such an approach comes with potential risks: the project becomes more about soothing egos than doing what's right, decision making takes longer, innovation doesn't happen in groups. But a group (and again, this is perhaps naive, but not without its merit) committed to a successful project will take steps to mitigate those risks.

General Process for Building a Diagram

Many of the documents described in this book use diagrams, visual representations of ideas or concepts. Since the early days of web design, these pictures have proved to be the best way to document some of the abstractions design teams have to work with. Although each of the documents in this book relies on a different process to create it, there is a general method you can follow when creating a diagram. (This is more or less the process I use. Your mileage may vary.)

- **Do a situation analysis.** Three things will shape your approach to diagramming an idea: the purpose of the drawing, where it fits into the process, and the audience. These factors are discussed in detail for each deliverable.

- **Make a list of all the pieces of information you want to capture.**
  Again, this technique is described in detail in each of the chapters. The pieces of information are called "elements" or "dimensions" or "data points." They represent a small part of the story, and the purpose of the diagram is to tie all these pieces of information together.

- **Plan the drawing on paper, capturing as many elements as possible.**
  The sketch should provide a good plan for how you're going to accommodate all your information.

- **Transfer the paper sketch to a drawing application, like Adobe Illustrator, Microsoft Visio, or OmniGroup's OmniGraffle.** Usually, it's best to start in black and white and just focus on layout.

- **Figure out how you want to use color and start experimenting with it.** With flowcharts, for example, color is good for grouping related steps or paths, or calling attention to certain elements. One approach is to go back to your list of elements and identify one or two that can be best represented through color.

- **Refine your visual language.** The visual language is the set of shapes and conventions you've applied to the list of elements. At this point, you'll have a sense of where your visual language is working and where it's not working. Specifically, diagrams may appear too busy to be readable, or may not have a coherent story. When you refine the visual language, you're looking for opportunities to make sure the main messages are clear. You're also looking to strip away excess information—visual noise that doesn't hold much meaning or contribute to the story.

- **Write your copy.** Start labeling the elements of your drawing before you forget what they mean, and add additional blocks of copy.

- **Identify the weak points.** Send the drawing to your printer and mark it up. You'll want to refer back to your situation analysis at this point for the sanity check. By now you're so engrossed in the drawing, you need to take a step back. Ask yourself whether the drawing answers the basic questions about flowcharts: Where does the user start and end? What are the major steps in the process?

- **Revise the drawing in the drawing application.** Transfer your comments to digital form.

- **Check your work.** Make sure you've got all the details your audiences expect. This may be a good time to do a peer review. You could, for example, show your work to a project manager. He or she should know the audience as well as you do and can serve as a good sounding board. Another technique for testing your work is to brainstorm some questions that people looking at the diagram might ask.

- **Adjust.** With comments from a third party in hand, you're ready to make the tiny adjustments to ensure that everything looks just right. With flowcharts, especially, lining the elements up on a grid can make the drawing look polished even if you don't have a lot of detail. Don't ruin a nice document by failing to line your data up right.

- **Add supporting information.** A professional-looking document includes a title, a date, attributions, and perhaps a version number. Diagrams floating in the middle of the page don't do anyone any good if they don't have some basic contextual information.

General Tips for Presenting Deliverables

The second half of each chapter focuses on using the deliverables because even the best-looking flowchart or the most detailed usability report is not worth the paper it's printed on if you can't use it. Each chapter provides detailed advice on how to plan and conduct meetings around the documents, and what to do if your meetings go awry. Here are some general thoughts:

- **Establish and communicate a purpose.** If there's one overwhelmingly consistent piece of advice throughout the chapters, it's that you should establish a purpose for your meeting or presentation. Somehow people think that bringing a document to a meeting automatically establishes an agenda and purpose, but a meeting to review a document is no different from any other. Of the handful of techniques for capturing a meeting's purpose, creating a list of questions is perhaps the easiest. After all, you're bringing people together to discuss an issue and what better way to get the discussion going than with a list of questions? Remember that the deliverables in this book are tools to communicate ideas, vehicles for discussing them, not ends in and of themselves. Your purpose, therefore, shouldn't be focused on the document, but instead on the content. For example, a deliverable-focused purpose would be "to review the deliverable and get comments." (If you think that's obvious, ask yourself how many meetings you've been to where that was the agenda.) A better purpose would be to address a list of questions about the idea itself—for example, "This navigation scheme tested well, but it's a new direction for the organization. Can you see anything that would make it difficult to populate with content?"

- **Decide what you want to get out of the meeting before going into it.** A meeting purpose can be different from what you want to get out of the meeting. Even if your purpose is to answer some questions about the web site design, your agenda might be to show stakeholders that you're getting conflicting direction from different areas of the organization. You don't need to keep this underlying message a secret from meeting participants, but it's important to recognize that while all meeting participants have a common purpose, they might not have a common agenda.

- **Think through participant expectations, agendas, and questions.** Once you know what your own agenda is, think through the agendas of everyone else who will be in the room. You can refine your message and your agenda by imagining all the questions you'll be asked. For example, in politically charged projects, every stakeholder may have one or two pieces of content or features they would like to see prioritized. They may come to a brainstorming meeting needing to get these things off their chest. Instead of listening to you or participating in the conversation, they'll spend the whole meeting thinking about their own agenda items. One technique for dealing with this situation is to give people time at the beginning of the meeting to air these issues. Usually, they're not as controversial as imagined, and if you lead with a more comprehensive outline, you have an excuse to move past any unnecessary discussion. Having diffused this pent-up politics, you can move along to the main purpose of the meeting.

- **Invite the minimal number of people possible.** Nothing ruins a meeting more than people who aren't supposed to be there. Too many bodies at the table can make a meeting lose its focus or get caught in the maelstrom of competing agendas. Too many bodies can be difficult to manage, and difficult to steer through the meeting. Let's face it, sometimes you need to be honest with yourself about whether you're one of these people.

- **Send materials around before the meeting.** Perhaps this seems counter-intuitive to you, but sending materials around in advance of the meeting means you can dig into the meat of the documents without having to spend too much time on background. Participants show up to the meeting with intelligent questions and you can focus on what's important. Some people think that sending the materials around can backfire by revealing the punch line to some elaborate story. Keep in mind that you're designing a web site, not telling a joke. If you're really concerned that people will miss the point of your deliverables without you to narrate, tell them during the meeting that you'll get to their questions at the end. You'll take some time up front to walk them through the whole document, and perhaps your presentation will answer questions they have.

- **Write up an account of the meeting.** It never hurts to capture the decisions made during the meeting. Even if you don't compose formal meeting minutes, send around an email with your "take-aways." This gives you some accountability and the participants a chance to correct any misconceptions you might have had.

- **Take pride in running a good meeting.** It's almost better than preparing a good document: that feeling you get when people get up from a meeting and say, "That was a good meeting." You've ended early and you've made progress. These are the two things people look for in a meeting. Don't try to do anything more.

- **For new clients, assume the first meeting won't go well.** You don't have to tell any of them that you're testing the waters, but writing off your first one or two meetings to "getting to know you" might help ease your own anxiety. Presenting documents or conducting brainstorming with a new team or new clients can be daunting. Before getting to the good stuff, get to know your clients by holding a, shall we say, less meaningful meeting, where you might present a relatively simple document. This can give you a good sense of their working style and their collaboration style. They may rip apart your deliverable, but at least you'll know what kinds of things they're looking for.

PART I

User Needs Documents

User need documents
- ▶ Personas
- ▶ Usability Test Plans
- ▶ Usability Test Reports

The people who will be visiting and interacting with your web site provide important context to the design process. By understanding them—their motivations, their goals, their habits, their expectations, their assumptions—you can create a successful design.

The design community is constantly coming up with new methods and techniques for understanding users. Regardless of the approach, this process usually ends in generating a profile of the audience, also known as personas. These profiles are important because they help everyone on the team have the same understanding of the target audience.

Besides seeking to understand users independently of the web site, you may want to see how the audience responds to the design itself. Conducting a usability test is a project in and of itself and can vary in size or purpose depending on your needs. There are two documents associated with usability testing: One document for planning the test and another document for reporting the results.

CHAPTER TWO

Personas

pər·so'·nəz (n.)

A summary representation of the system's intended users, often described as real people. Any project can have one or more personas, each representing a different kind of audience for the system. Also known as: user profiles, user role definitions, audience profiles.

Personas describe a site's target users, giving a clear picture of how they're likely to use the system, and what they'll expect from it, among other things. In the late '90s, personas became a popular way for design teams to capture information about customers. Like many other types of deliverables in the designer's kit, personas came from a different field altogether: marketing. While marketers were perhaps more interested in what messages would speak to their customers, design teams adapted the document to capture information relevant to their needs: user goals, scenarios, tasks, and the like.

Good personas make everyone happy. They give design teams an effective, accessible way to describe user needs and stakeholders a common language for talking about their customers. Personas mean that no one on your team will have to say "I think our users want this" or "If my mom were a customer she would want that." They paint a multidimensional picture of the audience in terms that allow design teams to evaluate the effectiveness of their designs.

Personas aren't born from nothing, hatching like Aphrodite from the designer's head. Instead, personas are the product of research into the target audience and the complexity of the personas depends on the depth of research. Research techniques vary from surveys and market research to interviews and ethnographic methods. There are shelves of books and articles on the best research techniques, but the purpose of this book is to describe the best approach for capturing all that information.

There's no standard format for personas across the industry and different gurus have offered different approaches. Regardless of what approach you select, personas should have a couple of things in common: expressing what users need and what they expect.

Personas at a Glance

Some personas paint richly detailed descriptions of a system's users, creating a quasi-biographical portrait of a composite person, based on research data. Others simply offer a brief sketch of each type of user. Over the course of this chapter, we'll discuss the merits of these various approaches, and how to tailor your personas to the needs of your particular project. Meanwhile, here are a few examples.

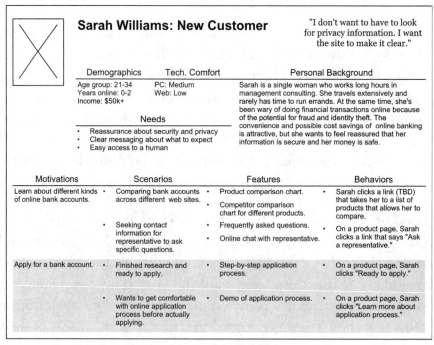

FIGURE 2.1 This persona gives a highly detailed picture of a typical "new customer" for a banking web site.

Sarah Williams: New Customer

"I don't want to have to look for privacy information. I want the site to make it clear."

Motivations	Scenarios	Features	Behaviors
Learn about different kinds of online bank accounts.	• Comparing bank accounts across different web sites.	• Product comparison chart. • Competitor comparison chart for different products.	• Sarah clicks a link (TBD) that takes her to a list of products that allows her to compare.
	• Seeking contact information for representative to ask specific questions.	• Frequently asked questions. • Online chat with representative.	• On a product page, Sarah clicks a link that says "Ask a representative."
Apply for a bank account.	• Finished research and ready to apply.	• Step-by-step application process.	• On a product page, Sarah clicks "Ready to apply."
	• Wants to get comfortable with online application process before actually applying.	• Interactive demo of application process.	• On a product page, Sarah clicks "Learn more about application process."
Check on status of application.	• Visits site daily until application is approved. • Receives email indicating that application is approved.	• Email updates of application status. • Secure RSS feed of application status.	• Sarah opts into an email reminder. • The site remembers Sarah has applied and gives her a link to "application status."
Learn how to use online banking.	• Awaiting application approval and wants to get up-to-speed on online banking functions. • Application approved and ready to learn more.	• Interactive demo of online banking functionality.	• On the application status page, Sarah clicks "Learn more about online banking."

FIGURE 2.2 This simpler persona provides just the basics of a user's needs and behaviors, focusing less on "biographical" information, and more on how the user will interact with the system, and how the system will support her goals.

YourBank.com: Customer Profiles

Customer	Quote	Description
New Applicant	"Don't make me hunt for the privacy policy. Make it clear in every step of the way."	New Applicants approach online banking with caution. Most are people who are already offline customers who want to try our online products. Their highest priorities are ease of use and reassurance about security and privacy.
Basic Account Holder	"There's only a couple things I need to do: check my balance and pay my bills."	Basic Account Holders aren't necessarily our newest customers. They may have been with us for a while, but limit the types of transactions they do with us. Their highest priorities are reliability, keeping things simple, keeping things inexpensive, and avoiding "spam." They generally have one or two accounts with us.
Advanced Account Holder	"Responsiveness. If I take the time to get in touch with the bank, I want them to respond within a day."	Advanced Account Holders are similar to Basic Account Holders, but they are happy to be informed about new products. They tend to be our early adopters and buy products that provide conveniences they can't get offline. They may have two, three, or four different accounts with us.
Previous Customer	"If I leave a bank, it's not because there are better products elsewhere. It's because their customer service did something to annoy me."	Customers who leave us haven't left online banking. They seek out competitors who meet their needs better. Before becoming Previous Customers, they were Advanced Account Holders. It's rare for a Basic Account Holder to leave us.

FIGURE 2.3 This quick-and-dirty set of personas gives only a name, a quote, and a brief description.

Persona Overview

Purpose—What are personas for?

Personas focus design activities by helping the team prioritize system features and content that best support the audience.

Audience—Who uses them?

Since ultimately personas help direct and inform design decisions, the design team is the primary audience, although stakeholders may weigh in on their creation and engineers may find them useful for providing context for their work.

Scale—How much work are they?

You may have as few as two personas or as many as a dozen, but the work involved in each will scale on another dimension as well: the level of detail provided.

Context—Where do they fall in the process?

The design team generally prepares personas at the beginning of a project since the customer segmentation strategy—the way the team models the audience—will drive much of the process. With user groups identified at the beginning, the design team can gather requirements and design activities around those groups.

Challenges

It's easy enough to make people up, but summarizing what you actually *know* about your audience can be tough. In some ways, the most important work of doing personas comes before you even start building them. To be truly successful, personas must draw from research into a system's intended users, including observations, interviews, focus groups, usability tests, surveys, and other interactions with actual users. The sketchier your information about your users is, the less detailed the personas will be.

Another common pitfall in building personas is dealing with companies that have done business successfully for years without formal documentation of their customers. They may have informal ways of referring to different customer groups, which may not be relevant to your efforts. Part of the persona process is helping organizations learn a new way of talking about their customers. Most commonly, organizations segment customers by the products they buy, even though there may be other differences that are more relevant to the user experience.

For example, the sample personas throughout this chapter describe customers for an online banking site and focus on the types of accounts they have. There are numerous ways, however, to cut up the audience of a banking service: by the amount of money they have in the bank, by whether they use physical branches or not, by the amount of interaction they expect to have with bank employees, or by the average number of transactions per month, just to name a few. If the reason you're segmenting the customers is because that's the way it's always been done, then you need to explore other options. A segmentation model may have worked for one way of doing business, but new ways of doing business call for new conceptions of the audience.

Creating Personas

The main choice you'll be making as you construct your personas is how much information to include for each one. Generally, there are three layers of detail to consider. The most basic personas will only include the first layer, while the most elaborate persona will flesh out all three layers.

Layer 1: The Bare Minimum

Personas can be rich with data, but without these basic elements they are essentially meaningless.

Name

Personas are summary representations of people. People have names. Therefore, your personas should have names, if for no other reason than to make it easy to talk about them with other project participants.

Real names, like those you'd find in the White Pages, are useful because they create a vivid picture, something real for stakeholders to associate with their customers. Real names turn formerly abstract conversations into slightly more concrete ones.

On the other hand, keeping stakeholders and other project participants focused on the important issues—goals, motivations, needs—may be difficult. A name that describes the persona's general role or purpose may help maintain focus. Either way, the name should be short and distinctive, even when describing the purpose: "The Learner," "The Infrequent Customer," "The Worrier," "The Multiple Account Holder," and "The Competitive Researcher," for instance.

These names describe what's bringing these particular user types to the system in the first place by focusing on purpose and objective.

TIP ▶ Real names and role names are not mutually exclusive. Feel free to use both.

Motivations and needs

Customers with common motivations form a user group—described as a persona—where the individual in the persona represents a typical member of that group. All the personas together represent all the reasons why someone would use the system.

Typically, motivations are expressed as what a particular user wants to get out of interacting with the system, but motivations may also reflect what users want to get out of interacting with the organization itself, or what they want in general. For example, a motivation for someone using a banking web site might be "wants to compare different types of mortgage products," or "wants to apply for a checking account."

Each persona must also express the user's needs, in other words, their expectations in interacting with the site. Often, needs are directly related to motivations—showing what a user needs in order to accomplish the goal—in which case the persona must reflect this relationship. Needs are not necessarily unique to the user groups. Your users may all have the same set of needs, differing only in the relative importance of each need.

While it can be difficult to decide how much information to include about your user's motivations, what's critical is that your motivation descriptions sufficiently help the designers understand why the users are there. If the research into your users reveals additional levels of details, you can try to capture them here, but they may be better documented elsewhere to keep the personas concise.

This description of the user's motivation provides good detail:

```
Sarah needs to get a checking account and wants to compare the
different kinds of accounts available. She's especially worried
about minimum balances and additional fees.
```

This one, on the other hand, needs some help:

```
Sarah is researching checking accounts.
```

Scenarios

Scenarios are more-or-less realistic scenes that set the stage for an interaction between a web site and a user. They allow project participants to picture the use of the system beyond the system itself, helping them understand how the system fits into their customers' lives.

Scenarios also help project participants identify what information users might have in-hand when they approach the site. For example, a user checking on flight status information should have the flight number, but may not in every scenario.

One part of the design process that is frequently neglected is how people use the information they get out of a system. From the system's point of view, it's "spit out some bit of information and the process is complete." But this is rarely the case for the person using the system. The information is a trigger for making a decision—"the flight is delayed, so I can leave later" or "my package still hasn't shipped, so I'd better call customer service."

One common user persona might be "the Worrier." Anyone who has done online banking has played this role at one point or another. Here's a typical Worrier scenario for a financial services site:

```
The Worrier is out shopping when his or her credit card is
declined. Upon returning home, the user goes to the customer
service URL on the back of the credit card to determine why the
card was declined. The Worrier expects to see instructions on
how to access his or her account and from the account how to
determine why the card was declined.
```

For each scenario, the persona should identify what the customer's next step will be.

TIP ▶ Based on your research, identify a set of circumstances behind each motivation; this will inform your scenarios. If your research methodology included spending time with users, you may already have a sense of the kinds of tools and documents they use in these circumstances, and how they will use the system output.

This scenario paints a picture of the circumstances in which the target audience will be using the system:

```
Sarah is a new college student and is getting a checking
account for the first time. She knows her Social Security
```

number, but has no other information. She's expecting to go to the bank tomorrow to tell them what kind of checking account she wants to open.

This scenario description, while accurate, does not establish much context:

Sarah is a college student looking for her first checking account.

Layer 2: Further Details

With the basics in place, consider adding more information to help solidify the relationship between the users and the system.

System features

System features spell out the site's content as it applies to the motivations of your personas. You may already have a sense of the features and content the site will include. In this case, you can align these elements with the persona's motivations to show which features will help users meet their needs.

Often, this process makes it much easier to spot the features that do not support any user needs, which will help the design team justify removing these features from the system.

By the same token, laying out the system features in this way will help designers see if some motivations do not have any features to support them. Stakeholders then learn where they should invest resources to ensure that their customers are getting everything they need.

Example:

"About Checking Accounts" area of web site

Behaviors

By describing expected behaviors, you bridge the gap between motivation and feature, answering the question: What does the user need to do to make use of particular content or functionality? Elaborating these behaviors can help the design team determine whether they're burdening the user with too many decisions, for example.

Typically, behavior descriptions use verbs like "clicks" or "goes to" and speak in the present tense to paint a realistic picture of how a persona will use the system.

Alternatively, behaviors can describe what happens after the user has engaged the system, illustrating what users will do with the information they get.

Example:

```
From the home page, Sarah clicks "About Checking Accounts" and
sees a grid comparing our different checking products. She
picks two accounts that seem like a good fit for her and writes
them down to take with her to the bank.
```

Quotes

Using quotes from users adds a personal touch without the distraction that comes with additional layers of personal detail. You can use actual quotes from your research participants to remind stakeholders that this information has a foundation in research.

Examples:

```
"I don't mind researching banking stuff online, but I'd rather
do all the transactions in person."
```

```
"These days picking a checking account is like trying to pick
toothpaste. Have you seen the shelves of toothpaste in the
grocery store?"
```

Layer 3: Personas in the Flesh

The first two layers contain all the essentials and more for describing users, but you may find the following data points useful for creating a real picture of your target audiences.

Demographic information

A holdover from its predecessor the marketing segment, demographic information is meant to describe the whole category of user, detailing, for example, the range of ages each persona might include.

By including demographic information in the persona, however, you are mixing genres. The persona is meant to be a summary *representation* of a group of users—a description of a *single* user (whether concrete or abstract) that best represents a set of needs. A persona should be described as a "35-year-old woman," for example, rather than as a "female, between the ages of 35-50." The purpose of a persona is not to describe the tendencies of a group of people defined by age, sex, race, and income, but instead to describe the behaviors of a specific person who represents a class of needs and goals.

If your stakeholders can bridge the gap between marketing segment and user persona without too much discomfort, best to leave out demographic information unless it has a significant impact on use. Even if it does, better to spell out particular user needs in the motivations and scenarios sections than expect the design team to interpret demographic information.

Technology comfort level

This bit of information is a favorite among first-time persona builders, but the real value of this information is its implications. A user's comfort level with technology should be translated into actual needs. Knowing that some people have never used the web to shop before, for example, does not necessarily help the design team. On the other hand, knowing that a particular user group will still seek contact with a human because they do not feel confident in giving certain information online does have a direct impact on the design.

Personal background

Personal background information can flesh out the user and make the persona more accessible to stakeholders and designers. Such information can include "day in the life of" descriptions or an overall relationship to the task at hand. In the case of our college student, for example, Sarah's personal background may indicate that she's never been good at managing money and her parents did not prepare her well for dealing with budgets and bills.

The personal background information is an opportunity to tell a story about the user, but it transforms the persona from a summary set of needs to a real—albeit fictional—person. It's the difference between a representation of a user and a typical user. On the other hand, too much information can be distracting.

Photograph

The maraschino on the persona sundae is a photograph. Like personal background, a photograph can help stakeholders stop thinking about their customers as a singular anonymous mass and understand that there are distinct groups of people with particular needs.

Still, photographs often come with risks. Using photos of actual users taken during research activities, for example, may present legal problems. Be sure to secure permission from research participants before using their picture in any materials. Of course, there are plenty of stock photography sites that can provide good images for this purpose. A Google Images search on "headshot" presents an abundance of material.

Building Your Personas: The Basics

The first step in the process of building personas (that is, after you've done the user research on which you'll base them) is understanding the context in which you're creating them. Throughout this book, this is known as the situation analysis. This process is more or less the same for every deliverable: Consider where you are in the project, the target audience, and the purpose of that deliverable. In the case of personas, this process will help you identify what content you'll want to include, and what you should omit.

Timeline: When personas happen

Ideally, personas come at the beginning of a project. They can supplement other documents that capture user needs or—in a pinch—stand on their own, and they're an especially quick way of documenting users for projects with short time frames.

At the beginning of a project, you may find yourself in one of two different situations. In the more typical situation, you already have a list of the kinds of content and functions available in the system. This list exists because you're redesigning an existing system or the stakeholders have a wish list of features. In this case, including these features in your personas will help put them in context.

In the less typical situation, you are creating a new system from scratch and have no idea what kinds of features to include. This situation impacts persona design because you can only summarize what you learned in research: what motivates the users in different scenarios.

Audience: Who's looking at the personas

With an understanding of the position in the project, consider who will be using the personas. The format for personas need not vary by audience. Personas capture a particular breed of requirements, and every project participant needs to make sure her or his work addresses those requirements. Still, some of the people using personas may need special adjustments.

Although it's been the better part of a decade that user experience professionals have used personas in their work, they're still relatively new for many clients, customers, and stakeholders. If you're introducing the *idea* of personas by introducing the actual personas, you may run into some resistance. To address this audience, sometimes it's a good idea to create personas from lists of questions rather than lists of user needs, thereby testing how much stakeholders really know about their customers.

Questions about the user's experience, for instance, can trip up stakeholders who don't really know anything about their customers. "Which is more important to users, product summary information or product technical specs?" is one example.

It's often just as revealing to phrase questions as if addressed to the user about his or her experiences, asking, for instance, "What information do you use to decide whether you'll buy a product?"

Both kinds of questions show how the users themselves—and not internal stakeholders—must drive design decisions.

Purpose: The role of personas

In the typical situation, personas help capture user needs and create a framework for making decisions about the design. Still, your situation may be anything but typical.

Depending on the personas' purpose in the project, their contents may emphasize different kinds of information. Some of these different purposes have been mentioned above in conjunction with the context and the audience. This is because the purpose is driven by these two factors. Other purposes are spelled out in Table 2.1.

A word of caution: These worst-case scenarios are spelled out because you may find yourself in them one day. Project circumstances change and the project plan you laid out may not be the one you get to follow. Or there is no project plan. Or the stakeholders have changed. There may be any number of reasons your situation is not best-case. That being said, if you have a choice, you should use personas for what they were meant for: capturing user needs. Table 2.1 shows how you can modify personas to address different needs in the project. Even though you can do it doesn't mean you should. The preferred textbook approach offers a more typical technique for addressing particular situations. It's also meant to make you feel a little guilty for abusing your personas.

TABLE 2.1

How Different Situations Call for Different Personas

Situation	Adjusting Your Persona to It	Preferred "Textbook" Approach
Justify use of personas	Create personas with a series of questions to illustrate to your team and stakeholders that there is a lack of information about your users. If you can, show how the answers to these questions will tie directly to design decisions.	Building skeletal personas with questions instead of answers is probably the best way (in document form) to show that you're missing crucial information.
Recruit for usability test	If you need to recruit people for a usability test, you can use personas to zero in on the types of people to recruit. Focus the personas on demographic information and emphasize scenarios that can help feed the screening process by identifying the kinds of behaviors you want to test.	You really should be using a screener for recruiting. A screener is a list of 10 to 20 questions you give to a recruiting firm. They ask prospective participants these questions to see if they're appropriate for your test. Perhaps you can write the screener so that it can evolve into a persona.
Rationalize existing design decisions	Emphasize behaviors to illustrate how a user would behave in the system as designed. When employed to show the inadequacy of certain stakeholder recommendations, you may need a mechanism for demonstrating that certain needs are not met or that designs would encourage behaviors that do not support motivations.	The best way to show the merit or inadequacy of a design is to build a functional prototype and test it.
Clients not buying into personas	Hey, it happens. Some clients find references to real-world customers scary. If clients aren't budging, keep everything in the personas but the person—describe user needs, tell stories, identify behaviors. A persona, after all, is just a way to collect all these things under a meaningful shorthand heading. If it's not meaningful, don't use it. It may be easier for your clients to work with and prioritize a more granular set of data— like a list of user needs. With these smaller items prioritized you can create logical groups out of them (e.g., high-priority needs) without giving it a scary label like "New Customer," or the even scarier "Joe."	Of course, you should get buy-in for the concept before presenting personas in the first place. Focus on the value to your team and how they help ensure a well-designed product.

Continues

TABLE 2.1 *Continued*

How Different Situations Call for Different Personas

Situation	Adjusting Your Persona to It	Preferred "Textbook" Approach
No time or resources dedicated to persona creation	Some information about users is better than no information about users. If you recognize the need for documenting user needs but have been given neither time nor money to do it, try building "power personas." Identify your user groups and write three sentences about each one. Focus on typical use scenarios and avoid personal details. Name each one with a role (like "First-Time Customer") and include a picture. In the context of this purpose, the picture helps humanize the user without resorting to elaborate personal backgrounds.	Build time into project plans for documenting user needs.
Identify extraneous content	Since a persona should just show information relevant to a particular user group and its needs, there's no convenient way to show that certain existing content does not support users. Instead, build a summary page that divides content into piles: content that supports a user need and content that does not. If you have a limited set of user needs you might group the content under each one.	Personas are not ideal for pointing out useless content, but a separate related document can be presented in conjunction with personas. You can create a checklist of major content areas to show which ones address user needs and which don't.
Show how existing segmentation models are inadequate	Organizations frequently have informal schemes for thinking about their customers that they used before you showed up. Building personas around the entrenched user model can show that it does not really show differences between users. In this case, build a document that lines the user needs up side by side to show how similar the groups are, or that the distinctions are not sufficient for determining content needs.	Building a set of fake personas is perhaps the best way to show that your needs require a different approach to segmenting customers. It is, however, an unfortunate waste of time.
Show skewed business priorities	User experience professionals can lean on personas and other user-needs documentation to make a point about business strategy, especially since in many arenas, the justification for certain business decisions is out of our control. In this case, consider showing how business decisions will impact the design of the system.	Employ a business strategist to develop a sound business strategy prior to design activities. (Sounds easy, right?) That being said, however, there are trends in today's business world toward employing design methodologies—including persona creation—to set business priorities. Because of this trend, the industry is seeing an evolution of the persona format.

	New Customers	Basic Account Holders	Advanced Account Holders
Checking Products	✓	✓	
Product Comparison Chart	✓	✓	
Frequently Asked Questions	✓	?	
Online Help	✓	✓	✓
New Product Announcements		✓	✓
Privacy Policy	✓		
Savings Products	✓	?	
Investment Products	✓	?	?
ATM Locator	✓	✓	✓
Investment Planning		?	✓
Retirement Planning		?	✓
Lending Products	✓	?	?
Credit Cards	✓	✓	✓
Interest Rates		✓	✓
Corporate Information	✓		
Credit Management		○	○
Access to Online Banking	?	✓	✓
Online Banking Functions	?	✓	✓

FIGURE 2.4 This simple table shows whether existing content meets the needs of different kinds of users. Check marks indicate that existing content is suitable to the needs of a particular user. Question marks indicate that the existing content does not meet the needs of a particular user group. Circles show that the content does not exist. This simple approach can be enough to illustrate that current content is geared toward one type of persona and the team has to put some effort into meeting the needs of other users.

Persona contents: Getting down to brass tacks

Up until now, you've just been thinking about the *kinds* of information you want to include. You've also thought about your situation, the context for creating personas. Now it's time to identify the information itself, such that is suitable to the situation. Once you have determined the content, the final step will be to compose all this information into a document design of your choosing. Having all the content in front of you in some rough form, however, helps you define the format. By writing all the content in rough form first, you can also double-check that your set of personas is mutually exclusive and collectively exhaustive—that it truly represents all your users.

Say there's one piece of information that appears in all your personas, for instance. Most likely it's either irrelevant or it points to an inadequacy in the way you've grouped your users.

If this information is relevant to all user groups, but by differing degrees, you might try a "moon phase" chart—also known as Harvey balls (no kidding)—to express different degrees of shared properties.

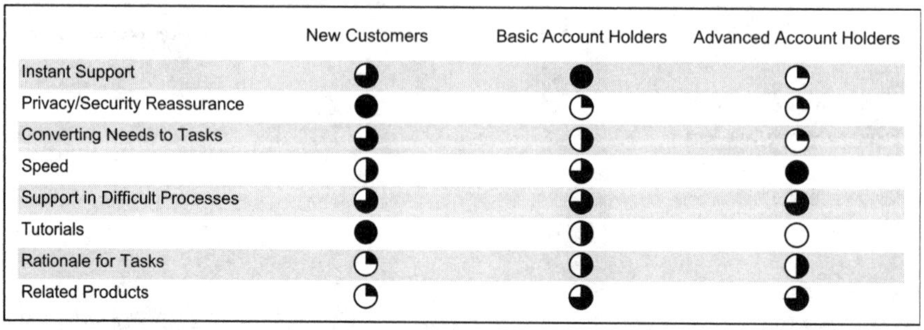

	New Customers	Basic Account Holders	Advanced Account Holders
Instant Support	◑	●	◕
Privacy/Security Reassurance	●	◔	◔
Converting Needs to Tasks	◑	◐	◕
Speed	◔	◑	●
Support in Difficult Processes	◑	◑	◑
Tutorials	●	◔	○
Rationale for Tasks	◔	◑	◐
Related Products	◔	◑	◔

FIGURE 2.5 This chart using so-called "Harvey balls" illustrates how a single piece of information applies to all personas, but by different degrees.

With a rough notion of the content, you can think about how you want to lay out the personas. They usually appear in one of three formats.

TABLE 2.2

Three Different Layouts for Personas

The Narrative:	The Table:	The Quick-and-Dirty:
Best for stakeholders who are not so concerned about the technical details of user needs and will buy into the process by being drawn in through story.	Best for designers who need an easy way to compare designs to user needs. Also good for project plans that afford little time to develop personas.	Best in situations where personas lack sufficient research to back them up.

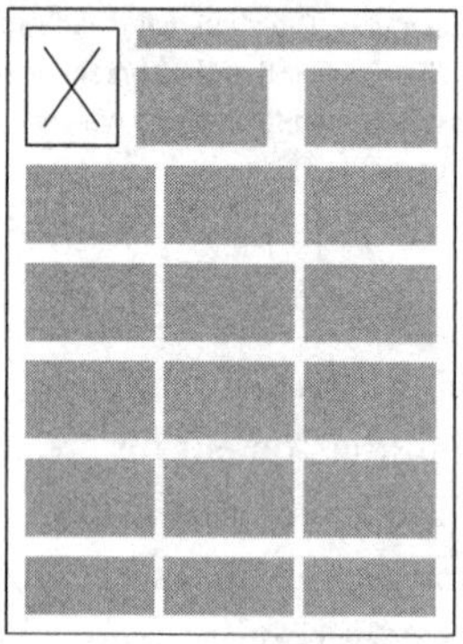

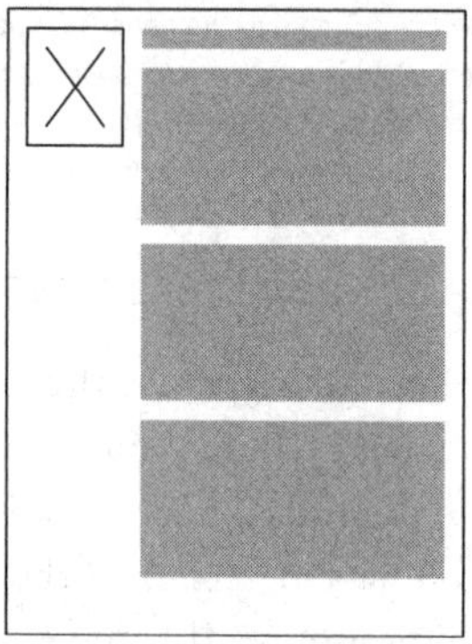

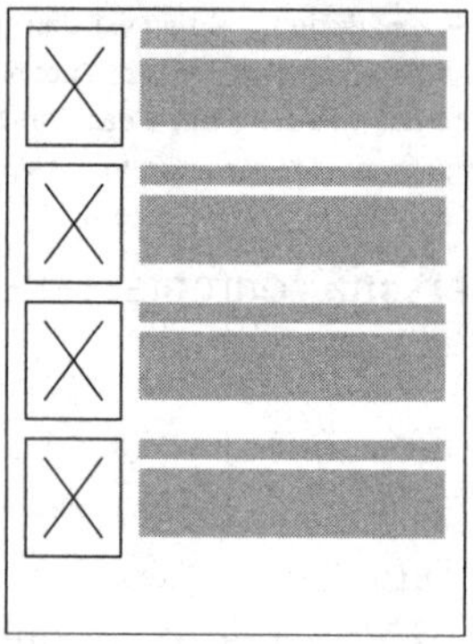

Polishing your personas: A few tips

You could hand in a short stack of pages that represent your target audience and be done with it. But your research no doubt includes some extra details you'd like to share. Or perhaps you've done some analysis on how these target audiences relate to the business overall, or to each other. By book-ending the personas with a little extra detail, you create a self-contained package of essential information.

Introductory summary pages

Because personas can represent a significant departure from the institutional conception of the target audience, stakeholders may be caught off guard by diving into the details of the first persona right away. To ease them in, you can use an overview that describes the personas at a high level: showing the name and goals of each one without any details. This overview can be useful, too, as a means for tying the entrenched institutional segmentation to the new approach.

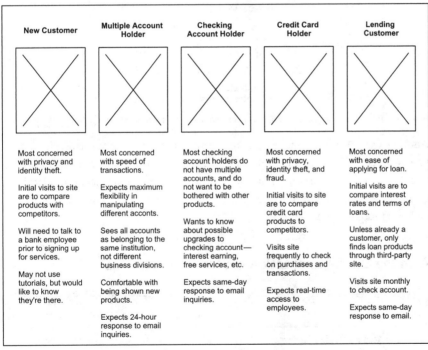

New Customer	Multiple Account Holder	Checking Account Holder	Credit Card Holder	Lending Customer
Most concerned with privacy and identity theft. Initial visits to site are to compare products with competitors. Will need to talk to a bank employee prior to signing up for services. May not use tutorials, but would like to know they're there.	Most concerned with speed of transactions. Expects maximum flexibility in manipulating different accounts. Sees all accounts as belonging to the same institution, not different business divisions. Comfortable with being shown new products. Expects 24-hour response to email inquiries.	Most checking account holders do not have multiple accounts, and do not want to be bothered with other products. Wants to know about possible upgrades to checking account—interest earning, free services, etc. Expects same-day response to email inquiries.	Most concerned with privacy, identity theft, and fraud. Initial visits to site are to compare credit card products to competitors. Visits site frequently to check on purchases and transactions. Expects real-time access to employees.	Most concerned with ease of applying for loan. Initial visits are to compare interest rates and terms of loans. Unless already a customer, only finds loan products through third-party site. Visits site monthly to check account. Expects same-day response to email.

FIGURE 2.6 This persona overview makes it easy for stakeholders to compare and get to know the system's various personas.

To give a high-level view of where personas fit into the system or the business, you can plot them on the marketer's favorite graphic, the two-by-two.

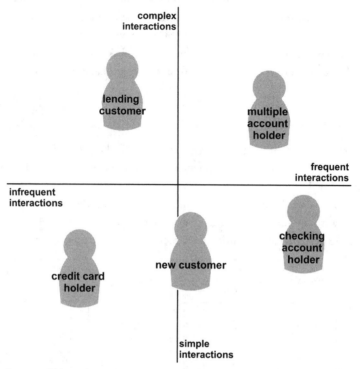

FIGURE 2.7 This two-by-two shows how different personas cover the spectrum of user types.

Another way to summarize users is to create a mapping to institutionalized user models. Besides helping stakeholders translate from an "old" way of thinking to a "new" way, this approach can also show that your model accommodates everything from the old model and beyond. Your document might include a table that looks like Table 2.3.

TABLE 2.3

Aligning Old Segmentation Model with Personas

Old user group(s)	Persona representing group
New Customers	Sarah Williams (First-Time Customer)
Checking Account Holder, Savings Account Holder	Jean-Marc Smith (Basic Account Holder)
Credit Card Customer, Mortgage Customer	Lisa Jones (Lending Customer)
(none)	Adam Jefferson (Multiple Account Holder)

Illustrating relationships between user types

Depending on your segmentation model, the personas may have relationships between them that are worth describing to your stakeholders. For example, some sites expect a natural progression of users from new customers to seasoned customers and will treat each stage of growth differently. You can incorporate these relationships into the personas themselves, or on a summary page.

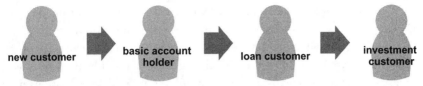

FIGURE 2.8 A graphic like this on your introductory page can show that a user may change personas over time—and not in a scary way.

Your personas may also reflect an object-oriented view of users where some user groups are "parents" of other groups. For example, the New Customers group may include two subgroups: First-Time Customers and Customers New to Online Banking. Showing these relationships can be useful if, for example, most of the users have the same set of needs but there are dramatically different scenarios drawing two groups of users to the site.

FIGURE 2.9 A family tree of personas can show that some personas are subtypes of others, sharing some of their characteristics, but not all of them.

Because personas can be so new for your stakeholders, though, persona relationships may be more trouble than they're worth. If your stakeholders are already skeptical about personas, adding detail and data to the mix will not help them answer the question "So what?"

Making Your Personas Bulletproof

As useful as personas are, there are several ways in which they're likely to cause trouble. Here are a few of the most common problems you'll run into, and how to prevent them.

Ensure maximum value

The value of personas is measured only by how useful they are during the design process. It's easy for the enthusiasm of project teams to wane as they enter the throes of wireframe revisions and prototyping. The importance of understanding your users, however, never diminishes and can rear its head when you least expect it. Frequently, we're called upon to make design decisions in the eleventh hour of the design phase. Personas can come in handy at this point because they can guide these decisions, avoiding the kind of completely random, bleary-eyed shots in the dark so frequently associated with these moments.

To avoid relegating personas to a dreary life on the shelf, there are a few things you can do. By incorporating the personas into subsequent deliverables, for example, you show how they support design decisions down the road. You might incorporate them into a site map, for instance, to show how certain categories were escalated to meet the needs of particular user groups. For wireframes, you might include the headshot of the persona representing a particular segment and suggest how a person from this segment might react to the wireframe.

One trick some user experience professionals use is to print the personas up large on posters and tack them up around the office. (This would have been inappropriate during the author's tenure at the United States Postal Service, where the only people tacked up on post office walls were wanted in several states for larceny and fraud.) If this is what it takes to keep users top-of-mind for your project team, suck up the Kinko's printing costs and break out the thumbtacks.

Do the research

Although this is really a methodological risk, it deserves some discussion, because you can't make a persona without something to base it on. This situation occurs more often than we like to admit. In these situations, you can leverage whatever third-party research is out there and create personas as if this were your own research (giving credit to your source, of course). The documentation in this case needs to include caveats indicating that this analysis is based on incomplete information. The purpose of the personas in this case is to drive further research.

Figure 2.10 Some teams print their personas out big and post them around the office. There is perhaps no better way of keeping customers top-of-mind. In this photo, courtesy of Todd Warfel and CXtec, the team has hung personas up in a conference room along with other inspirational materials.

Represent reality accurately

Though it's tough to admit, it's possible that our personas do not accurately reflect the customers. This could be a methodological issue—like the one above where there wasn't enough data to construct a complete picture—or a documentation issue, where the way you've chosen to display the results from the research does not accurately capture the users.

The main cause here is too much abstraction: taking the results of user research and smoothing them over so much as to lose the nuances of user situations. If you fear losing detail by overgeneralization, consider adding persona subtypes that fit into the general "family" of the general personas.

For example, the banking site may recognize that there are two types of new customers: those with experience in online banking and those without it. This distinction represents more than just technical savvy. Seasoned bankers may look for different kinds of information and be faster to make a decision, while those who haven't banked online before may take more time to commit. If the bank's business strategy calls for addressing both kinds of customers, the design team will need both personas.

Regardless of the number of personas you create, reference the raw data frequently to make sure that everything you learned is captured in the personas. One way to do this is to draw on quotes or other evidence from research activities to support the things you say about users.

TIP ▶ If there's any doubt about whether users are accurately represented in your personas, be sure to leave room in your personas to include direct evidence—like quotes from participants—from research activities.

Keep personas lean

Background stories, photos, and real names are nice, but they can distract from the purpose of the personas. Stakeholders may focus instead on these details, which don't speak to need or motivation and which ultimately do not provide any relevant information to the project team. Keep an eye on the time as you flesh out the demographic details of your users and decide how much time you want to spend on this part of the persona.

Presenting Personas

Personas are people—abstract summaries of people, but people nonetheless. You are hosting a party. These people are guests. Introduce them. Remind your guests of honor (the stakeholders) how they might know them and what they have in common—perhaps even why they invited them in the first place.

The users of the system will have goals that support the goals of the stakeholders. As host, your job is to show them how these apparently divergent interests have something in common.

The Meeting Purpose

When collaborating with your project team on personas, there are three different kinds of meetings. First, there's the buy-in meeting, where you're selling either the personas themselves or the idea of doing personas. Then there's the feedback meeting, where you're soliciting input on a set of personas in some state of completion. And finally, there's the brainstorming meeting, where you're starting with a (mostly) blank slate and generating the content of the personas together with your project team. Different meetings call for different kinds of presentations—here's a rough guide to what to expect, and how to prepare.

The buy-in meeting: Selling the idea

The buy-in meeting should happen only at the very beginning, when you are seeking approval on doing user research and building your personas, or at the very end, as nominal approval for a product that you have developed with the participation of the project team.

To get buy-in for the approach, devise lists of questions written in such a way as to be difficult for the internal stakeholders to answer. These questions may also be answered differently by different groups within the organization. It's a bit of a dirty trick, but doing this can help show stakeholders that the institutional conception of the audience is inconsistent or incomplete, and that we need to go outside the organization to conduct user research. By further tying these questions to specific design questions, you can show how user research directly affects the design of the interface.

To introduce the notion of a persona, you might capture these questions in the form of a persona. The goals section, therefore, would contain questions that help pinpoint the user goals. The scenarios section would contain questions that encourage users to spell out the situations they find themselves in when they attempt to use the system.

Getting buy-in for personas faces several difficult obstacles: Either stakeholders do not accept the premise that user research is a good thing, or they do not think the segmentation model is appropriate. In either case, creating personas as a way of getting buy-in to do user research is a bit of a catch-22, and requires some (if not substantial) investment in activities whose value is not recognized.

By now, however, you've identified the need. If the need is to get buy-in for the process, you may create straw man personas just to demonstrate their function in the design process. These straw men can be deliberately and obviously incomplete to demonstrate the need to do user research. They can also show how personas provide the kinds of distinctions that will drive design.

In a buy-in meeting, different participants will look for different things. Stakeholders, for instance, want to know that the time and resources dedicated to building these personas were worthwhile; they need to be shown that the personas represent customers who make sense in the context of their business. Designers, meanwhile, need to see that personas provide a useful set of criteria for making design decisions, which they'll later be able to trace back to elements of the personas. And finally, engineers will want to see that the needs and requirements in the personas will lead to realistic and buildable systems.

The feedback meeting: Getting input from the team

Feedback on the content of the persona itself may be inappropriate if the stakeholders or other team members did not participate in the research. You may have to push back on suggestions to change the personas when the suggestions have no basis in the research you did. The team members may, however, offer different interpretations of the data, which could call your conclusions into question.

Because the way the team thinks about the customers is crucial to the success of the project, it is important for everyone to have the same conception of the audience. By developing the personas over a series of meetings with participation from everyone on the project team, you can ensure that all participants see eye to eye on the audience.

In this type of meeting, your team members and stakeholders are there to provide input on the personas, and you'll need to structure the meeting to accept this input. Different project team members will offer different kinds of input, but stakeholders can help you prioritize the personas based on their relative value to the organization.

The brainstorm meeting: Building personas together

Brainstorming meetings, in which research is nurtured into fully fledged models of the audience, help ensure that everyone has the same idea of who the audience is. One of the more difficult situations to deal with on a project is when each person says "I think the users want...." When team members each develop an image of a customer segment, they invariably add features based on personal biases. This means that when one person is talking about the New Customer segment, she has a different notion of what that segment implies than does someone else on the team.

As brainstorming meetings progress, the team will move from reviewing research data to constructing an image of each customer segment. The initial meeting's structure might be methodological (see below), tracing the research process, while subsequent meetings may focus on the structure of the personas, followed by meetings to flesh out each one based on the research.

How to Structure Your Meetings

You have the most control over how to structure these meetings. Spend some time considering the best agenda, driven by what you want to accomplish and the personalities of the participants.

A conversation surrounding personas lends itself to three kinds of structures. You might discuss the personas in order of priority—in other words, by order of their importance, their value, or risk to the company. Or you might choose something like a "family resemblance" presentation, where personas are discussed in related groups. Finally, some people will describe the steps taken in creating their personas, in a chronological account of how they came to be.

The priority order approach

Despite the temptation to describe your process for building personas, you're better off diving right into the most important persona first.

In a commercial system, there are some customers that are inherently more important than others because they have a greater impact on the business. Usually they represent substantial income or costs.

In noncommercial systems, systems with many different kinds of customers, or in situations where business priority is undefined, the personas may be presented in order of risk, where risk is determined by the customer group you know the least about, or the customer group that will be most vocal, or the one that will be most directly impacted by changes to the system.

The family resemblance approach

Instead of presenting each persona separately, you can drive the discussion around the other dimension—user needs—identifying all the needs up front and then describing how each persona stacks up against each need. Make this an interactive whiteboard session where you list the needs across the top of the board, the personas down the right side of the board and build up a moon phase table (see Figure 2.5) as the meeting progresses. That is, discuss each need in detail and then identify the intensity of the need for each persona.

Because it may be difficult to dive right into describing the users in terms of needs, a short introduction to the segmentation model can help kick things off, and during this preamble you can use examples of each type of user to help set the stage.

The steps followed approach

By using a methodological approach to presenting personas, you explain the process for creating the personas, from research to analysis to synthesis. The personas themselves come at the end, the product of your rigorous methodology. By far, this is the most popular meeting structure. For some reason, consultants and designers of all types like saving the best for last.

Unless there's some burning need to describe the methodology, use one of the other two structures, incorporating methodology as a set of talking points toward the end.

But if you must use a methodological approach, use an agenda that starts with the high-level basics, including an overview of the personas, the main findings from the research, and the research methodology. By putting a high-level account of the important points at the beginning of your presentation, you set the stage and the agenda, and avoid the risk of missing your conclusion because the meeting got interrupted.

In addition to discussing the personas themselves, the presentation must address the reasons for grouping the audience in a particular way, the methods for gathering and analyzing data, the limitations to the research methods, and must provide an overview of the raw data. If you did not use formal research methods to define your personas, you will need to spell out the source of information for building your personas. In this case, you can identify each source and what they had in common and where they differed. Depending on your purpose, this can be a lot to cover.

The major risk with this approach is that you open yourself up to methodological criticisms, which would subsequently invalidate the results. Using a beginning-middle-end approach to presenting this kind of work is problematic anyway. The project team may want to save the punch line for the end, but invariably the stakeholders are never as impressed with the conclusions as the team is.

What to Expect When You're Presenting

It's just as hard to mitigate the following risks as it is to recognize that they're happening. Generally speaking, make sure you know what you want to get out of a presentation and be cognizant of the things that will prevent you from achieving those goals. This section describes some common meeting pitfalls.

Keep meeting participants engaged

We've all been here: You're walking through your personas (or any concept, for that matter) and your audience is not engaged. They ask no questions and provide no feedback. When faced with this risk, you must make it clear what the potential impact of personas is on the final product. Offer examples of the kinds of design decisions you might make based on the personas. Show the people involved how user needs translate into real design decisions. Suddenly the personas—their purpose anyway—become quite real.

Keep the agenda on track

Like the team assigned to create the personas, the people reviewing the personas may likewise become absorbed with the details behind the fiction, such as a photo or a user narrative. By spending too much time on age/race/sex/home-life conversations, you miss the notion that this person can be *anybody*, and that what makes them relevant in the context of your system is how they're going to use the outputs and what they will put into it. In this situation, the irrelevant detail can serve as a springboard to talk about a more relevant scenario.

Make use of research

The purpose of a persona is to avoid conversations that begin "I think the users want..." or worse, "What I would want to see...." One way to avoid this is to distribute copies of the research results before the meeting. This allows you to point to it and remind participants that the personas are a friendly way of summarizing data from your research.

Facilitate corporate culture change

Stakeholders may gravitate toward talking about the users with the old mind-set, with an institutionalized way of segmenting them that is irrelevant for designing the system (for example, foreign customers and domestic customers). To mitigate this risk, you need to remind them that for the purposes of this conversation, personas are the preferred means for talking about users. Your intent is not to invalidate the old segmentation model, which might be useful for other activities in the organization. Instead, you want to talk about the customers differently, in terms of a set of needs that impacts the system design.

Such groupthink is frequently inevitable, but can be addressed by giving participants readily accessible translations from old model to new and by using easy-to-remember names for the segments in the new model.

Personas in Context

Personas are a great way to capture user needs, but they cannot stand on their own. Ideally, your personas must fit into the overall design process.

Using Personas with Other Documents

As far as user needs go, personas only tell part of the story. Combined with other documents, however, they can help spell out a set of requirements for the system. Personas and other user-needs documents set the stage for a successful design process, feeding information to subsequent deliverables to help justify design decisions. This section describes how to build bridges between personas and other documents.

Documents describing what users need

Personas are both abstractions and summaries; they don't address every nuance of every user group or every system requirement. They are dependent on a segmentation model, a way of grouping customers that can also bias those user needs. Done correctly, personas should give the team a language for talking about users that focuses on actual user needs. They should also provide a structure for capturing requirements and for involving users throughout the design process. But personas, while necessary, are insufficient for providing a complete picture of what the system should do, how it should behave.

Combined with usability testing, personas become a much more powerful platform for doing design.

TABLE 2.4

Using Personas with Other User-Needs Documents

Document	Relationship to Personas
Usability Test Plans	Personas can help define a strategy for recruiting participants in the usability test. You can incorporate the personas in the test plan by describing how you'll represent each type of user in the test.
Usability Reports	Depending on the type of usability tests you conduct, you can use the scenarios and needs described in the personas as the basis for the tasks in your usability tests. The reports can then be structured by persona.

Documents establishing strategy

Personas are among the first documents you create in a project, and they set the stage for the overall approach to designing a system. They should, therefore, tie directly into strategy documents. The strategy documents, in turn, set the stage for specific design decisions, and decisions made in the strategy should be traceable to personas.

For example, imagine a system where users must evaluate incoming forms from customers, like an application for a business loan. The evaluation of the form passes through several stages: a primary review, a secondary review, and a final review. During each review, the user is looking for something different. Imagine, for example, the primary reviewer is most concerned about completeness and internal consistency, whereas the secondary reviewer's purview is compliance with various disclosure regulations. Although they're looking at the same information, the purpose of their evaluation varies. The strategy could establish different ways of structuring the incoming form, in other words, design decisions traceable to these different personas. When the actual structure of the information becomes documented in the design documentation—wireframes and the like—these structural decisions will be justified all the way back to the personas.

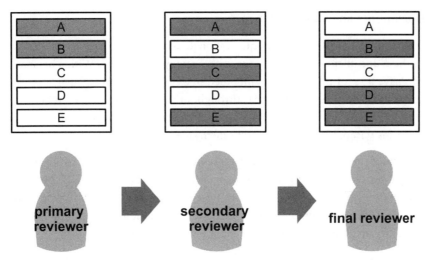

Figure 2.11 In a strategy document, personas can help establish that information priorities vary from user to user, even within the same document.

Table 2.5

Using Personas with Strategy Documents

Document	Relationship to Personas
Competitive Analysis	When comparing the features and content of competitive sites, you can use personas as a means for structuring the comparison. A competitive analysis can describe how different sites address the needs of the same kinds of users.
Concept Model	Describing the underlying model for the concepts that form the foundation of the system, the concept model may not draw on the personas for requirements. On the other hand, the concept model needs to address all the content and features available in the system, and must therefore demonstrate that it can accommodate all user needs. Depending on its level of abstraction, the model may have greater or lesser direct relationship to the personas.
Content Inventory	Unlike the other two, this is not a high-level document. Tying to users may be unnecessary. On the other hand, relating content elements to use cases can be a better account of the effectiveness of the model.

Documents showing design

Personas are a great way to interject rationale into the design decisions captured in these documents, just as they are with strategy documents. With a persona, you have a set of requirements embodied in a single label, like Amanda or New Employee. If you've used personas throughout the life of a project, you can utter these names to any member of the team and instantly call up a set of needs and scenarios without having to describe them one by one.

In each of these deliverables, you can use persona names to show how particular design decisions support particular user needs. Even if you don't spell out the connection (and if your personas have become well entrenched you won't have to) by simply including the label near the relevant design element, you demonstrate that the user needs played a role in making that decision.

TABLE 2.6

Using Personas with Design Documents

Document	Relationship to Personas
Site Map	Show how different areas of the information structure cater to different user groups. Alternatively, correlate user needs with information areas by calling out needs instead of persona names.
Wireframes	Use the personas to put yourself in the user's shoes and react to the screen structure. Headshots of user personas with thought bubbles can show how different user groups might perceive and react to the content priorities on the screen.
Flowchart	Like site maps, flowcharts allow you to show how structural decisions directly support user needs. Alternatively, you can show how the user changes after going through the process.
Screen Designs	Personas can set up conversations about screen designs by reminding team members and stakeholders of the kinds of requirements that went into the design. You can include a persona summary page at the beginning of these presentations. (You did do a persona summary page, right?)

Figure 2.12 Put these guys on a wireframe and the project team can discuss how users from different groups might react to a particular screen.

The Big Picture: Why Personas Matter

Without personas, there is no common language for talking about what users want. Project participants with particular agendas may try to squeeze them into the design by saying things like, "Users really want to see..." or "This content is more important to users." They may even be able to rationalize it with some commonsense explanations, like "The pricing information is most important because users make decisions to buy based on price," or "Password requirements for user accounts should be very strict because our users want to protect their personal information." Without personas, you're likely to hear things like "If my mother came to the site, she would not understand any of the jargon."

All these are perfectly reasonable assumptions, but they are not based on research. It's easy to imagine competing explanations that are equally plausible. Conversations like these go nowhere and lead to designs no better than those conceived in a vacuum.

In creating personas, the design team creates a common language with which to talk about end users and what they need. They also give you an out: If team members start speculating about personas, you can stop the conversation, point to the personas, and refocus the conversation around what is known.

Vacuous claims about user needs can lead to scope creep. They can lengthen project timelines by encouraging development of features that are not supported by user needs. They can lead to unnecessary compromise.

Personas may be just a fad in the design industry. Like any good tool, they're the subject of a good deal of backlash, and everyone has an opinion about their utility. Though personas aren't rendered obsolete by new technologies, detractors see them as a hindrance to the design process, quashing momentum if there's no user research.

At the same time, some practitioners tell stories about organizations incorporating personas into all aspects of their business. The personas described in this chapter focus on system design, but with only a few tweaks could become a strategy tool for other uses. Like any tool, the adoption and use will be driven by the organization's willingness and your ability to create something that fills a real need.

Ultimately, the purpose of a persona is to help the design team make decisions about design. The persona takes as input observations about users and structures those observations in a meaningful way. Whether the organization of data is called a "persona" or not, without it the design team is working with a collection of observations out of context. They do not know whether some observations were limited to particular kinds of users, less important than others, or pure flukes.

By providing structure, we can identify priorities that facilitate decision making, not confine it. Constraints without structure are easier to ignore, because they're harder to incorporate into the decision-making process, and can lead to meaningless design.

CHAPTER THREE

Usability Test Plan

yū'-sǝ-bil'-a-tē test' plan' (n.)

The usability test plan describes the goals, method, and approach for a usability test. The test plan includes several different components, from profiles of participants to an outline of a discussion with users. The test plan described here incorporates test objective, test logistics, user profiles, and the script.

Usability testing is an essential part of the web design diet. In a nutshell, it's a technique for soliciting feedback on the design of a web site. Usability testing is usually conducted on one participant at a time, and attempts to have participants use the site in as close to a real-world setting as possible. Different people have different approaches to usability testing but two things remain consistent—the documents describing what you will do during the test (the plan) and what came out of the test (the results report). This chapter describes the test plan—the document you prepare in advance of testing—and the next chapter describes the report.

There are several aspects of a usability test that need planning, and some people give each its own document. Other usability researchers create a single test plan, addressing all aspects of the test in a single document. This chapter will treat usability test plans as single documents, but will indicate where you might split the document if you need to have several deliverables.

Test Plans at a Glance

Test plans contain three main types of content: the purpose of the test, the logistics and methodology, and the script.

Unlike some of the other documents in this book, the test plan is usually long because it needs to be explicit about your method and what you're going to ask participants.

Version History	1
Test Objectives—Why We're Testing	2
Logistics—Timing, Location, Participants	2
Test Script	3
Pre-Test and Follow-Up Questions	7

FIGURE 3.1 This table of contents for a simple test plan shows the high points: objectives, logistics, and essential scenarios. This plan may be appropriate for an informal test with a handful of users.

Version History	1
Overview	1
Test Objectives	2
Methodology	3
Overview of Scenarios	5
Testing Facilities and Schedule	5
User Profiles	6
Screener	7
Pre-Test Questions	8
Post-Test Questions	9
Scenarios and Tasks for User Group 1	10
Scenarios and Tasks for User Group 2	17

FIGURE 3.2 When usability tests become more complex, so, too, must their plans. This test plan has separate sections for facilities, methodology, and user profiles. It also distinguishes between user profiles—high-level descriptions of the target audience—and the screener, as well as from a series of questions for recruiting participants. Finally, this test plan also has two sets of scenarios, one for each group of users.

Test Plan Overview

Purpose—What are test plans for?

As much as we'd like to grab a few people off the street, sit them in front of our work, and shove a microphone into their faces, usability testing requires a little more planning. The purpose of the test plan document is to lay out the approach for a usability test. Test plans help set expectations for the kinds of feedback the design team will receive and help everyone agree on the aspects of the design that need testing. The test plan also prepares the team member who will be conducting the test, establishing a direction for his or her conversations with end users.

Audience—Who uses them?

Everyone on the team benefits from usability test plans. The person conducting the test gets the most benefit by far because the test plan will direct conversations with end users in a meaningful way. Even if you're not conducting the test yourself, your involvement in preparing the test plan will ensure that your concerns will be addressed during testing.

Scale—How much work are they?

The usability test plan is one of those documents that always takes longer than anticipated to prepare. You can put a simple one together in a couple of hours, but feedback from the team will inevitably identify additional concerns— everything from logistical problems to additional questions for users. Because usability testing directly involves customers, stakeholders usually want to get involved, which can extend the timeline for putting a plan together.

Context—Where do they fall in the process?

The real question here is when to do usability testing, and that can vary depending on your methodology. Most people save usability testing for the end of the project, or do it at strategic points throughout the design process. The bottom line: Whenever you schedule usability testing, you must allocate some time to put a plan together. Keep in mind that the organizational roadblocks to planning a test are significantly lower than those for conducting a test—the prospect of talking to customers can give some stakeholders cold feet—so it might be weeks or months between the planning and the doing.

Format—What do they look like?

For better or worse, the usability test plan hasn't evolved much in the last 10 years. Unless you're working with a particularly innovative team, you'll find that usability test plans are straight prose documents, usually prepared in a word processor.

Challenges

Though planning a usability test is fraught with challenges—logistical decisions, keeping the scope of the test in check, varying the script for different user groups—the main challenge with the test plan itself is creating a multipurpose document. This document will be used for discussing the plan with stakeholders and team members, and for conducting the actual test.

Perhaps the easiest way around this challenge is to prepare two separate documents—the test plan and the test script. Preparing two documents, however, comes with its own set of risks. Two documents means related content in two different places and two version histories to track. Perhaps these are trivial issues for you. Over the years, however, I've found it easier just to combine the documents.

Creating Test Plans

If you had to conduct a test tomorrow, there are three basic elements you'd need (beyond a group of users, a place to conduct the test, and—oh, yeah—a set of designs to test). The simplest test plan—described in the elements of layer 1—consists of a set of goals, a description of the logistics and method, and a set of questions to ask the participant. As stated, these are pretty broad categories, and therefore suitable for informal testing. The more formal the testing, the more details you'll need. Fleshing out the test script is described in layer 2. Further details around the logistics, described in layer 3, seem somewhat extraneous but your stakeholders may demand them.

Layer 1: When You Need to Test Tomorrow

The basic elements of a usability test answer three questions: What do we want out of this test, how will we conduct the test, and what will we ask users during the test? With those questions answered, you've got the barest information necessary to make a test happen.

Test objectives

In planning a test it's easy to let things get out of hand. Without any direction, you'll find yourself asking users questions of increasing irrelevance. Explicitly stating a direction in the test plan, as in other documents, allows you to keep the design of the test on track. The script should be derived from the objectives and everything you ask the user should take you closer to meeting your objectives.

Unfortunately, people designing usability tests frequently gloss over this part because (1) it's hard, and (2) they want to dig into the script. Consider this: Your script is meaningless unless it is working toward a specific purpose.

Because the test objectives drive the discussion between the test facilitator and participant, you can make them pretty specific. Too often, the test objective looks something like this:

```
To determine whether our web site is easy to use.
```

You'll forgive me if I refer you to the Wikipedia entry on "duh." You can use a simple strategy to make your objectives more specific—think about why people are coming to your site. (If you created the personas described in the previous chapter, this should be easy.) By basing test objectives on user motivations, you get objectives that look more like these examples for a fictitious health encyclopedia:

```
To determine whether people who come to the site with a spe-
cific illness in mind are satisfied with how they located
relevant information.
```

```
To determine whether people who are doing research on behalf
of another person can easily refer someone else to the infor-
mation they find.
```

```
To understand how people who have just been diagnosed with an
illness want to revisit their research.
```

These objectives may be used together—nothing says your test must have only one objective. Once you've written up a couple, you can do a quick litmus test. If you state the objective in the form of a question, is it an answerable question? To take the first (bad) example, the test designers could ask themselves "Is this site easy to use?" which would not be an easy question to answer. On the other hand, you could probably easily answer the question "Are people who have a specific illness in mind satisfied with how they found relevant information?"

Test logistics

Your plan needs to describe the who-what-when-where-how of the test, if for no other reason than to make sure you've thought of everything you need before recruiting and scheduling participants. Even the most basic tests have lots of questions that need answering: Where will you be conducting the test? How many people do you need to recruit? When will the tests take place? Who from your team is involved? What roles will people play? The list goes on. The more you have planned out, the less you have to worry about when the test happens.

For stakeholders and team members who have never participated in a usability test (or at least one organized by you) the test plan gives a good picture of what's going to happen. The logistics section is also a good place to describe a high-level agenda for the test itself—sort of an outline of the test script. If each participant is scheduled for an hour, you can describe how you break up that hour.

Another topic you might cover in the logistics section is methodology. There are several different kinds of usability testing methods, and this section is your opportunity to define and defend the one you've chosen.

Finally, your stakeholders may want to know what happens after the test, in which case you can include a description of the type of analysis you will do. Another approach is to describe the outputs—the documents and artifacts that are by-products of the test. For an informal test your outputs may be the raw notes and a short report. For more formal tests you may have additional outputs, like audio and video recordings, or more detailed reports, like an observations report and a recommendations report.

Test scenarios

Test scenarios run from the general to the specific. For example, in some cases your scenarios may be as straightforward as "present screen to user and ask for impressions." In other cases, you may want to ask the participant to imagine himself in a specific situation and use the web site to address the situation: "You have just come down with the flu and you want to see if any of your symptoms put you at high risk."

The list of these scenarios forms the test script. Layer 2 describes a more detailed test script, but at the basic level the purpose is to give an impression of what the facilitator will ask the user to do.

Layer 2: Further Background

If you've got a little more time to put into planning, there's plenty more detail you can add to provide a clearer picture of what the testing is for and what you'll do during the test.

User profiles and screener

Although the logistics element from layer 1 should reference the kinds of people you'd like to recruit, you can always provide more detail. The more complex the test, the more detail you'll want to give because you may be testing different user groups. Defining profiles for each group allows you to effectively design an appropriate test for each group. If you've done user personas (described in the previous chapter) you can draw straight from those. Here's a user profile for a parenting web site:

```
The Day Job Parent needs to work outside the home. He sees
his kids in the morning, maybe drops them off at the bus
stop, and then sees them again in the evening, when he comes
home from work. The Day Job Parent may steal a glance at this
web site during a lunch break, seeking advice on specific
child-rearing problems. He may spend a bit more time on the
site in the evening after the kids are in bed. In the Day Job
Parent's house, both spouses work. They are both familiar
with Internet technologies, and have shopped and researched
health issues online.
```

High-level descriptions of users are one thing, but actually finding people who meet those criteria is another. If your test is formal—that is, you're recruiting a large number of people outside your immediate user group—you need to put together a screener. A screener is a set of questions to ask potential participants to see if they fit your needs for the usability test.

Some screener questions are pretty straightforward, asking about experience with using the Internet or shopping online. Some will be more specific to your particular application. For example, for the fictitious online health encyclopedia, your screener might seek out people who have recently been to the doctor, or who visited a health site in the last three months. Such questions will help narrow the pool of applicants to those who best match your target user group.

Usually, recruiting from the general public is done by a recruiting agency. They have a large list of people to draw from. If you're using an outside agency, you'll need to provide as much detail in the screener as possible. Indicate when a particular answer to a question should eliminate a potential participant. Indicate quotas for particular answers. You may want, for example, half your participants to have visited a health site in the last three months, and half to never have visited a health site. Recruiting methodologies aside, you need to communicate the makeup of your ideal group of participants to the recruiter. A screener is the best way to do this.

How long have you been using the Internet? (Less than 3 years, abort screen.)

When was the last time you made a purchase online? (More than 1 year, abort screen.)

In your household, do both parents hold jobs outside the home? (Need 4 respondents for each "yes" and "no" answer.)

In your household, what is the age of the oldest child? (Need 4 respondents for less than 10 years old and 4 respondents for greater than 10 years old.)

Figure 3.3 In this excerpt from a screener for a web site on parenting, the usability test needs advanced Internet users only. The group of participants will vary by the age of their children, and whether both parents work or not.

Pre-test and post-test questions

Usability testing best practices suggest that you ask users questions before and after the actual test. At the beginning of the test, before showing participants any screens or prototypes, you can establish their expectations with respect to the web site and their general level of experience. You can clarify their motivations for using your site and flesh out your profile of them.

The format for these questions will vary depending on your methodology. Some usability testers ask the questions of the user in person, recording their answers by hand. Others give participants a questionnaire that they can answer separately. (This approach allows the facilitator to spend less time with each participant.) If you decide to let participants answer the questions on their own, you may want to separate these questions into a different document because it will be something you hand to them. In that case, you may need to format it differently, and—if the participant is to answer the questions without intervention from the facilitator—you'll certainly want to be explicit about directions.

Pre-test questions can help you get a handle on the user's expectations and experience before seeing the site for the first time. Questions after the test can gauge overall impressions and allow general pain points and suggestions to surface. Formatting for pre-test and post-test questions can include open-ended questions and questions with predefined responses.

Examples of open-ended questions:

```
We're developing a new system to support your sales process.
What are the most challenging tasks in the sales process
for you?
```

```
The web site we're building is called FluffyPuppies.com. What
do you think you'd find on this web site?
```

```
What system do you currently use to manage your family
videos?
```

Examples of questions with predefined responses:

```
On a scale of 1 to 7, where 1 is strongly disagree and 7 is
strongly agree, how would you rate this statement: I found
the web site easy to use.
```

```
What level of Internet user are you? Beginner, Intermediate,
Advanced
```

```
How long have you been involved with the sales process?
```

Regardless of how you deliver the questions to the participants, you should write the questions exactly as you intend to ask them. This can help ensure that you ask the question the same way every time.

The script

Layer 1 calls for defining the scenarios for the usability test, though it leaves the format pretty open. For the second layer, you can add more detail, depending on the complexity of the test. You can look at the script as a hierarchy of information. At the highest level are the scenarios, which re-create situations in which participants might actually use the product. Each scenario includes a series of tasks, and each task describes what will be read to the participant and the background material for the facilitator. The task or scenario may also include specific follow-up questions and notes to the people developing the prototype.

Scenario: User Researching Medical Issues at Lunch Hour

Over the weekend, you spoke to a friend of yours who indicated he had been diagnosed with diabetes. On Monday, you decide you want to learn more about what your friend is going through, so you spend some time during your lunch hour researching it. Since you don't have much time, you won't read everything you find, but you know you'll want to go back to it later.

Task 1: Find Information about Diabetes

You decide that you're specifically interested in learning more about various causes for diabetes.

Expected actions:

1. *From home page, click on "Diseases and Conditions"*
2. *Click on "Endocrine Conditions"*
3. *Click on "Diabetes"*
4. *Click on "Symptoms and Causes"*

Follow-up Questions

1. *Were you able to find information about Diabetes where you expected?*
2. *What other information would you expect to see on the Diabetes page?*

Task 2: Store Information in Personal Library

Since you won't have time to review everything you find, you want to save it for later.

Expected actions:

1. *Click article of interest*
2. *Click "Save for Later"*
3. *In dialog box, enter name for "Saved Articles List"*

Follow-Up Questions

1. *Under what circumstances would you use the built-in "Save for Later" feature?*
2. *How would you normally store a link to review it later?*

FIGURE 3.4 This excerpt from a usability test plan shows each element of the test script. Each part is formatted to make it distinct from the others. Facilitators need to know at a glance what should be read aloud to the user and what is instructional for them.

Layer 3: Adding Further Detail

You may have seen tests that go into even more detail than described in the first two layers. In some cases, this information is important because it reflects a larger-scale test. In other cases, the value of this information is measured only by your team's and client's need to have it spelled out.

Background

Your test plan can provide an overview of the project and the product being tested. The background describes the purpose of the product and offers a high-level business case for it. This section of the test plan can be used to rationalize the testing, or describe the design process to date. There are two main purposes to this content: First, it makes the plan internally comprehensive, a stand-alone document. Second, background information helps make stakeholders who care about this sort of thing more comfortable with usability testing. If you don't have a need for either of these, the background section may not be essential to conducting a good usability test.

Functional details

If you are testing a prototype of the site you may need to provide instruction to the facilitator that describes how it should behave during the test. Prototypes are notorious for being hopelessly incomplete at the time of testing and the facilitator can easily misstep if not adequately prepared. In a test plan, the functional details should be embedded in the script adjacent to the relevant scenarios. Figure 3.4 shows how functional details might be embedded with the rest of the script.

For example, in running a test on an internal web application designed to support a specific business process, the facilitator will need some direction about how the application is supposed to behave. For a scenario where the user needs to check on incoming responses from users, the test plan might include directions like: "The user must click the checkboxes next to the incoming responses before clicking 'Export to Text File'. Clicking this button before selecting responses will lead to an error."

Expected behaviors

In addition to functional details, the script may also include notes to the facilitator describing the expected response from the participant. This helps the facilitator gauge whether the participant is going in the right direction. Depending on your methodology, you may want the facilitator to steer participants right if they stray too far off course.

Of course, expected behaviors should appear adjacent to the relevant scenarios. At the same time, they should be formatted to distinguish them from the part that gets read aloud to the participant. (Giving them the answer during the course of the test just wouldn't be fair, would it?) Depending on the facilitator's comfort level with the prototype, you may need to be very explicit about the expected behaviors.

TABLE 3.1

Comparing Explicit and Non-Explicit Expected Behaviors

Explicit	Non-Explicit
User clicks checkbox next to responses	After users select responses, they should click Export to Text File and select the Attachments option. User clicks "Export to Text File" Export options dialog box appears User clicks checkbox for "Export with Attachments" User clicks button "Export" Browser window appears with text file

Preparing a Test Plan: The Basics

In simplest terms, the function of a test plan is to tell people what to do in anticipation of and during a usability test. It is a set of instructions, grounded in project-specific objectives. Like any document in this book, the test plan will be shaped by a situation analysis—an assessment of the purpose, timing, and audience for the document.

The why and when of usability testing

For most other documents in this book, the situation analysis calls for assessing the purpose of the document itself. In this case, the question isn't "Why should I do a test plan?" as it might be with wireframes or personas. Instead, the more relevant question is "Why should I do usability testing at all?" because if you're doing a usability test, you need to do a test plan. Like any good business meeting, you need to go in prepared, and a test plan gives you that preparation.

Still, the answer to that question—"Why do usability testing?"—will define the content of the test plan. Usability testing is an essential component of design, but it can't be done for the sake of itself. To understand how the purpose of the test affects the content of the test plan, we need to look at the two main kinds of testing: formative and summative. Formative tests take place during the design process, allowing the design team to do research on early versions of a design as it's taking shape. Summative tests occur at the end of the design process, with a more or less final product.

Plans for formative tests: You'll find that most formative testing is to assess the usability of a specific part of a web site—the home page and high-level pages, the checkout process, or the navigation labeling. The test plan needs to recognize that participants will only experience part of the entire interface. It may be more rigidly scripted to focus on specific issues and avoid users' missteps into unfinished parts of the interface.

Plans for summative tests: When conducted with a final product, usability testing can be more open ended. Rather than identifying particular tasks, your script may focus more on the post-test questions to glean the participant's opinion of the product.

Adjusting the test plan for your audience

The two main audiences for usability test plans are the project stakeholders and the test facilitator—the person doing most of the orchestration during the test. There may be other players in the test—people taking notes, people managing the facility, people working the recording equipment—or there may be one person who does it all. The facilitator may be someone on your team (i.e., you) or it may be a contractor or freelancer you've hired for this purpose. In the latter case, the script needs to be as specific as possible.

Frankly, even if you're doing the test yourself, making the script specific can be very helpful. During the test you'll be thinking about so many things at the same time—what the participant is doing right then, whether the recording devices are working, what will happen when the user clicks a button or link—that you won't want to have to worry about what to do next.

A specific script is also useful for stakeholders. By being explicit about what the facilitator will say to the participants, the script can help set the stakeholders' expectations, especially if they've never been involved with usability testing.

If the facilitator is outside your project team—a contractor you brought in just for tests, for example—your test plan may need to be explicit in other areas as well, like the purpose of the test, the test procedure, and the project background. It's easy to take this information for granted when you're working with the same set of people throughout the process. But for a new or unfamiliar team, a fully fleshed-out test plan can help build a common understanding of the project, the methodology, and how they fit together.

Making test plans unboring

The situation analysis—understanding the who, when, and why of usability testing—helps define the contents of the test, providing direction for what kinds of information you need to provide and how much detail to give. With these decisions made, you'll need to think about how to format the document itself. Although this isn't a document heavy on the visuals, there are still several considerations for formatting.

Prose or bullets: Items like test objectives, background, and method can be described in straight paragraphs or through bullet points. The decision is more than aesthetic. The primary consideration is your audience, since you can communicate the same message with either bullets or prose. Bullets will be more effective if you do not need to go into a lot of detail. The objectives for the imaginary test at the beginning of this chapter might be rendered in prose like this:

Users researching health information online are a committed and persistent audience. Despite their keen interest—or maybe because of it—they are especially picky about the web sites they'll use to find information. A web site should not just have the most up-to-date information. It needs to be easy to find, written well, and in a format that gives users lots of flexibility in how they use it. The purpose of this usability test is to see how well our site lives up to the expectations of our users, by putting potential users in mock scenarios and observing the effectiveness of the web site design.

Specifically, we want to learn whether people with a specific illness can quickly find useful information. They should be able to locate it quickly and it should be compelling enough

to make them want to stick around. This test will also measure whether the site makes it easy to refer other people to
information—our users typically are doing research on someone else's behalf. Finally, we recognize that our users don't
come to the site once. They return again and again to learn
more or to focus on a new aspect of their condition. This
test will identify how the design can be improved to more
effectively meet this need.

Distinguishing "say aloud" from instruction: There are two types of
information in the script—things to expose to the participant and things that
give the facilitator background on a particular task or scenario. In some cases,
the facilitator needs to read things out loud to the participant; in others, the
participant must read to him- or herself. Figure 3.4 illustrates all the different
parts of a usability script.

Making Test Plans Airtight

Here are a couple tips for making sure you cross all the t's and dot all the i's in
your test plan. The best strategy, however, is not in document preparation, but
in the planning itself. If you've made your testing methodology airtight, your
test plan will follow.

Save the script for last

Before digging into the script details, you should make sure the test's objectives
and logistics are more or less nailed down. By saving detailed script development until after these other pieces are in place, you ensure that your work on
the script is compatible with the test objectives and with the methodology. For
example, if you're conducting a test on a semifunctional prototype, that may
limit the number and type of questions you'll ask participants. If you do not
have the time, budget, or personnel to develop the prototype further, those facts
will establish boundaries for the tasks participants can perform.

Format the document appropriately

Consider how the facilitator will use the actual document during the test. Even
if the sessions are being recorded, for example, the facilitator may want to take
notes on the script itself. Different facilitators have different preferences, so ask
yours what he or she wants. (If you are the facilitator, make sure no one catches
you talking to yourself.) A document designed to be a note-taking tool will

look different than one that's simply a series of prompts. If the test includes pre- and post-test questions for participants to answer on their own, perhaps these can appear on separate pages so they can be easily removed and distributed.

Risks in Creating Test Plans

When putting your test plan together, you may run into a couple different obstacles. Realizing these shortcomings during the test itself is way too late, so you'll want to diagnose and mitigate these risks as early as possible.

Incomplete script

A script can be incomplete for any number of reasons: The read-aloud part does not adequately describe the scenario, the expected behaviors aren't explicit, there are crucial scenarios missing. The single best remedy for these problems is to conduct a dry run, which takes the usability test out of the abstract and into the real. Anything missing from the plan appears quite starkly when in the thick of a test. If you don't have time to test the test, as it were, you can also cross reference the script with the user profiles to identify potential holes in the scenarios. You can do a cheap version of the dry run by reading the scenarios aloud to colleagues and seeing if they understand them. A set of expected behaviors is simply a set of instructions for doing a particular activity on the web site. Hand someone the list of expected behaviors for a scenario and see if they can follow it to the goal. These are low-impact ways to diagnose potential holes in the script.

Document unusable for testing

It's one thing to review a test plan in a meeting and quite another to bring it into a testing situation. The content of the document may work, but the formatting may not be appropriate for use during an actual test. Again, the best way to mitigate this risk is to do a dry run of the test. By putting everyone (the facilitators and note-takers) and everything (the web site or prototype and the test plan) through its paces, you can establish whether the document format is suitable.

Presenting Test Plans

In a sense, the usability test itself is a presentation of the test plan. The test plan is the agenda for the facilitator's meeting with the participant. But this is not the kind of presentation we're talking about here. Instead, this section will provide strategies for preparing and doing presentations with the test plan as a deliverable, as work product. Like any documentation review, the structure and agenda for the meeting should be driven by the meeting's purpose.

Meeting Purpose

There are a few main reasons to review a test plan with the project team and stakeholders. In a high-level meeting, your aim is to get buy-in for the overall approach, while at the other end of the spectrum, you may want to do a dry run of the usability test, digging into every detail.

Securing buy-in

If your stakeholders do not have much experience with usability testing, you may need to stage a buy-in meeting to review the overall process with them. You could hold a session that provides an introduction to usability testing in general, but this won't be as meaningful to stakeholders as a test plan that deals with their particular product. In this kind of meeting, you must go through every aspect of the plan, but you do not need to go into a great level of detail on the script. Instead, spend even amounts of time on the objectives, the methodology, and the script.

Soliciting input

Once your stakeholders are comfortable with the idea of usability testing and the approach you're taking, you can solicit input on the script. There are two kinds of input you need. First, you need to know if your range of scenarios covers every possible use of the system. Second, you need to know what to get out of each scenario. If you're already familiar with the system, you should be able to do most of this yourself, but the stakeholders may have some input.

Testing the test

The best way to get input on a test plan is to do a mock test, running through each step of your plan with a participant who might be another member of the team not directly involved with the design. Doing a dry run of the test is a good way to ensure that the scenarios aren't too goofy and that you can do everything you need to in the given amount of time. A dry run can uncover potential logistical issues—for example, transitioning from one scenario to the next—or identify major holes in the script where scenarios or instructions for the facilitator should be.

Meeting Structure

A test plan isn't a hard story to tell, especially if the project team has bought into the idea of usability testing. While other documents in this book lend themselves to different meeting structures, the only decision you'll need to make for a usability test plan is how much time to spend on each section.

If you have only one meeting to review a test plan, make sure you cover each part—don't leave anything out—but you don't need to go into great detail on the logistics and methodology. If your stakeholders aren't big "detail people" you can also just hit the high points of the script, describing what scenarios you're testing and how those correspond to the different functions or areas of the web site.

Effective presentation of the test script

If you've provided a lot of information in your test script, as in Figure 3.4, you need to decide how you will go through all the details during your review meeting. For the majority of reviews, describing the scenario and stating what will be read to the user may be sufficient. In these cases, you can gloss over the other information. If the scenario is especially complex, you may want to go through every detail. Additionally, if you're meeting with developers who will be building the product to test, you may want to spend more time on the expected product behavior—what the web site does in response to user actions.

Presentation Risks

Regardless of which method you choose to present the script, you may find that the meeting starts to get out of hand. Specifically, you may find your pristine usability test suddenly soiled by competing agendas—stakeholders or team members may want to add pointless and out-of-scope questions and tasks to the test. You may also find the review of the test derailed by questions about usability testing in general, or your methods.

Scope creep: Losing sight of objectives

When presented with the opportunity to talk to actual end users, some stakeholders and team members are like kids in a candy store. They may start suggesting questions and tasks—reasonable though they might be—that are outside the scope of the test. Some stakeholders may use the post-test questionnaire, for example, to solicit feedback about other areas of their business. When this happens, the stakeholders need a reminder about the purpose of the test.

The flip side of this coin is that the suggested questions and modifications may fall within the scope of your script, but the script has become so long that there's no way to get through it all in the time allotted. This is a good indication that your objectives are not specific enough—they're not serving as an effective filter to keep the test focused.

Usability newbies

Inevitably, you'll be presenting your test plan to a roomful of stakeholders, one or two of whom aren't familiar with usability testing. They may start questioning the purpose of the exercise, or worse, your methodology (see below). If your discussion is derailed by these kinds of questions, you should whip out your usability testing elevator pitch—the three-sentence description that at once gives an overview of usability while shutting down this line of questioning. Don't have a usability elevator pitch? This is your reminder to come up with one, or just use this one, free of charge:

```
Usability testing is a means for us to gather feedback on
the design of the system in the context of specific real-
world tasks. By asking users to use the system (or a reason-
able facsimile) we can observe opportunities to improve the
design, catching them at this stage of the design process
rather than later when changes would be more costly. Usabil-
ity testing has been built into the project plan since day
one. We need to get through the plan because we have users
scheduled to come in next week, but if you want to talk fur-
ther about usability testing, we can discuss it after the
meeting.
```

Feel free to modify this to suit your needs. The message is clear: I want to help you understand usability testing, but now's not the time.

Methodological questions

Usability testing has been a popular technique for web designers for years, and yet we're still called upon to justify our methods. You may get questions about the kinds of data you're gathering or the number of participants, the length of the interview, or the format for follow-up questions. This is another opportunity to prepare three or four sentences on methodology, but you may have to have several prepared responses in anticipation of different kinds of questions. You know your stakeholders best, so confer with your team before speaking to the client, and brainstorm possible objections to the methodology.

Test Plans in Context

Using a Test Plan with Other Documents

Usability testing is often treated like a self-contained activity, despite its impact on many other design activities. The test plan itself, as a foundation for testing, may seem detached from other documents, but you'll need to think about the far-reaching implications of your test, and how the test plan can anticipate those implications.

Test plans and other user-needs documents

User-needs documentation—at least in the context of this book—is any documentation that contributes to or comes from research into your target audiences. The test plan is a keystone in design methods because it is the mechanism for testing hypotheses, the means for answering the basic question, "Does this work?"

There are two other user-needs documents described in this book—personas, profiles describing the target audiences, and usability test results reports, which document what happened during the usability test. These are appropriate book-ends for the test plan.

User Personas and Test Plans: User personas—the profiles of your target user groups—help you set up the test plan in two ways. From a very practical point of view, the personas tell you whom you must recruit to participate in the usability tests. The descriptions can form the foundation of your screener. Personas can also help structure the scenarios used in the test. Remember: The purpose of a usability test is to see how well a site design supports user needs. The scenarios in your test should be driven by what's documented in the personas, not in the site's functional requirements. One of the examples earlier in this chapter described a user group for a parenting web site, the Day Job Parent. This was drawn from (in our imaginary example) the personas created for the project. The script for the test would include scenarios that such a user might encounter:

```
Scenario 1: Quick Look-Up at Work. On your commute to work,
you recall a conversation you and your spouse had last night
about your daughter. You'd talked about how her grades had
been slipping at school. You decide to take a moment on your
lunch break to investigate possible causes.

Scenario 2: In-Depth Research at Night. After the kids have
gone to bed, you and your spouse get together at the com-
puter so you can share your research from earlier in the day.
You're hoping to get further information about some of the
causes you identified.
```

Test Results and Test Plans: The yang to the yin of the test plan, test results document the observations and conclusions from the test itself. Without test results, there's no point to the test plan, and without a test plan, you'll never get useful results. There are some direct parallels between the plan and the results: The objectives will hopefully not change, though you may have to adjust the method during the course of the test. The test results should build from the same objectives and account for any methodological changes. At the same time, when it comes to the script there may not be a direct correlation between the plan and the results report because your observations during the test may need analysis and interpretation that takes them outside the scenarios defined in the plan.

Test plans and strategy documents

Strategy documents capture essential information for the design process, but do not describe the design itself. This book describes three strategy documents—the competitive analysis, the concept model, and the content model—and anyone would be hard pressed to find direct relationships between a test plan and these documents. This isn't to say that usability testing isn't strategic, just that the kinds of things in the test plan aren't driven by the contents of any of these strategy documents. Even the test objectives, which might seem the most strategic, should focus on what you want to get out of the test, not goals for the entire project.

Test plans and design documents

The purpose of design documents is to capture ideas for the design of the web site. Documents like site maps or wireframes show different aspects of the web site's design from the user's perspective. Their relationship to the test results is obvious—the observations made during the usability test will strongly influence the design of the web site. The relationship between a test plan and design documents is a little more complicated because the design documents may be the things that are being tested.

Some design teams, if they don't have a working web site, will put design documents in front of users to gauge their reaction. The thinking here is that testing a representation of the final product is the next best thing to testing the product itself. If you employ a similar method, the test plan needs to be tied closely with the design documents to describe what kinds of questions you'll ask users. You might, for example, put a site map in front of someone and ask him or her to navigate to a particular section. In testing the screen design for a homepage, you might ask what features jump out at first glance. Wireframes documenting a checkout process can be an effective tool for testing the overall flow of the interface. Using paper to do usability testing is another science (or art form) entirely and may require supplementing the test script to provide further direction to the facilitator. There are a handful of books on this subject, including the widely cited *Paper Prototyping: The Fast and Easy Way to Design and Refine User Interfaces*, by Carolyn Snyder. In lieu of a working web site or prototype to test, design documents are the next best thing for soliciting feedback from end users. Compared to a full-fledged web site, building design documentation is quick and easy, which means that site maps and wireframes can increase the amount of audience participation in the design process. On the other hand, it can make the test planning process more complex.

The Future of Usability Testing

The test plan is a stand-in for the test itself, a representation of the test without being the test. So, when we talk about why test plans are important we're really talking about whether usability testing itself is important. (The sheer audacity and recklessness of wondering whether you can do a test without any planning makes that scenario impossible to consider.)

Can we imagine a design process that doesn't include any sort of testing? Will the backlash against the usability gurus be so great that designers begin to wonder why they ever bothered with testing at all? For many a designer, a world without usability testing may seem like a world without constraints, a world that thrives on innovation and creativity without compromise. In this world, of course, the designer rules.

But design is creativity with a purpose. By its very nature, it's not arbitrary or detached from a host of criteria. A good design meets a need, and does so better than any other product that's tried to fill that need. A good design fits effortlessly into those criteria without calling too much attention to itself (unless that's what the design is supposed to do). But knowing your constraints and designing to your constraints are two different things. The design process is, out of necessity, a dance between what could be and what must be.

For the web, this means putting designs in front of the people who will be using the site and checking that the design does what it needs to do. The gold mine is innovation inside the context of use, finding a novel way of doing something that immediately clicks with users. The crowning achievement of a design is the exclamation of an enthused user: "This is awesome!" (The exact exclamation will depend on your target demographic.) Without usability testing, however, we designers would never have occasion to hear these outbursts of joy that come from using a well-designed site.

CHAPTER FOUR

Usability Reports

yū'-sə-bil'-a-tē rē-pŏrts' (n.)

The usability report is the outcome of a usability test, whose results are compiled into an actionable format.

Usability testing documentation doesn't end with the plan. You've got more to do. Once you've conducted the test, you need to report on your results. The usability report accounts for what happened during the test, and is a tool for guiding the design team.

Since you can test just about anything, the report needs to reflect the circumstances of the test and the scope of its results. Testing the existing web site as a precursor to redesigning it does not immediately yield results on what should or should be done in the new design. Likewise, results from prototype testing do not immediately imply how to change the prototype to meet user needs. These tests simply report that a problem exists and the nature of that problem, not necessarily how to fix it. This isn't to say that usability testing does not add value to the design process. The point is that the report needs to be very clear about the implications of the results in the context of the test and the overall project.

Different design teams have different conceptions of the role of the usability analyst. Some teams ask their usability person to perform tests and report on what the users thought. Others ask usability people to play an active role in the design process, making design recommendations based on their observations during the test. This chapter assumes that there's a clear delineation between the observations made during a usability test and the interpretation and analysis of those results, regardless of who's responsible.

Usability Reports at a Glance

The main purpose of a usability report is to communicate the responses made by users over the course of the usability test. The bulk of the report, therefore, is observations, but a report also will include a summary of the test plan and the outcomes of the test.

Version History	1
Test Summary—What we did and why	2
Test Logistics—Where and when the test happened	3
Test participant profiles	4
Summary of observations—what we saw	5
General observations	6
Home page observations	7
Category page observations	9
Product page observations	10
Search results observations	12
Recommendations	13
Next steps	14

Figure 4.1 This table of contents shows the basic elements for a usability report. Though the observations are summarized at the beginning of the report, the bulk of the document is dedicated to providing a detailed account of what happened during the test.

Usability Reports Overview

Purpose—What are usability reports for?

A series of usability tests yields hours and hours of data—actual users talking about their experience with your product. Since not everyone has the time to sit through all these tests, the usability test report is meant to highlight the main findings.

Audience—Who uses them?

The usability test report is a widely read document because everyone wants to know what users think. The design team, however, gets the most value out of the report because it contains information that directly contributes to their design work.

Scale—How much work are they?

The size of a report depends entirely on your usability testing methodology. There are some factors that can increase the scale of report preparation, including the use of quantitative measures (like the amount of time it takes to complete a task), the number of tests, the number of different user groups (testing ten users is different from testing five users in two different groups), and the amount of information collected before and after the actual test. Some stakeholders may demand two versions of the report: one version produced quickly to capture the essential observations and allow the design team to move forward without much delay, and a second, more in-depth report.

Context—Where do they fall in the process?

There's not a lot of wiggle-room here. If you've conducted a test, a report inevitably follows. See the previous chapter for a discussion of when to conduct tests.

Format—What do they look like?

Usability reports come in all shapes and sizes. Some teams are comfortable presenting them as large written documents while others use a slideshow approach. The main advantage to creating a slide show with Microsoft PowerPoint or Apple's Keynote is that these applications allow you to mix text and images very easily. When presenting results from the usability test, lining up screenshots and other tools from the test with the observations from the user can be very powerful.

Challenges

Preparing a usability report entails three main challenges and the most serious of these is accessibility. As usability testing and analysis seeks to establish itself as a science, its reports tend to become mired in technical jargon and complex explanations. Unfortunately, the reports themselves become unusable, an ironic twist that's only funny if you're not the one paying for the report.

With the challenge of accessibility comes the delicate balance between being comprehensive and being clear. The more detail you include, the more you need to explain, and the more difficult it is to craft an accessible and understandable report. At the same time, you don't want to generalize too much because that can encourage your audience to have a skewed view of what actually happened during the test.

This points to the third major challenge of creating usability reports: distinguishing between observations and recommendations. Throughout this chapter, "observations" will serve as the building blocks of the usability report. When you're conducting a usability test and you identify an issue, this counts as an observation. The purpose of the report is to give an account of everything you observed. Attempts to explain why usability participants behaved in a specific way during the test are interpretations (or explanations). Besides observations and interpretations, there are recommendations and suggested fixes for problems observed during the test. Because the lines between these concepts can be blurry, the challenge is to make the distinctions clear. You want to avoid stakeholders and other team members mistaking something the user did in the course of the test with an idea you have to improve the design.

Creating Usability Reports

Like every other deliverable in this book, the usability report is described here as a series of layers, with the first layer being the essential elements—the parts of the document that make it what it is. A usability report hinges on the observations—the issues and problems you noticed during the course of the test—that make up the bulk of the first layer. The second and third layers add context and give you the chance to expand on the details of the observations.

Layer 1: For the Itchy Designer

If you need to get a report out quickly because your designers are eager to dig into the design, you can put a document together with these essential elements. The first layer focuses on answering three basic questions: What did you do? What did you see? And what do we do next?

Test summary

To address the first of these questions, the first couple of pages of your report should recap the test objectives, logistics, and methodology. Unless you're a stickler for details, a handful of bullets for each should do the trick: Remember, you've already sold the usability test, so the key here is to remind readers what you did and why you did it.

Basic observations

The next question to answer is "What happened?" Answering this question means recounting everything you saw and heard during the usability test, but since the report is meant to be a step or two up from a mere transcript, the observations show a bit of analysis. Your observations are a generalization of patterns you saw emerge during the test. For example, regarding a donation form on a nonprofit site, you might get the following responses from the four different users:

```
Sam: [After filling out the form, Sam scrolled down to
continue. It took him a few seconds to find the submit
button, and he moved the mouse around in circles before
landing
on it.]

Jim: So… I filled out the form, now what? Do I just push
return? [The facilitator asks Jim where he would usually find a
button to submit the form.] It's usually at the bottom of these
things… Oh, wait, I just scrolled and there it is.

Ella: [After filling out the form, Ella scrolls down and clicks
the submit button.]

Barbara: [Before filling out the form, Barbara scrolls down the
length of the page. The facilitator asks about this behavior.]
```

```
I dunno. Whenever there's a form to fill out, I scroll all
the way just to see what kinds of things they ask me for.
[The facilitator asks why.] Well, sometimes I want to make
sure they're not asking for information I don't want to give.
[Barbara fills out the form.] You know, I know there's a submit
button down there because I scrolled before, but it's kinda
hard to see.
```

These (admittedly loaded) responses might be summarized into this observation:

```
The donation form's submit button appears below the fold on
screen resolutions of 1024 x 768 and smaller. Its size and
position can make it difficult to see.
```

Clearly, the original responses have lots more detail. Depending on the format of your report, you can include these details, but boiling the responses down to a pattern keeps your report concise and actionable for the design team. If they need more detail, you can provide the raw data or recordings from the sessions.

If a problem is not so clear-cut, your description of the observation needs to hedge a bit, or qualify it. This is discussed further below.

A little context

Even the most basic usability report should provide some context for the observations. A list of observations may be comprehensive, but it won't be easy to follow.

The best way to provide context for the observations is to show the relevant screen. You can line up the observations next to the screen.

But even a screenshot isn't enough. There may be specific circumstances surrounding the particular screen that you need to differentiate between. For example, you may have tested several different user groups or used the same web page in several different tasks. A web site can contain pages that look similar and so require a little differentiation. A simple header is usually sufficient to draw a boundary around the context.

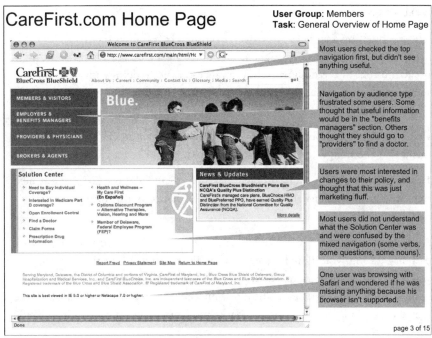

FIGURE 4.2 This page from a basic usability report lines observations up next to the relevant screens. The page includes a header to spell out the exact page and any other contextual information. In this case, the report is organized by screen, so the header includes the name of the screen.

This chapter assumes you'll be producing a document that combines images of the site with your observations, but this isn't absolutely necessary. If you had to, you could put together a spreadsheet with all the observations. In addition to the observation, each row in the spreadsheet could include contextual information, like the name of the relevant screen, its position in your site map or user flow, the name of the user group, and the task.

A	B	C
Home Page		
General Overview	Members	Most users checked the top navigation first but didn't see anything useful.
General Overview	Members	Users were most interested in changes to their policy and thought that News and Updates was just marketing fluff.
General Overview	Members	One user was browsing with Safari and wondered if he was missing anything because of using an unsupported browser.

FIGURE 4.3 Although it's best to show observations side-by-side with screenshots, this could do in a pinch. Note that this format preserves context by including relevant information in additional columns.

Next steps

The last question you need to answer, even in a bare-bones report, is "What now?" Though the answer might seem obvious—the design team takes this input and revises the designs—circumstances or methodology may call for something more subtle. Different teams work differently, but here are a couple ideas for what you might include in your next steps.

Priority: If some problems emerged as more dire than others, you can recommend that the design team focus on these first.

Brainstorming: Not every problem has a clear-cut solution, and so your next steps might recommend that the team get together to brainstorm potential design ideas.

Additional Testing: Unless your client is very much onboard with regular usability testing, you should recommend additional testing. At the very least, you'll want to test the incremental design changes. Until testing becomes entrenched in the corporate culture of your client, it is your duty as a user experience professional to push this agenda. (And, hey, the worst they can say is no.)

Layer 2: A Friendlier Document

The bare-bones report is fine if you're just working with the design team to take their work to the next level. Creating a client- or management-friendly report, however, is another story. (If you've got the kind of client who doesn't mind a quick and dirty report, count your blessings. At the same time, you should also be thinking about how every document you make contributes to your portfolio. You won't just be showing this stuff to your current client, and your next boss may be a stickler for detail.) The layer 2 elements make the document a little more human and allow it to stand alone, without your having to walk people through or explain very much.

Summary of observations

At the start of your document, you can summarize the observations you made during the test. This is yet another level of abstraction from the basic analysis you did for the observations. It doesn't need to be any longer than one paragraph or a slide's worth of bullets, and you can use it to highlight the particular problem areas. Because usability testing isn't all negative, you can also indicate what tested well.

Summary of recommendations

If your usability methodology calls for making specific recommendations to address the problems uncovered in the test, you can summarize them at the beginning of the report. This, along with the observations summary and a recap of the test plan, constitute the entire message of your report. If you keep these three topics concise, you can get through the basic gist of the report in a handful of paragraphs or slides. This executive summary is ideal for busy clients or project managers.

Even if you don't include detailed recommendations, you might want to include some high-level recommendations. Like the summary of observations, this summary isn't meant to be specific, but to provide an overview of the changes that need to happen to the design.

Severity level

Some of the things you observe during a usability test may be so dire that they prevent users from completing the task successfully. Other problems are minor annoyances that allow the user to complete a task, but affect the user's satisfaction with the web site. In this way, the problems with the site may be graded in terms of severity.

The effect of severity level on your design process is up to you and your team. Some teams use it to prioritize which problems to address first, while others use it to make a judgment about whether to launch the site. Still others use it just to see "how badly" they did.

Whether your team makes use of severity level or not, your stakeholders may be interested in the information because it adds further structure and categorization to the seemingly endless stream of observations. Including severity level in your report can help structure the presentation of the report—you can spend more time on those observations graded most severe. Some tips follow for determining severity level.

User quotes

In many ways, it's a good idea to put quotes from the users on the first layer of your report. People love seeing what other people say, and these quotes can be more meaningful than any observation or quantitative analysis. Getting them requires going through recorded material or transcripts, which can be somewhat time-consuming.

The easiest way to roll user quotes into your report is to attach one to each group of observations. If you're using a slide show to present your findings, this is especially easy because you can just put a quote on each slide.

Layer 3: More Context

Though a usability report containing all the information described above will be thorough and friendly, there are a few other things that you might include. The value of these items depends entirely on your usability methodology, your client, and your project team.

Quantitative data

Some usability methodologies call for recording quantitative data during the course of the test. You might time users to find out how long it takes them to complete a task, or you might count the number of errors they make on each task.

Quantitative data can be presented independently of the observations. You might conduct a statistical analysis of time on task, for example, to show which tasks took longest, and where users were most inconsistent in completing a task through standard deviation.

If you've done a pre- or post-test survey that collects quantitative information, this should be presented independently of the observations as well.

You can also run quantitative data alongside your observations as a means for providing further context or emphasis. You might show which problems led to the most errors by users, or which ones contributed most to the time it took to complete the task. This approach makes the data more meaningful by showing how it directly relates to the observations.

User profiles

The incremental change between the report and the test plan is that in the former, you know what actually happened so you can include some more detail, such as who exactly participated. For example, your test plan might call for six users meeting particular criteria. In the report, you can name the users and describe how they met the criteria. A usability test report for a nonprofit web site seeking donations and recruiting volunteers online might spell out the particulars of their usability test participants like this:

```
Sam, frequent online shopper, currently donates to causes by
phone or mail
```

Jim, very frequent online shopper, donates to causes every few
years through web site

Ella, frequent online shopper, active eBay participation,
volunteers with local soup kitchen, no monetary donations

Barbara, occasional online shopper but expert Internet user,
donates online yearly to causes

Remember, these are the actual people who participated. For more continuity,
these descriptions might reference the personas document, if it exists.

A Short Aside (i.e., Rant) on Quantitative Data

Layer 3 might seem like a strange place for quantitative data, and this is
where my biases come out. Quantitative data is interesting, but not necessarily instructive. It can round out an observation, but it's not actionable.
Knowing that it took a person 3.7 minutes to complete a task doesn't immediately imply what needs to happen to make the design "better." Also,
objectively speaking, it's difficult to say whether these numbers imply the
need to make a change.

Many user experience professionals still operate in environments where
getting to do a usability test at all is an accomplishment. For quantitative
data to be meaningful, it must illustrate comparisons. And to make comparisons, you would need to conduct at least two tests: One test benchmarks
the current web site and the second test, conducted against an improved
design, compares it to the benchmark. Through this comparison, you can
show where the new design improves upon the old and where it does not.
But not every environment offers the resources or flexibility to conduct
multiple tests. Quantitative data is also difficult to collect. For many people, quantitative data can be a barrier to entry, a reason not to do testing
because they don't have the capacity or resources to do data collection and
analysis. These days, we need to empower people to do usability testing
and remove reasons not to do it.

Finally (and this really is my last point on this topic), usability testing methods are already a little alien to our clients. Generating numbers out of sample sizes of six to eight users is a little fishy, to say the least. Attempts to
make a design tool scientific seem, to me, misguided. Usability methodology
should seek not to be more scientific, but instead more useful to the people
who rely on its outcomes: the designers.

Tactical recommendations

The basic purpose of a usability report is to account for what happened during the usability test sessions. As an additional layer of information, you can make recommendations for how to improve the design based on what you saw. In this context, there are two kinds of design improvements you can recommend:

Best-practice improvements: Sometimes you may observe a pattern that makes the solution painfully obvious. The submit button that users keep missing because it's too small is a classic example. The solution may be so obvious that you wish that you could replace the button during the test itself, just so you don't have to watch anyone else stumble over it. If the solution is staring the design team in the face, you might want to roll it into the report next to the observation. Format recommendations to distinguish them from observations—it should be clear that this is a recommendation from the usability team, not an observation.

FIGURE 4.4: In this excerpt from a usability report, a best-practice recommendation is included next to an observation.

User-recommended improvements: During the course of the test, participants might make statements starting with "It would be better if…" or something similar. You may feel obligated to report some or all of these suggestions—some methodologies even call for soliciting them—which might help the design team, even if they don't take the suggestions verbatim. To keep things aboveboard and honest, you should always attribute the ideas to the users who contributed them, unless an idea was suggested by more than two users, in which case you can be more general.

Composing the Report: The Basics

Because usability tests yield a plethora of data, it is important to take a step back and consider your specific situation before setting anything down on paper. Answers to questions like "Who will be using the report?" and "What is the purpose of the usability test?" can shape the report itself.

Before you start: Assessing the situation

As described in the previous chapter, usability tests fall into two main categories. Formative tests are conducted during the design process to identify incremental improvements. Formative tests may be conducted against pieces of the product or web site. Summative tests are conducted on a finished product to provide an overall assessment of the site's usability. Your report will look different depending which of these tests you're running.

Reports for Formative Tests: Formative tests appear throughout the design process, punctuating the development with test sessions to validate and verify design decisions. Your team can perform any number of tests during the process, and those tests can be as comprehensive or as targeted as necessary. What formative tests have over their summative cousins is a specific set of objectives. If a test is being run during the design process, it's to uncover problems and help give designers some sense of direction.

This impacts the format of the report because the document must address those immediate needs. Any other information that comes out of the test is nice and should be reported, but plays a different role. While the report focuses primarily on the data that gives the most direct feedback to the matters at hand, it can handle any other information in a manner appropriate to the audience. Designers with a deadline might not care about the other results, whereas clients who eagerly soak up new information about their customers may want to spend as much time as possible on this information.

Reports for Summative Tests: A summative test appears at the end of the process and its role is less design-y and more strategic. By conducting a summative test, you are providing an overall assessment of the product's usability and giving the client a crystal-ball view into what they might expect when they launch the product. Hopefully, the design process has included formative tests; otherwise the summative test might uncover factors that question the viability of the product altogether.

The report for a summative test should put the observations into two contexts: The client needs to know, first, what to expect upon launch, and second, what to build into the project plan for subsequent releases. By setting the client's expectations, you help them plan their technical support needs and prepare for the kinds of questions they might receive via email. More importantly, the summative test establishes a starting point for subsequent releases, helping the client prioritize the features and changes.

Organizing the report

After the introductory material, your report will contain a brain dump of all the observations you made during the test. No doubt this mess of data will benefit from a little structure and there are a handful of organizing principles you can use to bring order to the chaos.

Task-based structure: In this approach, you group the observations by task, presuming this is how you structured the usability test. This structure documents each task, the "right" way for users to accomplish the task, and then each of the problems they encountered when doing so. Since tasks can be further grouped into scenarios or objectives, your report can follow a fairly straightforward structure. This approach makes the most sense when the tasks and scenarios are discrete chunks with their own sets of usability problems. If you have a lot of redundant usability problems, it may be better to organize your report by screen.

Screen-based structure: Some web applications use a single screen for multiple tasks. Many modern approaches to web design minimize the number of screens, allowing users to accomplish many things within a small set of screens. (This design philosophy follows the general trend to make the web behave more like a desktop application.) This approach is best when there is a lot of overlap in the observations between tasks because they share screens.

In this case, your report should simply have a section for each screen, starting with the main screens—those in your application where the user will spend the most time—and working toward the least important screens. Alternatively, you can order the screens by severity—those screens with the most problems go first.

The following lists show how you might use these approaches to organize a usability report for a health insurance site. Each list represents sections of your usability report.

TABLE 4.1

Two Approaches to Organizing Usability Reports

Task-Based Approach	Screen-Based Approach
Applying for a policy	Home page
Finding a doctor	Members page
Downloading a claim form	Search results page
Filing a claim	Doctor search form
Checking claim status	Forms download screen
	My Account screen

Distinguishing user groups: One important twist will be the users, especially if you divided the users into distinct groups. You may observe different patterns of usage in different groups. Or, you run a variation of the test against each group of users, perhaps because each group will be responsible for doing different tasks, or because you want to test two different designs in the same test. The impact on the organization of your report, therefore, depends entirely on how you incorporated the groups into your test.

It is important to communicate how the user groups impacted the results. If the results sets are completely different for the same test, you'll want to show the results side by side to compare. Similarly, if the results are the same for two different designs, you'll also want to compare these side by side. On the other hand, if you're conducting two different tests—where the variations accommodate the differing needs of the user groups—organizing the results by user group makes more sense.

Incorporating user groups into the screen-based approach example above might yield a slightly different organization for the usability report. Here's a list of sections for a usability report that takes user groups into account:

```
Home page
Audience-specific category page
Search results page
My Account screen
Plan comparison screen
Screens for members:
        Doctor search form
        Forms download screen
Screens for employers:
        Sales rep search screen
        Order materials screen
```

Focusing on Usability Observations

Since the heart of the usability report is its account of the observations made during the test, these data points deserve some special attention. To keep your observations in context, it's best to present them along with a screenshot of the relevant web page. Of course, you'll also have to consider more general observations that address the entire site.

Display observations with screenshots and callouts

Your results are, in essence, commentary on the screen designs. The clearest way to communicate this commentary is to show the screen and point out the problems you observed.

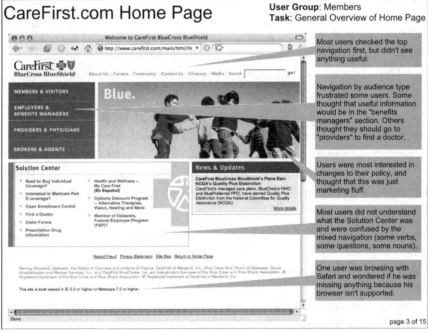

FIGURE 4.5 Clients and designers alike respond positively to the simple screenshot-and-callout approach to displaying observations. Even though the callouts may obscure part of the screen, they clearly show the context of the observation.

Another way to report observations is to show the screen with reference points—numbered dots at the locations relevant to the observation. Though this might be a cleaner presentation—no arrows stretching all over the screen—it can be a little harder to follow.

FIGURE 4.6: Besides keeping the screenshot cleaner, this approach gives you more room to describe the observation without having to confine yourself to a callout box. Your designers might like this approach best because it preserves the screen design and potentially offers more description.

If you're not afraid of taking a screen element out of context, you can crop your screenshot to show just the relevant area, and place the observation adjacent to it. This approach is clean and allows you to point out specific areas of the page clearly. On the downside, you'll have to prepare many more images for the report, which can be time-consuming.

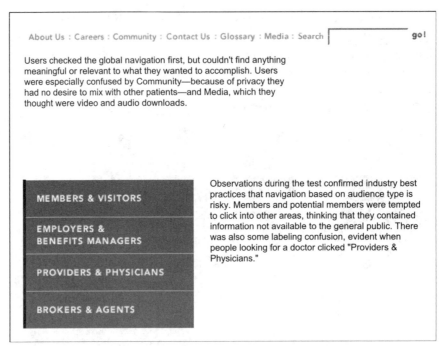

About Us : Careers : Community : Contact Us : Glossary : Media : Search [   ] go!

Users checked the global navigation first, but couldn't find anything meaningful or relevant to what they wanted to accomplish. Users were especially confused by Community—because of privacy they had no desire to mix with other patients—and Media, which they thought were video and audio downloads.

MEMBERS & VISITORS

EMPLOYERS & BENEFITS MANAGERS

PROVIDERS & PHYSICIANS

BROKERS & AGENTS

Observations during the test confirmed industry best practices that navigation based on audience type is risky. Members and potential members were tempted to click into other areas, thinking that they contained information not available to the general public. There was also some labeling confusion, evident when people looking for a doctor clicked "Providers & Physicians."

Figure 4.7: Lining up a bunch of these screen excerpts in a report may get a little messy. No doubt about it, though, you'll have a lot of flexibility in how you lay out the report if you're just dealing with cropped screenshots. At some point in the report, however, you may want to show the screen in its entirety.

Distinguish between different kinds of observations

Some of your observations may apply across the whole site or reflect generally on the whole page. You can represent these more general observations the same way as specific observations, but without arrows pointing to areas of the page.

Figure 4.8: These two observations are relevant to the same page, though one deals with a specific area of the page and the other is more general. Notice that the specific observation has an arrow coming from it while the general observation is just a box.

Even more generalized observations may need their own section. You may have observed, for example, that users like seeing a "save" button so they know for certain that their work is committed to the server. If you've created a more automated web form that automatically saves or saves data when hitting return (or Enter), the users may not be comfortable with the interface. Rather than repeat this observation throughout, you can include it in a "general observations" section at the beginning or end of your report.

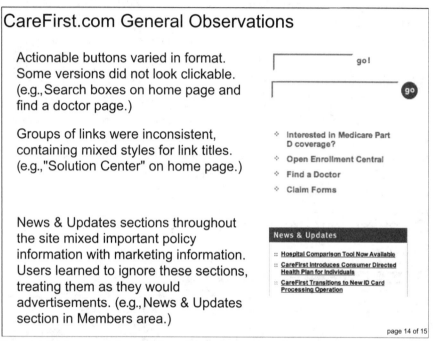

FIGURE 4.9: This is a general observations page for CareFirst.com. Though it doesn't include a screenshot, it lists several issues that came up throughout the usability test. To help readers understand the observation, each one comes with an example and a page reference in the report itself. You could combine general observations with the screen excerpt technique above. The screen excerpt can provide the example of the general observation outside the context of a specific screen.

Crunch the numbers

One of the elements of layer 3 is quantitative data. Though I made my feelings about this kind of information pretty clear, you may find it useful to supplement your observations.

In *The Handbook for Usability Testing,* author Jeffery Rubin divides the world of usability metrics into two main types: performance data and preference data. Performance data covers things like how much time it takes for users to complete a task or how many errors they make. When you're trying to glean whether users like a web site, you're looking at preference data, which can include responses to survey questions or the number of complaints made during the test.

Rubin's book offers excellent advice on narrowing the scope of data collection based on the objectives of your test. When you're done looking at *The Handbook*, though, come back here to work through how you'll present your information.

Quantitative Performance Data: Rubin further divides performance data into two types: time, and counts and rates. Time data shows how much time it took a participant to do something—complete a task, comprehend information, recognize and fix an error. You can also simply count the number of occurrences of things like errors, skipped steps, accessing or asking for help.

You can present any of this information in the usual ways: a table of times or rates, or a series of bar charts showing the time on task for each user. The value of this format will depend on your audience but you should also consider the relevance and meaning of this approach. Unless you're shooting for particular benchmark times or rates ("Our users were able to check out in 176.29 seconds!") straight quantitative data is meaningless.

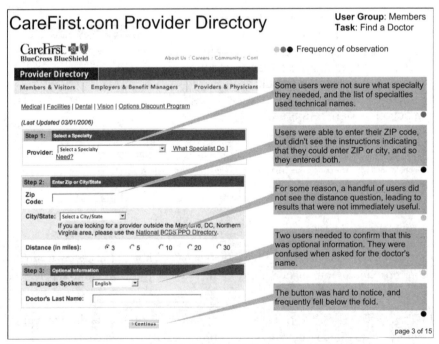

FIGURE 4.10 The observations on this screen have been enhanced with simple counts to show how many times the error occurred. The darker the dot, the more it was observed. Each observation is also accompanied by a little stopwatch to show how much time the usability issue contributed to the overall time on task.

Instead, consider building a relationship between the quantitative data and the qualitative data—the observations you made during the test. Placing visual representations of quantitative data adjacent to the observations can enhance both pieces of information.

Quantitative Preference Data: Preference, by its very nature, is subjective, and any measure of it must be taken with a grain of salt. It's much easier, for example, for users to express a preference between two possible options. Ask them how much they like something without the benefit of a comparison, however, and they're more concerned about pleasing you (or making themselves look good) than answering objectively.

Subjecting quantitative preference data to rigorous statistical analysis always seems a little irresponsible, too. It would take an expert in statistics (if you don't have one among your inner circle of friends, you should hang out in coffee houses near the local university) to say for certain whether a particular set of data is crunchable. But if you've asked users to rate how much they like a particular feature on a scale of 1 to 10 and then average those scores to say that people liked the feature "68 percent," something's not quite right.

Much of the preference data you collect may be outside the scope of the observations. Unless you're counting, as Rubin suggests, the number of times users offer unsolicited negative comments or the number of times users ask for help, most of the preference data will be collected in a post-test survey. The post-test survey might ask users about particular features or certain aspects of the interface.

If the questions are specific and ask users to make comparisons, you have more to work with. For example, asking users to rank a list of features in terms of which they would use the most yields data that allows you to show comparisons between features. You can also show relationships between features: People who picked feature A first usually picked feature B second.

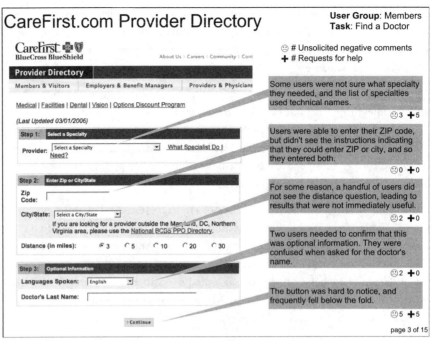

CareFirst.com Provider Directory

User Group: Members
Task: Find a Doctor

CareFirst
BlueCross BlueShield

About Us : Careers : Community : Cont

☹ # Unsolicited negative comments
✚ # Requests for help

Provider Directory

Members & Visitors   Employers & Benefit Managers   Providers & Physicians

Medical | Facilities | Dental | Vision | Options Discount Program

(Last Updated 03/01/2006)

| Step 1: | Select a Specialty |

Provider: Select a Specialty ▾   What Specialist Do I Need?

> Some users were not sure what specialty they needed, and the list of specialties used technical names.
>
> ☹3 ✚5

| Step 2: | Enter Zip or City/State |

Zip Code:

City/State: Select a City/State ▾

If you are looking for a provider outside the Maryland, DC, Northern Virginia area, please use the National BCBS PPO Directory.

> Users were able to enter their ZIP code, but didn't see the instructions indicating that they could enter ZIP or city, and so they entered both.
>
> ☹0 ✚0

Distance (in miles): ◉ 3   ○ 5   ○ 10   ○ 20   ○ 30

> For some reason, a handful of users did not see the distance question, leading to results that were not immediately useful.
>
> ☹2 ✚0

| Step 3: | Optional Information |

Languages Spoken: English ▾

Doctor's Last Name:

> Two users needed to confirm that this was optional information. They were confused when asked for the doctor's name.
>
> ☹2 ✚0

> Continue

> The button was hard to notice, and frequently fell below the fold.
>
> ☹5 ✚5

page 3 of 15

Figure 4.11 Counting unsolicited negative comments or requests for help can give you data to supplement the observations. As in Figure 4.10, the observations on this screen have been enhanced with icons to show where in this online form users became frustrated and started making negative comments.

Risks in Creating Usability Reports

Because the report is attempting to capture and summarize what happened during the usability test, information can get lost in translation. An observation that seemed harmless or meaningless during the course of the test can get blown out of proportion. Likewise, some of the subtleties of a major observation can get lost when documenting it.

Keep severity scores realistic

Because the purpose of a usability report is to bring to light the issues that came out during the test, the things you report may seem more important than they actually are. By simply including an observation in the report, you're already inflating its severity. Stakeholders can easily seize upon an observation that "sounds right" to them—or worse, confirms a bad design idea they thought of themselves—and blow it out of proportion.

Assigning a severity rating to observations can keep this inflation in check. The more objective you can make the ratings, the better. Of course, the severity of a usability problem is a totally subjective metric, but you can set some criteria for what counts as a major problem. Table 4.2 shows the most typical definitions.

TABLE 4.2

Severity Ratings for Usability Reports

Rating	Description	Example
High	Prevents the user from completing the task.	User could not find the submit button and believed the task was complete even though it wasn't.
Medium	Does not prevent the user from completing the task, but caused a significant distraction that the user noticed.	The system threw an error when the user clicked submit. Upon clicking back to the form, the user realized that he missed a checkbox that was required before moving forward.
Low	Does not prevent the user from completing the tasks, but caused a delay or an error that the user did not recognize.	The user knew he needed to click a submit button, though he could not immediately find it.

Balance accurate reporting with readability

A usability report is a delicate balance between reporting what happened and condensing several hours of testing into readable chunks. Too much detail, and the report loses its value. Too little detail, and the results are questionable. Your report should provide enough detail to show the nuances in the results—the users don't speak with a unified voice, some observations are not as severe as others, patterns of behavior may be artifacts of the test itself, just to name a few. Presenting observations as absolutes is a power to be used with great responsibility.

On the flip side, too much qualification and hedging render the results somewhat useless. If you don't feel comfortable drawing any conclusions about the site, stakeholders and designers alike will wonder why the usability testing was done at all.

One way to strike this balance is by assigning an observation a severity rating (keeping in mind the risks stated above). You can use any number of criteria to determine an observation's severity. So long as you use the same criteria for every observation, the severity rating allows you to prioritize the observations and indicate which ones deserve the most attention.

Used correctly, quantitative data allows you to qualify observations, to make statements like "Even though users consistently missed the submit button, it didn't prevent them from completing the task, and it wasn't the thing on the page that tripped them up the most. This drop-down menu of state names in geographical order from northwest to southeast, on the other hand..."

Presenting Usability Reports

Like a usability test plan, a usability report is a pretty easy document to walk through. When planning the presentation, however, you need to decide which parts of the report you want to emphasize and spend more time on. The emphasis will depend on whom you're presenting to, the contents of the report, and the purpose of the presentation.

Meeting Purpose

The purpose of presenting a usability report is pretty straightforward—people on the team need to know what happened during the usability test—and it's unlikely you'll get together for any other reason. That said, you may want to change the emphasis of the meeting depending on whom it's for.

Presenting findings to stakeholders

Experience shows that stakeholders are less concerned about specific design observations and more concerned about the overall tenor of the usability tests. They want to know whether the web site was successful, whether the users were helpful, and whether the participants had other questions or concerns relating to the organization. This isn't to say that the stakeholders have no interest in the results from the test, but that their interests are broader.

Don't spend any more time on the observations than you need to hit the high points. If there were a few things that users pointed out consistently, be sure to talk about those. Throw in an outlier—some unusual behavior unique to one user—because it helps show that you got a broad range of feedback.

With stakeholders you may need to spend more time on the pre- and post-test questions that shed light on the audience more broadly. Participant responses to these questions might also include their thoughts on the overall organization or other product lines or the brand in general. Hopefully, stakeholders won't put too much stock in these responses—it's difficult to capture a person's reaction to a brand in a couple questions after they've sat through a usability test—but you may need to clarify the limits of these questions.

Presenting findings to the design team

The design team will be more interested in the observations and—depending on the team—may demand solutions. When the people assembled in the meeting are there to learn about how to improve the design they'll want your help in getting inside the user's head and will appreciate focusing more on the observations.

Meeting Structure

When presenting a usability report to your stakeholders or project team, you should always start with the basics, reminding them of test objectives and describing the test method and logistics. The test method and logistics should include when and where the test was conducted, the structure of the test and the kinds of tasks you asked participants to perform, and a quick rundown of who showed up to take the test. Though most of this is a repeat from the test plan, you now know exactly what you did and who came. If you changed your approach during the test, or if the user profiles were not quite what was expected, now is the time to describe those deviations from the plan.

Before getting to the observations, you can also summarize them in a handful of bullet points. By summarizing the observations, you give yourself a platform to build from and set expectations for what's going to come next. If you can't get through the whole presentation, at least you've hit the high points.

If your report also includes some analysis, you can summarize that as well at the beginning of the presentation. With this approach, the meeting participants get the whole story in the first part. Having set up the big picture, you can dig into particulars. How you approach these depends, of course, on who's at the meeting.

Moving quickly through observations

You might choose to blaze through the observations, spending only a few minutes on each screen or task and mentioning each observation without going into detail about exactly what the user did. You'd use this approach when the meeting participants are not directly impacted by the usability observations, or when they're there to simply get a tour of the report and will read it in more detail on their own time.

Moving slowly through observations

Some designers don't like sitting in meetings, and would rather read your report from the safety and comfort of their desks and then make the design changes implied by the usability test. Some, however, like hashing things out collaboratively. If this is the kind of designer you have on your team—or the kind of designer you want to encourage—you'll spend more time on each observation. The meeting participants will want to hear stories and this is your chance to describe the nuances of the observations. Maybe everyone had trouble understanding a form, but every user tried something different to make it work. These kinds of details may be lost in your report, but they're ideal discussion points for a longer meeting.

Pulling out the problems

Of course, you don't need to structure this part of your meeting as one of two extremes. The middle ground is to breeze through the minor problems and dwell on the more serious problems. Is there one part of a process flow that tripped up every user? Did users struggle to get past the home page? Were users reluctant to sign up or register? These problems might impact more than just whether users can complete tasks, but also whether the business model of the web site is viable. You can use the bulk of your meeting to explore these showstoppers.

Presentation Risks

As you run through your presentation, no doubt your client or team members will come up with some tough questions. Although these can derail the meeting, a little preparation goes a long way. One major complaint about usability test reports is that too much time elapses between the test and seeing the results. You may want to nip that one in the bud even before you plan the presentation.

Report findings ASAP

One of the greatest challenges with usability reports is that stakeholders do not get to see the results immediately following the usability test. They may not understand that it takes some analysis to put the report together. If you can buy yourself a few days, this may be all the time you need to put a report together. If stakeholders are applying pressure, you can compromise by holding a usability test debriefing, in which all the people who observed the test can get together with those people who did not and talk about what they saw.

This compromise meeting is not really a presentation of the report, but it may be a crucial client management tool to give you time to put the "real" report together. The risk, of course, is that there's no analysis in the debrief, so the observations will be out of context and you might miss something. The stakeholders have to understand this risk, and know that after further analysis you might identify other priorities.

Be objective and honest

Usability testing, as practiced by most people, is an inexact science and more often than not there is room for interpretation in the observations. During your presentation of the observations, be careful to distinguish between what happened and your interpretation of what happened. For example, users of a web application might consistently miss a submit button. You don't know why they missed it—perhaps it is too small, or the contrast isn't right, or perhaps it doesn't look clickable enough—but you might have asked users why they missed the button.

In reporting this observation, you can say that people consistently missed the button and then offer several explanations why. Unfortunately, the nature of usability testing is that you may never find an exact explanation, but the team may need to agree on one in order to develop a solution.

Prepare for questions about design

"So what should we do?" You may face this question after running through the litany of problems with the web site design. If you haven't decided upon your role as usability person, now is the time to do it. Some usability analysts are comfortable with offering solutions. Others see a clear dichotomy between uncovering and diagnosing problems and solving them.

If you fall into the second camp, you might feel funny about offering potential solutions, as if it were outside your responsibilities. If the "I don't solve, I just identify" shtick doesn't work with your team, you may need to have some ideas in your back pocket. Difficult design problems do not have just one answer, so force yourself to think of a couple different approaches for each main design problem. In the case of the button that people keep missing, you might offer a couple explanations and then solutions derived from those explanations. One explanation might be that the button is lost on the page because there are so many other clickable elements. Another explanation is that the button may be too small and too far away from the action to make it visually relevant to the rest of the page. Having offered these explanations, you can then suggest some solutions.

Usability Reports in Context

Usability testing can be a difficult process, fraught with logistical, methodological, and political concerns. These difficulties, however, are also usability testing's greatest appeal: It brings everyone on the project together. The report serves as a gathering place, so to speak, a landmark that everyone must participate in and understand.

Say what you will about getting everyone on a project involved in something, but there's something strangely satisfying about getting everyone on the same page, about working from a single common platform. The scope of a usability report can vary from a simple step in a larger process to a starting point that largely sets an agenda for the next stage of development.

Using a Usability Report with Other Documents

As part of the design process, the usability report is the linchpin between different phases of the methodology. With each usability report, you learn a little bit more about how your audience will respond to the web site and what about the design works and what doesn't work. Because the report serves as a connection between one phase and the next, it needs to cooperate with other documentation.

Usability reports and other user-needs documents

Within the framework of this book, usability reports are classified as user-needs documents because they provide a picture of the user. In the case of the usability report, that picture of the user is described through the use of the web site, framing attributes of the user as observations.

The report can work well with other user-needs documents. Personas can provide a framework for describing the participants in the usability report. Your report is stronger if you can show how the people you recruited to participate in the test reflect previously established profiles. Stronger still is a report that challenges those initial profiles because it demonstrates a willingness to grow with new information.

The other user-needs document described in this book is the usability test plan, the sister document to the report. The report needs to recap the plan, to remind the project team of the test's approach and purpose.

Usability reports and strategy documents

Although there may be opportunities to draw connections between your usability test and what you've learned about competitors or the underlying concept model, the focus of your usability report needs to be the usability test. While it is important to keep your documents relevant to each other, the context for the usability report is set by the design documents.

Usability reports and design documents

Though it's unlikely you'll need to mention design documents explicitly in the usability report, there are a few exceptions.

Wireframes: There are a couple occasions where you'd use wireframes in place of screenshots. If in your usability test you used wireframes instead of the actual web site to do testing, you'll need to use the wireframes in the report to provide context for the observations.

Another use of wireframes in the report is as a substitute for screens when the screens would prove too distracting or compete with the data in some way. Even if wireframes are not faithful representations of the screen, they can be useful. Imagine, for example, that your wireframe uses no layout—it only shows the pieces of content on the screen and their relative priorities without representing the page layout. Your usability tests might include results that show which content users actually gravitated toward. This can show a nice contrast between the conceived priority and the actual priority.

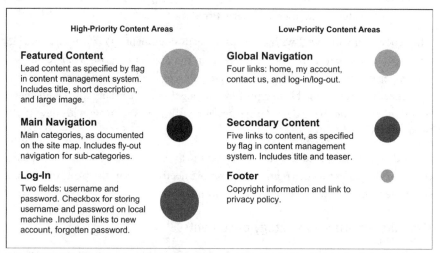

High-Priority Content Areas

Featured Content
Lead content as specified by flag in content management system. Includes title, short description, and large image.

Main Navigation
Main categories, as documented on the site map. Includes fly-out navigation for sub-categories.

Log-In
Two fields: username and password. Checkbox for storing username and password on local machine .Includes links to new account, forgotten password.

Low-Priority Content Areas

Global Navigation
Four links: home, my account, contact us, and log-in/log-out.

Secondary Content
Five links to content, as specified by flag in content management system. Includes title and teaser.

Footer
Copyright information and link to privacy policy.

Figure 4.12 This wireframe represents the site's home page in terms of content areas and relative priorities without prescribing any layout. Usability results—what content got the most attention from users—are displayed as dots of different size and intensity. The size of the dot shows what users looked at the most and the intensity of the dot shows their likelihood of interacting with it. You could do this with the actual screen, but your data might compete with the design, making it difficult to interpret, and the actual screen might not provide as interesting a context as the wireframe.

Site maps and flowcharts: These documents show potential paths users can take to get through the site, but usability testing always demonstrates that users tend to find the strangest (if not the shortest) distance between point A and point B. Like wireframes, site maps and flowcharts (called "flows" collectively) may be used in the usability test in lieu of a prototype or set of web pages. In this case, you'll want to include these diagrams to show how the participants reacted to them.

But flows can also provide context for presenting results. Imagine that a web site allows multiple paths to its collection of documents, and one of the things you're interested in is the path typically chosen by users. A site map is ideal for displaying this information, and can even serve as a foundation for comparing different user behaviors, as in Figure 4.13.

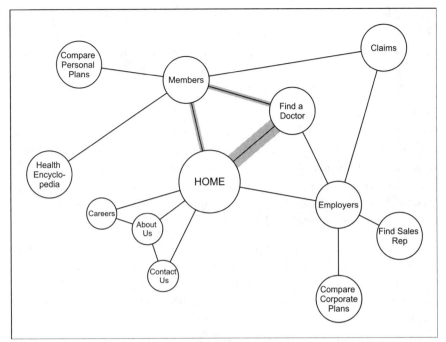

Figure 4.13 During this usability test, participants had to navigate to a document deep inside the web site. The majority of users found the same path, but a handful of users took an alternate path. The number of users is represented by the weight, or thickness, of the line. This simple graphic can convey a lot of information.

Getting Inside Their Heads

The conclusion of the last chapter implied that usability testing will live forever, in some form. Far be it for me to change my mind in the space of a chapter, but it's important to consider what form it will take.

Done right, usability testing is a great way to see whether a web site works, but it has some serious methodological concerns to overcome. Placing users in an artificial environment—outside the very place they'll use the site, sitting next to someone they'll never see again, responding to questions no one has ever asked them before—means that usability testing in its current form is a design technique trying to be a science.

Many user experience professionals these days advocate getting out of the lab, that is, shedding the artificial environment and going to where people actually do use the web. No doubt this scares some of you as much as it does me. If we have a hard enough time finding the time to schedule a couple days of testing and getting a good selection of users to come to the lab, won't it be more difficult to visit their homes and offices? The answer is most likely "yes," but the bigger concern isn't logistical; it is, again, methodological. This kind of testing is not appropriate for every situation.

In fact, the evolution of the web and the web design process points to more immediate access to usability results. More and more web-based services launch so-called "beta" versions of their sites—mostly finished, but still requiring some fixes and enhancements. Some sites live in what the industry calls "perpetual beta." Like the house up the street whose owners are constantly renovating, these sites are being tweaked daily. Basic assumptions about how the web is built and used are undergoing a major shift.

Early adopters of this methodological shift are probably not doing usability testing the way you and I are doing it. They're probably planning the initial site carefully, putting it out there, soliciting feedback, and issuing new "releases" every day in response. And now we get back to the point of this chapter: understanding how people use a web site. When you do a usability test, sitting with actual users, you get a rich array of data. The people who are building "perpetual beta" sites don't have access to that same depth of information. The next stage of usability testing needs to be a convergence of these two ideas: rich data with near-real-time response

When that happens, usability reports will look much different, but they will contain much of the same kind of information described in this chapter.

PART II

Strategy
Documents

Strategy documents
- ► Competitive Analyses
- ► Concept Models
- ► Content Inventories

Strategy documents provide additional context for the design, but the connection to the final design may not be a straight line. You may look at competitors to get a sense of how other web sites address the same issues, or you might build a conceptual model of the business to facilitate your understanding of how the organization operates. You may need to construct an inventory of all the content on the site so you know what the design needs to accommodate.

CHAPTER FIVE

Competitive Analysis

kəm-pě'-tə-tǐv' ə-nă'-lǐ-səs (n.)

A web design competitive analysis shows the differences between the site you're working on and comparable sites. The differences highlighted and the sites compared in the document depend on the purpose of the analysis.

Every industry has its own version of the competitive analysis and its function is clear: to line up your product with other products and show where yours falls short and where yours is superior. Each industry brings a different spin to this old favorite and user experience design has its own set of criteria by which to judge competitors.

Take the simple competitive analysis shown in Table 5.1.

TABLE 5.1

Simple Competitive Analysis

Criteria	PETCO.com	PetSmart.com
Products	No specific products, links to product categories and specials	Home page features six products
Search box	Upper-left-hand corner, adjacent to primary navigation	Upper-right-hand corner, between primary navigation and account navigation
Navigation	Primary navigation organized by pet. Additional navigation for retail services	Primary navigation organized by pet. Additional navigation for account management
Contact information	Linked from left-hand navigation	Linked from top navigation
Shopping functions	Links to shopping cart, account management, and order status	Links to shopping cart and account management

This tiny competitive analysis looks at the home page contents of two prominent pet-related web sites. The table shows how each site's home page stacks up in different categories. Despite the simplicity, this table includes the two main pieces of a competitive analysis: the competitors and the criteria to compare them by.

Competitive Analyses at a Glance

Because competitive analyses vary along only two dimensions—competitors and criteria—you'll always see some mechanism for showing two or more sites side-by-side with the differences highlighted. The specific nature of those differences will vary depending on the criteria selected. At the same time, these documents can also vary by quantity—some are larger than others because they show more contexts or more competitors.

Competitive Analysis Overview

Purpose—What are competitive analyses for?

Most often, the competitive analysis helps the design team and its clients position their product in the landscape of offerings. It helps determine what customers are used to and best practices in everything from interface design to features offered. Though not the best driver of design decisions, the competitive analysis can provide a baseline understanding of what works and what doesn't.

Audience—Who uses them?

A competitive analysis is flexible enough to address the needs of just about anyone on your team. The contents may vary depending on who the main audience is. Designers may be more concerned about how individual features are represented and prioritized while stakeholders may want a broader view, for example, of the range of features offered.

Scale—How much work are they?

Because the level of detail can vary, competitive analysis can be very easy or very time-consuming. A comparison of terms (say, "log in" vs. "log on") can take minutes, while the simple spreadsheet can take a couple days, and a full-fledged report will consume a couple weeks. The scale depends simply on the number of criteria and competitors. The more of these in your study, the more time it will take to research and put together.

Context—Where do they fall in the process?

Like most other strategy documents, the competitive analysis is usually prepared at the beginning to lay the groundwork for the rest of the design process. Occasionally, if the team finds itself stuck on a particular design problem, it may conduct a competitive analysis midway through the design process to help solve the problem.

Format—What do they look like?

Competitive analyses can be as simple (and ugly) as a spreadsheet, or as elaborate as a poster. Some are written up as reports, while others are presented as slide shows. There really is no standard format, and yours will be determined by the audience, purpose, and the amount of data you have.

Figures 5.1 and 5.2 show two sample competitive analyses. The first is as simple as can be: a spreadsheet with the competitors along the top and the criteria down the side. The second is more complex, showing different kinds of comparisons for each competitor.

	A	B	C	D	E
1		PetSmart.com	Petco.com	DrsFosterSmith.com	LucytheWonderDog.com
2	**Navigation**				
3	Primary Navigation Categories				
4	Global Navigation				
5	Account Navigation				
6					
7	**Catalog**				
8	Merchandizing				
9	Sale Items				
10	Seasonal Items				
11					
12	**Content**				
13	Product Use				
14	Training				
15	Health				

FIGURE 5.1 This simple spreadsheet can be the starting point for any competitive research. Whether it remains the ending point as well is up to you. Though it captures all the information adequately, it may not be appropriate for presenting results to stakeholders or other team members.

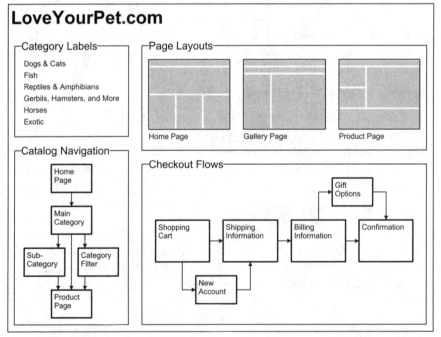

FIGURE 5.2 This page is from a more complex competitive analysis, where the research explored many different aspects of each site. Instead of presenting the data in one consolidated view, as in Figure 5.1, this report spreads the information over several pages.

Page Layouts

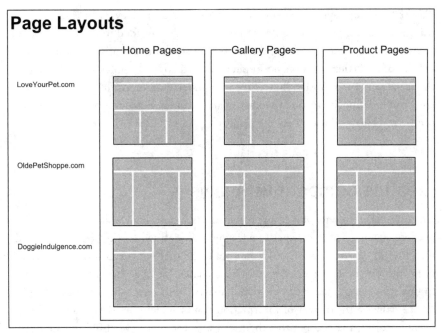

FIGURE 5.3 Like the previous illustration, this shows a page from a report. This report, however, is organized differently, dedicating each page to a different aspect of the analysis, and illustrating this criterion for each competitor. The display of the data in this example is much like the table in Figure 5.1 with a couple of key differences. First, the data is displayed as a series of pictures—a technique called "small multiples" which we'll discuss further later in the chapter. Second, since this is a page from a larger report, it focuses on one issue, rather than all the issues.

Challenges

In the entire process of creating a competitive analysis, preparing the document is the easy part. You'll have some tough decisions to make about the document—for example, whether to present a simple table or something more elaborate—but ultimately, this is not what makes the process challenging. Once you've established the criteria and the range of competitors, gathering the data is also fairly straightforward, albeit time-consuming. Drawing a box around your analysis, however, and establishing boundaries to define what's relevant to your project, is the more difficult task.

This will be a lot easier if you identify your purpose before you begin your analysis. A purpose statement can drive not only the types of information you collect about each competitor, but also how you present the data. That purpose may be as simple as "We're struggling with widget X in our site and we want to see how it is done on 20 prominent web sites." Or, it may be as complex as

"We're building a system to support user group Y and we want to find out how this group has been supported elsewhere." If you've decided to do a competitive analysis, spend some time with the team brainstorming about what you want to get out of it. Articulate a purpose statement and compare notes with the rest of the team to make sure they have the same understanding of the purpose. In the end, you'll define an agenda for the research and set expectations about how the information will be useful on the project.

Creating Competitive Analyses

The essential elements of a competitive analysis, described in layer 1, are the purpose statement, the competitive framework (defined by the competitors and the criteria), and the data itself. You might find that your data is too extensive to fit into one table. Layer 2 describes the challenges of scaling the document from a simple table to a more in-depth analysis. Finally, to flesh out the document further, a third layer of information can provide more details about the overall project, the competitors themselves, or the method behind the analysis.

Layer 1: The Basics of Competition

Though it may be worthwhile to provide lots of detail about how you approached the competitive analysis or the rationale for the lineup of competitors, the brass tacks of the document are much simpler. To boil a competitive analysis down to its essentials, you'd find only the objective—the purpose of the analysis—and the data—the comparison. Of course, the data needs some kind of backdrop to make it meaningful; this is where the competitive framework comes in.

The competitive framework

Even the simplest competitive analysis displays two critical dimensions: the competitors and the criteria, or what we'll call the competitive framework. The purpose of the competitive framework is to present the data in a way that makes it easy to compare the various sites across the different criteria.

When the competitive framework takes the form of a table, like the ones on the next page, the competitors run along the top of the table and the criteria along the side. The criteria can vary from the very general to the very specific. The first row of Table 5.2 offers a general comparison between navigation systems. Table 5.3 offers more specific comparisons.

TABLE 5.2

Comparing Pet Web Sites with General Criteria

	PetSmart.com	DrsFosterSmith.com
Home Page Navigation	Primary navigation is different pet groups. Offers secondary navigation around account management and retail locations.	Primary navigation is different pet groups. Secondary navigation groups include additional pet product categories (like new items or sale items) and account management.

TABLE 5.3

Comparing Pet Web Sites with More Specific Criteria

	PetSmart.com	DrsFosterSmith.com
Additional item categories	None	Sale items, new items, clearance items
Account management links	My account, shopping cart, customer service	My account, sign in, checkout, shopping cart, shopping list
Offline shopping links	Store locator, in-store services	Catalog quick order, request a catalog, toll-free phone number
Other pet services links	Pet care guides, pet-related articles	Pet care newsletter, information center, pet pharmacy

A different kind of competitive framework is known in MBA circles as the two-by-two. No, this isn't the Noah's Ark approach to comparing web sites. Instead, it plots competitors on a simple grid depicting only two criteria.

That right there is about 12 credit hours of most MBA programs. Notice that with a two-by-two, the number of criteria is shrunken down to two, so they tend to be broader. If you think these plots are based on actual numeric data, the graph has done an excellent job in turning subjective information (whether one pet-related web site is more specialized than another) into objective information. (In most MBA programs, this part is extra credit.) You could use real numbers and actually plot along the scale, but two-by-two presentations are ideal for very broad criteria that might not lend themselves to hard numbers. This type of graphic is useful to identify holes in a landscape. Competitors clustered around certain areas of the two-by-two can indicate that there are opportunities for your site to fill those holes.

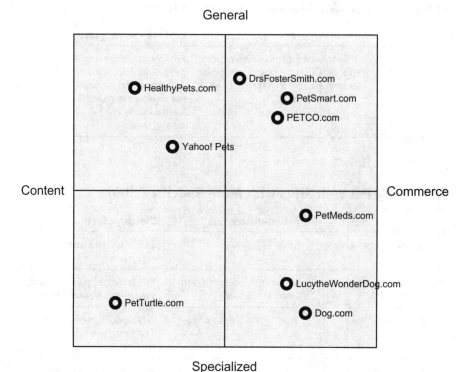

FIGURE 5.4 In this two-by-two, different pet-related web sites are plotted on a simple graph. In this case, the axes of the graph represent the scope of the content (commercial vs. advice/information) and specialization (number of pet types supported).

There's one other kind of competitive framework that appears in comparisons of different user experiences: the small multiples. This term belongs to visualization guru Edward Tufte. In Tufte's *Visual Display of Quantitative Information*, he writes: "Small multiples represent the frames of a movie: a series of graphics, showing the same combination of variables, indexed by changes in another variable." More plainly put, small multiples are a series of graphics that allow the viewer to easily compare similar sets of information. In the case of interface design for the web, this approach is most effective for comparing page layouts.

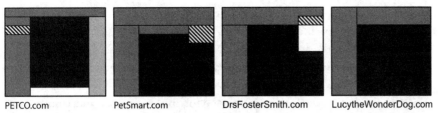

PETCO.com   PetSmart.com   DrsFosterSmith.com   LucytheWonderDog.com

FIGURE 5.5 These small multiples show the general layout of the product pages from three different pet web sites. The dark gray boxes show navigation, while the black boxes show product description information. Promotional information is represented by light gray, shopping cart information by diagonal stripes, and related products by vertical stripes. (In color, you'd have more options.) Finally, the white boxes show related noncommercial content. From these small multiples, it's easy to see that LucytheWonderDog.com uses a very simple layout and DrsFosterSmith.com prioritizes its advice content.

The data

Data is where the rubber meets the road in a competitive analysis. The data can be as simple as yes-no values, indicating whether a site meets a particular criterion, or it can be descriptive, going into some detail for each criterion.

Yes-No Values: You've seen these kinds of competitive analyses on infomercials where the product in question is lined up with "other leading brands." For each feature, the product gets a check mark while its competitors get an X, to show you how versatile the product is. When it comes to web sites, the straight yes-or-no comparison is most effective for considering features, in other words, whether a set of web sites has a specific feature or not. In such a comparison, however, the subtle differences between the competitors may be lost.

TABLE 5.4

Comparing Web Sites with Simple Yes-No Values

	PetSmart.com	DrsFosterSmith.com	PetMeds.com
Products on home page	Yes	Yes	Yes
Retail store locator	Yes	No	No
Expedited shipping options	Yes	Yes	Yes
Non-pet-type categories	No	Yes	Yes

Scores: Some competitive analyses score the competitors in different criteria. You'll see this approach in restaurant reviews where every place is scored on the quality of its food, the ambiance, the service, and the expense. For web sites, scores help give a little more substance to the comparison, though it may be difficult to generate the data. In this table, the sites are scored on a scale of 1 to 5, where 5 indicates the site does a good job in the category and 1 not so much.

TABLE 5.5

Using Scores to Compare Web Sites

	PetSmart.com	DrsFosterSmith.com	PetMeds.com
Promoting products on home page	4	4	5
Alternate modes to find products	2	3	4
Promoting noncommercial content	3	1	4

Notice that in this approach you'd have to define what it means to do well in each category.

Descriptions: Used more frequently than yes-no data or scores, descriptions specify how the competitors meet each criterion. Descriptions allow you to be more explicit about how the competitors stack up against each other, without resorting to potentially skewed numbers.

The two other formats for a competitive framework—the two-by-two and the small multiples—represent a different kind of data entirely. With plots on a graph or thumbnail images depicting screen layouts, the value is in the comparison. This isn't to say that data presented in a table isn't worthwhile as a comparison, but it can stand on its own. A plot on a graph, however, is meaningless unless it is lined up with other plots. The same is true for sketches of page layouts. Showing how much screen real estate is dedicated to navigation and content is pointless unless the reader has a basis by which to judge the amount of space. With two sketches next to each other, the reader can easily compare how one site uses its screen real estate with another.

TABLE 5.6

Providing Further Descriptions for Comparisons

	PetSmart.com	DrsFosterSmith.com	PetMeds.com
Product catalog	Though the home page does not show the depth of the catalog, clicking into each pet category reveals a list of about two dozen product types, specific to the pet.	Extensive catalog of all kinds of pet supplies, somewhat more obscure than PetSmart.com. Clicking into a category reveals many different product types for each pet. There's a separate category for pet pharmacy, which is subcategorized by ailment.	The catalog is limited to dogs, cats, and horses, and focuses almost exclusively on medication. Nonpharmaceutical items are categorized under "accessories" for each type of pet.
Navigation	The catalog links on the home page are limited to pet types. Other links take users to store information and account information.	The catalog links on the home page are limited to pet types and sale categories.	Primary navigation is through a long list of ailments and needs, like "heartworm" or "grooming."
Non-commercial content	Lots of noncommercial content but hidden behind two small links on the home page. This content does not offer any links into the catalog.	Extensive noncommercial content, with some linking into product catalog The pet care articles reference each other, avoiding dead-ends in navigation.	Noncommercial content located in "Ask the Vet" section. Site contains extensive frequently asked questions, categorized by product category (though not linked to the products!) and a link to a separate pet care site.

Your conclusions

No matter how small your analysis, you'll need to document the conclusions. Even if you're doing a simple count of how many hits "log in" and "log on" get on Google, the data can't stand on its own. You need to interpret the data in the context of your client and your project.

By putting your conclusion into words, you are establishing a partial direction for the design. The design team will take its cues for the design from these conclusions. When embarking on building a pet-related site, for example, the design team may seek out best practices from the competition. A cursory study of the landscape allows them to conclude that most pet-related sites use pet type (dog, cat, etc.) as the main navigation. A more in-depth study, however, leads to more detailed data—how sites specializing in one kind of pet categorize their content, how frequently sites use the same categories, the order of the categories (cats first or dogs first), how sites deal with uncommon pets (turtles). With data like this, the conclusions—and therefore design direction—can be better informed.

Layer 2: Tougher Competition

Competing in multiple events

In many cases, the simple bare-bones competitive analysis will suffice, but there will be some cases where your comparisons need to be deeper or broader: Perhaps the number of criteria makes a simple table unwieldy or you're comparing your site to different sets of sites. For example, imagine you're comparing the pet-related web site to other pet sites for navigation and design, but to major commercial sites for shopping cart and checkout functionality. As the scale of the analysis increases, you need a way to accommodate additional data in the document. There are two typical approaches: additional sections by criteria, and additional sections for each competitor.

Organizing report by criteria: Organizing your competitive analysis by criteria creates a collection of smaller competitions in different events, so to speak. You might compare a handful of sites across five different groups of criteria: home page design, interior page design, search functionality, features offered, and navigation. Figure 5.3 shows the results of page layout comparisons across three fictitious pet web sites. For each of these categories, you'd create a separate competitive analysis but use the same competitors throughout. This approach allows you to identify the best players in specific categories and across all categories, but it can also create a disjointed picture of the user experience. In other words, because of the analysis, it is difficult to see the user experience of each competitor in its entirety.

Organizing report by competitor: On the other hand, you could add data to your document by creating a separate section for each competitor. In this case, the competitive analysis reads as sort of a rogues' gallery of sites, each one having a separate profile. Within each profile, the site is described with various criteria. This approach offers a holistic view of the user experience for each site, but it is more difficult to compare that site to others. Figure 5.2, at the beginning of this chapter, shows a page from a competitive analysis organized by competitor.

The purpose

Regardless of how you organize your competitive analysis, with size comes a potential lack of focus. As you expand the reach of your analysis, either by adding more criteria or more competitors, you don't want to lose sight of why you're doing the analysis. Including a statement of purpose in the document itself is a great reminder, and also helps the document's audience understand the context for the analysis.

Layer 3: Adding Further Detail

Competitive analyses with just elements from layer 1 usually stand well on their own, but you may want to add some flesh to the bones. Perhaps the most interesting information you can add is a description of your method for analyzing the competition.

Your methodology

Spelling out your process can help address any possible methodological inadequacies, especially for stakeholders who take these things seriously. What's most worthwhile is rationalizing the selection of competitors and criteria.

The range of competitive web sites out there will vary, of course, depending on the site you're building. The number may seem finite because your site is in a niche category and all the competitors are known players. The number may seem infinite because the web is vast and there are lots of sites competing for attention. You'll have to narrow it down some way, and whatever way you choose makes for worthwhile content for your document.

At the same time, there are infinite criteria by which to compare sites. They can be as broad as the main navigation categories, or as narrow as the label on a button in a particular area of the site. You've made conscious decisions to include certain criteria—maybe they are a standard set used by your client or your company, maybe they were defined ahead of time by the stakeholders, or maybe you devised a special list just for this project. Whatever your methodology behind determining the criteria, this is excellent fodder for your competitive analysis.

Analyzing the Competition: The Basics

Like any deliverable in this book, the competitive analysis must start with a situation analysis: a hard look at the purpose, the timing, and the audience for the document. These aspects of your situation will drive the document's contents and design.

The competitive drive

There are many reasons why you'd want to compare your site to others out there, but unless you make that purpose explicit in the competitive analysis, your data is meaningless for other people reading it. Even if you're doing a competitive analysis that won't see the light of day, establishing and documenting its purpose helps keep the competitive analysis in check and avoids "analysis paralysis," too much thinking and not enough doing.

For the purpose, the best place to start is the motivation. Doing broader competitive analyses—comparing competitors across multiple contexts—usually comes from a need to get a sense of the landscape and industry best practices. The value here is knowing what the cost of entry is for a site like yours—knowing what the minimum expectations will be for users who are used to your competitors.

More narrow competitive analyses—those that look at one specific set of criteria—are usually motivated by a particular design problem. In these situations, you can treat the analysis almost as a science experiment, where the statement of purpose establishes a research question or a hypothesis. Labeling is a typical design problem that can be addressed with a quick competitive analysis. In this case, your purpose would be something like: "To identify what labels are used most frequently among our competitors for product navigation categories."

A timeline for analysis

A competitive analysis is one of those funny documents that usually appears at the beginning of the overall process, but can easily appear at any time. Some methodologies call for a competitive analysis as a standard step at the beginning, whose purpose is simply to understand the competitive landscape before the design process begins.

If your team was tasked with building a new online pet store, you might look at some of the sites already mentioned in this chapter. The sites themselves vary: Some sites focus more on dogs and cats or specialize in medications. Doing such a comprehensive analysis allows you to make some strategic decisions about how your site meets needs not already met—perhaps a site that specializes in pet reptiles or in plush toys for dogs. It may help you determine a competitive advantage, like having noncommercial content about pet health that can cross-sell items from the catalog.

An early competitive analysis can help set the stage, but it may also skew your other decisions at this stage—which features to include and which features will have the highest priority, for example. Though the competition can provide good information about these ideas, those decisions should also be driven by user research. A competitive analysis at the beginning of the design process may be incomplete. Until you do user research, you won't know what features and issues are most salient.

Like concept models (described in the next chapter), which can serve as tools for understanding the problem at hand, a competitive analysis may never see the laminate top of a conference room table. It might only provide an overview of the landscape for you and your most trusted team members. Such informal analyses may be appropriate later in the project timeline, too, when the design is well under way and you have some specific issues in need of a benchmark. Of course, in doing a competitive analysis later in the process to clarify specific design issues, you can uncover other issues that would have been useful at the beginning of the project.

Suppose you've established a strategic direction for your site—specializing in plush toys for dogs—but now need to decide on a labeling scheme for the product categories. An informal analysis of the competition can give you a sense of what labels your audience may be used to. (Establishing whether your audience is the same as that of PETCO.com, for example, is a different exercise entirely.)

Ultimately, the content of the analysis depends more on the need than where it appears in the process. Still, it's safe to say that early competitive analyses tend to focus on strategic issues, while those late in the process generally try to shed light on specific design issues.

It's about the fans

Conflict, tension, resolution: These are what draw spectators to a competition. Unfortunately, no web site competitive analysis will be as compelling as the Olympics or Tour de France. Still, there are people who do take a keen interest, and definitely want to know how the drama will end.

The audience for the competitive analysis will affect the presentation of its data. If your competitive analysis must be readable by people beyond the immediate team, you may need to create it as a self-contained package, requiring no specific knowledge to understand it. In this case, your document might need descriptions of the criteria, an explanation of why the analysis is being done, an overview of the conclusions, or all of the above.

On the other hand, a competitive analysis serving as an internal benchmark does not need to have as much context or description built in. If driven by the need to give the team an overview of the landscape, the document can forsake context for speed of delivery.

Prepping the data

The purpose of a competitive analysis is to show consistency between sites—thereby establishing industry practices (good, best, or otherwise)—or to show marked differences—identifying where some sites stand out. Inconsistencies can indicate that one particular site has developed an innovative solution to a common problem, or that the industry has not settled on a singular approach.

In the early days of e-commerce, for example, a consistent shopping cart model had not yet emerged. Eventually, the industry arrived at a de facto standard—nothing set in stone, but something that most users came to recognize. Newer online features—like the ability to add tags to content to make it easy to find later—are still trying to find their feet as far as design. Different sites do it differently, and showing these differences is the key to good competitive research.

Your data, therefore, needs to paint a clear picture and demonstrate these comparisons. When compiling it, you should think about visual mechanisms to show distinctions and similarities. With yes-no data and scores, this is pretty straightforward, but with descriptions, it becomes a little more complex. To add some depth to the information and make the data jump out a little more, you can assign keywords to the descriptions, or code them to indicate whether the site's approach is good or bad.

Site A	Site B	Site C
Content lives under two layers of categorization. Users must select a main category and then a sub-category before seeing a list of content.	Content is categorized with metadata and users can enter search terms to find content, or use a system of links to filter content.	To find content, users must enter relevant search terms. They can narrow down search results by clicking on metadata.
Navigation Categories Content lives under two layers of categorization. Users must select a main category and then a sub-category before seeing a list of content.	**Metadata Filters** Content is categorized with metadata and users can enter search terms to find content, or use a system of links to filter content.	**Search and Filter** To find content, users must enter relevant search terms. They can narrow down search results by clicking on metadata.
Navigation Categories Content lives under two layers of categorization. Users must select a main category and then a sub-category before seeing a list of content.	☑ **Metadata Filters** Content is categorized with metadata and users can enter search terms to find content, or use a system of links to filter content.	**Search and Filter** To find content, users must enter relevant search terms. They can narrow down search results by clicking on metadata.

FIGURE 5.6 Here are three rows from a competitive analysis. The descriptions are exactly the same throughout, but the presentation changes slightly: The first row just shows the raw data, while the second row adds a headline. This makes the competitive analysis easier to read. In the third row, the description includes a small icon to indicate a technique that would be appropriate for the author's own project.

Tips for Effective Competition

A competitive analysis can generate a lot of raw data, and sifting through it can be daunting for team members and stakeholders who want to reach the bottom line. The best thing you can do for your competitive analysis is nail down your conclusions and spell them out early in the document. These conclusions will look different depending on whether you're looking at a specific design problem or trying to get a sense of the overall competitive landscape.

For specific design problems

In the flurry of collecting data, you may get carried away with presenting all of it in an effective way. If you've set up the competitive analysis effectively and gathered a comprehensive set of data, you should have a problem statement that's driving the analysis and a response to the problem statement. Table 5.7 shows an example.

TABLE 5.7

Problem Statements and Responses

Good Problem Statement	Good Answer
Our site has a feature for allowing customers to add tags to our products. What interface elements do other sites use to support this feature?	Sites with tagging features overwhelmingly use a simple text field and ask users to separate tags with spaces. Since tagging is relatively new, nearly every competitor includes a "what is this?" link adjacent to the text field. Upon pressing Return (or Enter), the user gets immediate feedback from the interface that their tags have been added.

If your competitive analysis was motivated by several different design problems, be sure to have a conclusion for each one.

For landscapes and overviews

When you're looking at the competition just to get a sense of what's out there, you may not have a specific design problem in mind. This doesn't mean you can't come to conclusions, however. After nosing around the competition a bit, you should have a handful of key take-aways—essential messages that the team should keep in mind as they move forward with the design process. You might organize these take-aways by context, identifying one or two bullet points for each of the design areas you looked at.

TABLE 5.8

Key Take-Aways for Pet Store Web Sites

Category	Take-Away
Navigation	Pet type is the primary navigation, even on sites where the catalog is limited to certain products (like medications).
Search	Search results tend to offer both product listings and category listings. There are no advanced search options.
Product Categories	Within each pet type, products are listed either by type (e.g., leashes) or need (e.g., training).
Checkout	Of the pet sites looked at, none offered any sort of special checkout.
Shipping	All shipping options available

With Every Competition Comes Risk

Table 5.9 shows the results of a competitive analysis. It lines up a conclusion (in the first column) with observations from the competitive sites. Without each other, the data and the conclusions are meaningless. Data provides support to the conclusions and conclusions give purpose to the data. In this example, the clients were wondering whether any pet supply sites have successfully moved away from using pet type as primary navigation, and whether product types (e.g., leashes) or needs (e.g., training) were most appropriate for product categories.

TABLE 5.9

Balancing Data and Conclusions in Competitive Analyses

Conclusion	PetSmart.com	PetMeds.com	LucytheWonderDog.com
Pet web sites always seem to use pet type as primary navigation, even on sites that offer a limited catalog. The exception to this rule is sites that specialize in one type of pet.	PetSmart's navigation categories are as close to industry-standard as they come, and their extensive catalog demands narrowing at this level.	PetMeds limits its catalog to medications for dogs, cats, and horses, but even this small group of pet types is used as the primary navigation. Since the catalog is smaller than a general store, however, PetMeds.com uses an additional layer of navigation on the home page.	Since LucytheWonderDog focuses exclusively on dogs, there are no pet type categories, and the primary catalog navigation includes product categories.
Even though it is semantically jarring, all sites freely mix product type with user need. Categories like "training" and "flea and tick control" sit next to "dog bowls" and "dog beds." Notably, sites tend to favor one type over another. So even though a site will use both product types and user needs as category, one type of category will appear more frequently.	Subcategories in PetSmart's catalog tend to focus more on product types for conventional pets, though there are a few user-need categories. More unconventional pets like reptiles, fish, and birds, however, tend to have more user-need categories. Overall product type categories dominate.	PetMeds is an interesting case study because two levels of navigation are spelled out on the home page, so it's easy to see how they categorize their products. The highest level of navigation is based on need, like "flea and tick control" or "grooming" or "bone and joint." There are a couple of notable exceptions, like "medications" and "accessories," which serve more as miscellaneous categories than anything else. The second level of navigation consists mostly of product types.	Unlike PetSmart, Lucy's categories for dogs include a few product types (like "shampoo") but mostly rely on user needs, like "grooming" or "dental" or "joint care."

This table demonstrates the balance between observations and conclusions—presumably, this table is a good balance. The risk in doing a competitive analysis is that you skew too much in one direction, missing the forest for the trees, or vice versa.

Start with your conclusions

If you have a lot of data—you spent a lot of time with many different competitors, looking at many different criteria for comparison—you might get caught up in trying to include all that information in your analysis, to the detriment of your conclusions. The solution here is methodological: Make sure you know your conclusions before starting to document your data. Then you can present your data in context of the conclusions.

Keep your data meaningful

You could also build a document with all generalizations and no data. In this case, you may be overly concerned about simplifying the data for your audience, and end up boiling it down to the point of meaninglessness. You may also find yourself unconsciously biased—wanting to prove a point but finding the data doesn't stand up to your hypothesis. The solution here is also methodological: Before starting the document, identify a handful of data points that support each conclusion.

Presenting Competitive Analyses

When planning a presentation, you must first determine the purpose of your meeting, and then how you want to structure it.

Meeting Purpose

In the context of user experience, there are two main purposes to a competitive analysis: justifying an overall strategy for the design and justifying a specific set of design decisions. Therefore, the purpose of your competitive analysis presentation will be one of these two things. To this end you might combine the presentation of your competitive analysis with the presentation of other strategy documentation or design documentation.

Providing justification for design

Besides describing each of the criteria you looked at, there are a couple of other things you should include in your presentation.

Balance competitive research with user research. When presenting results from a competitive analysis, compare what you found against what users have asked for. Your presentation should show where there is a disconnect between a competitor's site and your target audience, as well as instances where a competitor's site does a good job meeting user needs.

Have an opinion. You're the expert, and if your clients don't put you on the spot explicitly, it doesn't mean they don't want to hear your opinion. Express what you like or dislike about each competitor. Talk about what works for you and what doesn't work for you.

For designers, be explicit about design direction. If your presentation is strictly internal, your team members will want some kind of bottom line—a core set of take-aways they can bring back to their desks to help focus their efforts.

Providing justification for strategy

"Strategy" can mean a lot of things. When using competitive research to make overall decisions about the direction of the web site, the key to the presentation is identifying what role the research plays in your decision making.

Identify the focus of the research. Before diving into the specific differences between various competitors, you can provide some background by stating what it is you were looking for in the competitive analysis. Typical background questions for an overall strategy might relate to the industry baseline for a set of features, the scope and breadth of content available, or the balance between original content and advertising. By stating these issues up front, you've given the stakeholders some context for the presentation.

Identify the implications of strategic decisions. Since your pet-related web site wouldn't jump off the Brooklyn Bridge just because Pets.com did, you need more than just a competitive analysis to justify a strategy. In considering the strategic decisions of your competitors, you need to identify what kind of impact the same decisions in the context of your business would have. By stating explicitly the implications of strategic decisions, you'll go a long way toward putting the competitive analysis into context.

TABLE 5.10

Conclusions and Implications from a Competitive Analysis

Conclusions	Implications
Most pet-related commercial web sites feature a wide variety of products on the home page that rotate daily or weekly.	The site would need a system of business rules and a publishing strategy to determine which products would appear and how often they would change.
Most pet-related web sites use pet type as the main navigation categories.	We would need a publishing strategy unique to that pet type for each main navigation area.

Meeting Structure

Once you have a sense of the purpose of your meeting, you can decide upon an agenda. Competitive analyses are the kind of story that can be hard to tell because there are two main dimensions—the characters and the moral. There are pros and cons to each. Focus too much on the competitors, and the main message (the moral) is lost. Spend too much time on the conclusions, and your stakeholders might wonder whether you're just pushing your own agenda. Still, the meeting structure needs a spine, a central focus to keep conversation moving in the right direction, and this can be either one of these dimensions.

Competitor-driven story

It may seem counterintuitive, but since the competitors will form the basic structure of the meeting, you should actually start with an account of the criteria. Provide an overview of the criteria at the top of the meeting to set the stage and then dig into each competitor more specifically. Describe how each competitor measured up in each aspect.

This approach works well for laying the landscape and for addressing broader issues, like how each site serves the needs of its target audience. By taking the stakeholders on a tour of the competition, you give them a sense of what they're up against. This walking-tour approach helps answer broad strategic questions, such as which features are available on the site, what appears most prominently on the home page, and how the site prioritizes content, but not specific design issues, such as comparing the treatment of "add to cart" buttons.

Though a competitor-driven approach is best for discussing larger strategic issues, it can also work well for specific design problems. If you're looking at just one aspect of the design, your meeting can show how the particular design problem was solved for each competitor. When discussing a specific design problem, your meeting can end with the conclusions, drawing together lessons learned from all the competitors.

Moral-driven story

Instead of structuring your presentation in terms of the competitors and walking through all the issues for each competitor separately, this approach takes the opposite tack: For each issue, you talk about how each competitor stacks up against the others. To set the stage, provide a short overview of the competitors. You don't need to get into comparing them at this point, but instead describe why they were included in the study.

The presentation then focuses on your conclusions. For each conclusion, you'll first need to describe the criteria you looked at to arrive at the conclusion—in other words, what you analyzed on each site.

For example, you might conclude that the highest level navigation categories on a pet-related web site are usually pet-type, but that this isn't the only system of categorization used on the site. To support this conclusion, you looked at three different criteria: the navigation categories on the home page, the metadata attached to products in the catalog and other content, and the structure of intermediate "gallery" pages (galleries are lists of products or content that appear on the user's path between the home page and the product or content page). Finally, within each of these criteria, you make observations about each of the competitors. This structure is useful for both high-level strategy analyses and specific design problems: The content of the conclusions may be different, but the logic behind them is essentially the same. In this approach, the criteria do not disappear, but become a bridge between your conclusions and your observations.

Presentation Helpers: A Speaking Shortcut

The "Moral-Driven Story" section describes a simple conversational structure to follow while discussing a competitive analysis, from conclusions to criteria to competitors. It's a useful structure. When doing presentations, these kinds of "speaking heuristics" can be helpful if you're feeling stuck. If you don't know where to turn next, or if you feel like you're babbling, grab this template and go from there.

Presentation Risks

When presenting a competitive analysis, you might run into a few snags. You may have moments when the conversation is either derailed—a stakeholder brings up an issue that calls the methodology or the results into question—or gets way off topic. Here are a couple of ways your presentation might spin out of control, and how to reel it back in.

Maintain perspective

The worst way for a meeting to get off topic is to get too caught up in the competition. Although you've invited people to the meeting to discuss your site's competitors, it can be easy to lose perspective on the purpose of the competitive analysis. Symptoms of this problem include getting stuck on one particular design element in a meeting about strategy, or spending too much time talking about one competitor over others. Even though your competitive analysis is meant to address one particular design problem, you might find conversation straying from that design problem into other areas of the site, or your participants might start talking about more strategic issues.

If the conversation is productive, you may not see this as a risk at all. However, if you have a specific agenda and certain goals for the meeting, these kinds of digressions may not be productive regardless of how interesting they are. To get back on track, jump in and remind the participants of the purpose of the meeting. One way to help stop this problem before it happens is to write the purpose of the meeting on a whiteboard or flipchart at the very beginning. If someone attempts to stray too far, you can always point to the meeting purpose and look very stern. You won't be popular, but you'll be respected for running a good meeting.

Know the rationale behind your methods

As you present the results of your competitive analysis, you may run into troublesome meeting participants who question your methodology. They may raise questions about your selection of competitors or criteria, or your technique for capturing data.

There is only one surefire way to address this risk: Don't invite these people to the meeting. But, if that's unavoidable (and it usually is), the second best way to address the problem is preparation. Methodological questions are easy to anticipate, and if you think about your rationale before going into the meeting, you can usually quash these hecklers. (OK, maybe they have legitimate concerns, but you don't have to like it.)

Say you're building this pet web site, for example, and your analysis looked at a handful of sites. That might not stop one of your participants from saying, "I do all my online shopping at JeffersPet.com. Why isn't that in your competitive analysis?" If you've done your homework, you can respond with "Given the time constraints on the competitive analysis, we had to keep the number of sites down to four. We included DrsFosterSmith.com among our reviewed sites to represent the non-retail-store competitors. If, after our presentation, you think there are some aspects represented in JeffersPet.com that we missed, let's talk about it offline." Ah, the offline discussion, the Internet consultant's secret weapon.

Open your mind to varying interpretations

It's one thing for meeting participants to question the number of competitors or your method for scoring, quite another for them to poke holes in your analysis. Questioning your conclusions is a scarier risk than questioning the methodology, but in reality you may be less married to your conclusions.

In other words, once you've done the research for your competitive analysis, a serious concern in your methodology might mean throwing out the entire analysis and starting again. Questioning a conclusion, on the other hand, means revisiting the data for a different interpretation. If you're convinced of your conclusions, be prepared to defend them vehemently. If you're open to discussion about what the data mean, try spreading out the data and soliciting alternative interpretations. This could lead to worthwhile discussion.

Unfortunately, the only way to mitigate this risk may be to revisit the raw data. If you can rationalize your conclusion, you may not need extensive discussion (which would derail the meeting), but if you try to simply quash the criticism of your conclusions, your clients may start to question your integrity as a consultant. A vehement defense of ideas is one thing, but outright defensiveness is another. The bottom line is that you need to go into these meetings with the mental and emotional preparation to both unpack your conclusions and to go back to the raw data and observations if necessary.

Competitive Analyses in Context

The competitive analysis is a strategy document: It does not describe the user experience itself, but it's a stepping-stone to getting there. It's not an output of the design process but rather an essential input to it. However you employ your competitive analysis—whether for arriving at an overall strategy or for zeroing in on a specific design problem—you'll need to anticipate how it will fit into your process.

Using a Competitive Analysis with Other Documents

With competitive research, your aim is to establish a context for discussions about specific design problems or overall strategic decisions, like which features to include. Therefore, most of your competitive analyses will have to cooperate with other deliverables, which more directly document those decisions for your site.

Competitive analyses and user-needs documentation

User-needs documentation—at least in the context of this book—is any documentation that contributes to or comes from research into your target audiences. A competitive analysis can work with both aspects by helping to define an agenda for user research or put the results into context.

If you do your competitive analysis before talking to any users, you can use results of the analysis to identify issues you'd like to clarify through research. For example, in looking at different pet-related web sites, you might notice that the competitors use two different strategies for home page navigation. Namely, some home pages just use pet categories to get users into the catalog while other sites offer additional product categories (like sale items, or "new this week"). Your user research can attempt to shed light on these different strategies from the user's point of view. Your competitive analysis, therefore, can make reference to upcoming user-needs documents (like personas) that will elaborate on these particular issues.

On the other hand, you might save your competitive analysis for after you've done some user research or usability testing. In this case, the user research can set the agenda for the research into competitors. For example, in your pet web site project, suppose you start the process for upgrading the site by soliciting feedback from some of its users in a usability test. That test might reveal certain aspects of the site that are most important, functions or features of the design that users respond to either very positively or very negatively.

Imagine, for example, that the current version of your site offers extensive pet care advice that helps sell products from the catalog, and that users respond enthusiastically to this content. In this case, your competitive analysis might look at how other sites make use of advice content. This competitive analysis would use the usability test results as a rationale for examining particular criteria.

Competitive analyses and other strategy documents

Competitive analyses are strategic documents: They help define a design direction without defining the design itself. Other strategic documents described in this book are concept models—a tool for describing complex ideas that serve as the foundation for design—and content models—a tool for keeping track of all the content on the site.

Since each of these strategic documents aids the design process in a very different way, it's highly unlikely that they'd reference each other. Still, you employ these tools as part of the competitive analysis, using them to describe or highlight different aspects of the competitors' web sites. Put simply, you can do a concept model or a content model for each competitor as an additional means of comparison.

Competitive analyses and design documents

Even though competitive research can help drive design decisions, it's difficult to draw specific references between your analysis and a set of wireframes, for example. By the time you've gotten that far along into the design process, the information from the competitive analysis has already been absorbed into the design team's approach. As a result, the relationship between a design decision and a specific observation in the competitive analysis may not be explicit.

When competitive research addresses very specific design concerns, it should acknowledge the source of the design. For example, the design team behind the pet web site may be trying to decide where to locate the search box, a very specific design decision. A survey of competitors might reveal that they all put their search box at the top of the page, and the majority on the left-hand side. When putting a wireframe together for the new site, you could point to the competitive analysis by way of rationale. At this stage of the design process, however, such references are sometimes unnecessary.

Acknowledging the Competition

A competitive survey, no matter how rich the information gleaned from it, will always play second fiddle in the design process. After all, just because your competition does something doesn't mean you should. The competition is a good place to get ideas and to establish a baseline, a cost of entry. But the value of that information in making design decisions is limited at best.

Innovation moves fast online. Regardless of how the design process evolves, information about how other sites address the problems you face will always be valuable, because it keeps you abreast of the latest trends in technological change. With innovation comes a change in landscape. At the most basic level, your audience has to make a choice and it's our job as designers to make that choice easy, even when we don't understand all the factors that go into the decision.

When the commercial Internet emerged, retail stores faced a new kind of competition. Suddenly, competitors were lurking around every corner. This is still the case. What drives your understanding of the competition, therefore, should be a keen understanding of your audience. On the Internet, the competition is more than simply every other site trying to do the same thing you're doing. The competition is nearly any site that can attract and hold a user's attention. By knowing how your audience spends its time and how it makes decisions, you can anticipate how other sites or technologies are getting their attention, thereby expanding your survey of the competition.

CHAPTER SIX

Concept Model

kän'-sĕpt mä'-dəl (n.)

A concept model is a diagram that shows the relationships between different abstract concepts. You can apply the concept modeling technique in a variety of circumstances to explain different aspects of a web site. Also known as concept maps or affinity diagrams.

Concept models are highly flexible documents that you can use to show a variety of ideas at play in a given web site. At their simplest, concept models illustrate how different ideas relate to each other, representing the building blocks of the idea as nodes and their relationships as lines between them. Typically the basic ideas are expressed as nouns and the relationships as verbs, so the connections look like: NOUN-VERB-NOUN. Figure 6.1 shows a very simple one.

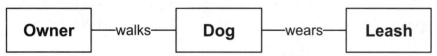

Figure 6.1 Simple concept models explain the relationships between different nouns in a particular context by linking them with verbs.

What's most important about a concept model, however, is that unlike other documents, it's as much about facilitating the thought process as it is about communicating ideas. It's as much for the creator of the document as it is for the consumers: an opportunity to wrap your head around complex ideas and relationships that, until you were hired by your client, you never had occasion to think about. The utility of the concept model is not so much in the output as it is in the getting there. It is very much a Zen deliverable.

Web sites, while very tangible, are typically built on abstract relationships: the categorization of products, the structure of a document, a business process, just to name a few. Even if these abstract ideas are not explicitly represented on the web site, it is important to hammer them out beforehand and make sure everyone agrees on them.

Concept models are not unique to web design or even software engineering circles. According to Wikipedia, concept mapping was developed by Joseph D. Novak at Cornell in the 1970s as a learning tool. It has since been subsumed into other formal methodologies, including the Unified Modeling Language, a system of documentation techniques for software engineers.

One of Novak's basic tenets was that learning involves incorporating new ideas into existing ones—that when we learn something new we do so in the context of stuff we already know. For the purposes of web design and underlying structures, the important thing is to help the project team understand how parts of the business (stuff they already know) will be incorporated into the web design (new ideas). The simplicity of a concept model makes it ideal for communicating these notions.

Concept Models at a Glance

Though most of the other chapters about deliverables in this book include three examples showing various levels of detail, the concept models that follow show how concept models can be applied to illustrate different kinds of concepts.

Although "traditional" concept maps label the connections between nouns with verbs, those used in web design do not always include these labels. In some cases this is because it's enough to know that there is a relationship between objects without knowing its specific nature. In other cases, it's because the concept models we build for the web have self-evident relationships. Typical relationships in modeling for the web—for example, part-whole relationships (one concept is part of another) or semantic equality (two concepts are the same)—are fairly straightforward.

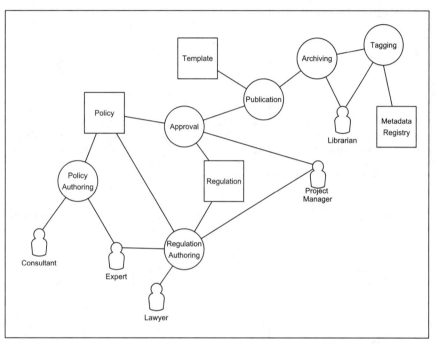

Figure 6.2 To explain the relationship between different documents in an organization and the processes and people required to produce them, this concept model distinguishes three kinds of nouns: processes (circles), documents (squares), and people (figures). The connections between them are nonspecific, so the reader is not given any information on the relationship between, say, a librarian and the archiving process.

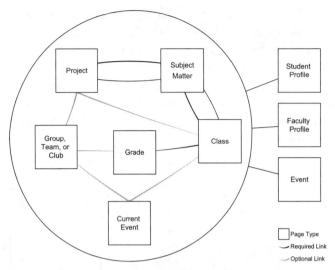

Figure 6.3 In this concept model representing a web site for a high school, the nouns all represent a type of page found on the web site. This is not a site map, per se, in that it does not show how users would navigate through the site. Instead, it shows the connections between pages. For example, every class page (e.g. Mr. Smith's Seventh Period Geometry) is linked to a subject matter page (Math) and vice versa. By contrast, some connections are not required. The Chess Club and Debate Team both use the "Group, Team, or Club" page type, but the Chess Club page isn't linked to anything in particular, while the Debate Team page is linked to a few different current events pages. It also shows that any of the pages in the large circle may be linked to a faculty (Mr. Smith) or student (Claire H., captain of the Debate Team) profile, or a specific event page (Senior Prom). I hated high school. Let's move on to something more interesting.

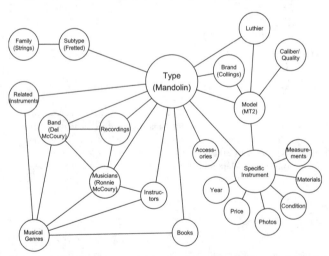

Figure 6.4 While this concept model doesn't show any more or less detail than the others, it does deal with a more specific concept. Instead of representing a broad view of the web site, it shows all the different kinds of data on the site and how they relate to each other. This concept model is for a web site selling musical instruments and illustrates the different ways of categorizing an instrument (the categories of categories) and the associated metadata for each instrument. (Metadata is special information attached to a document or some other object that helps describe what it is.) This concept model represents the relative importance of each concept by varying the size of the circles.

Concept Model Overview

Purpose—What are concept models for?

Concept models help the project team puzzle through and document the ideas that form the basis of the web site design. As demonstrated above, this can be as broad as the overall business process or as narrow as the categorization structure.

Audience—Who uses them?

Since the concept model is used to document underlying structures in the user experience, the audience will be members of the project team and stakeholders who'll use the concept models to help understand the basis of the web site design.

Scale—How much work are they?

Though the scope of a concept model is typically limited—showing only a select set of ideas and detail—the intensive part is developing the concepts. Since the model informs the rest of the user experience, decisions made here have far-reaching implications throughout the design.

Context—Where do they fall in the process?

Although it makes sense to do concept models at the beginning of the project—to establish a common vocabulary for the underlying elements and to lay the groundwork for the user experience—it can be just as useful to do the concept model later in the design process. In many cases, it's difficult to anticipate the underlying structure without first having thought through the user experience. When it becomes clear that the project team has different notions of the basic assumptions, that's a good time to take a step back and document those assumptions.

Format—What do they look like?

A concept map represents a single set of ideas. It usually appears on a single page and may be included with a larger deliverable, as part of the introduction to establish the user experience basics.

Challenges

Depending on which ideas you're illustrating, the concept model's main challenge is to explain abstract ideas as concretely as possible.

The main purpose of a concept model is to come to a common understanding of the site's underlying assumptions, so the concept model must explain these assumptions effectively. The challenge is not only to capture the assumptions, but to make sure everyone has the same understanding.

Creating Concept Models

Concept models are visually simple, despite representing abstract concepts. They're usually nothing more than circles or boxes connected by lines. Like other deliverables in this book, however, concept models will be described here in a series of three layers, each layer containing elements of the document with increasing levels of detail. In the case of concept models, however, layer 2 simply describes how to embellish the basic elements of layer 1. Layer 3 describes departing from the typical format and adding a third element, the backdrop.

Layer 1: The Bare Minimum

At its heart, a concept model consists of shapes connected by lines. As the examples at the top of the chapter show, these shapes can represent anything from business processes to metadata elements. I'll refer to these shapes—the boxes or circles or whatever—as nodes and the lines connecting them as, well, connections.

Nodes

The basic currency of a concept model is the node: the thing that's connected to other things. The simplest nodes are circles or boxes with a name. The node itself conveys very little information; its relationship to adjacent and connected objects is much more meaningful. Still, your choice of what constitutes a node is crucial.

Nodes as content types: A content type is a way of categorizing different kinds of documents appearing on the web site, like press releases or product descriptions. Although there may be relationships between these categories, you will no doubt need to include additional kinds of nodes—like people working on the content or processes that operate on the content—to spell out a concept from beginning to end.

Nodes as processes: Processes are connected to inputs and outputs, and the people involved in them. They should be labeled with the "–ing" form of a verb, like AUTHORING or PUBLISHING. Occasionally, larger processes will be labeled with the "-tion" form of the verb, like DISTRIBUTION.

Nodes as people or entities: One way to make the abstract more tangible is to include people or groups of people who are responsible for performing tasks related to the concepts, or who are somehow constrained by the concepts.

Nodes as data elements: Commonly linked to content types, data element nodes—which refer to individual pieces of information—can show which parts of a document are important to the user experience.

Nodes as groups or categories: The web site may have unique ways of grouping concepts together. For example, a social networking web site may have different groups of people represented by the connections between them: the immediate circle of friends, the friends of friends, etc. Figure 6.4 shows different ways of categorizing a musical instrument.

Nodes as events: It may be important to show how the concepts are related to an event. For example, convening the editorial board is required to determine the home page features.

Nodes as systems: Users may be required to consult a variety of systems to perform their tasks, or the web site you're building may need to grab information from other systems. The web site that sells musical instruments may consult a separate system for customer data, for example.

Nodes as other concepts: The flexibility of the concept model means that just about anything can be a node—time, location, feelings, qualities, judgments, technical standards, and much more.

Connections

In the simplest concept maps, connections are not differentiated from each other visually. A line merely connects two nodes to show a relationship between them. As described previously, this may be because the connection is self-evident or the nature of the connection is not as important as the connection itself. When in doubt, however, you should label the connections to make the relationships explicit.

Both common concepts and unique ones benefit from explicit labels on their relationships. With common concepts (like "time" or "people" or "documents"), the relationships are crucial to establishing the context and meaning of the model. When the concepts are unique to the project, the specific nature of their relationships may help with understanding these novel ideas.

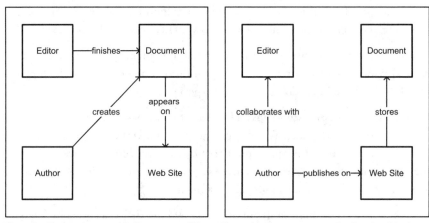

Figure 6.5 These concept models illustrate two different ideas with the same concepts by changing the relationship labels.

Layer 2: Adding More Detail

The great thing about a document this flexible is that there's an opportunity to show rich amounts of detail. Like any diagram, it's best to start with just the first layer in order to get an understanding of the concepts and the relationships between them. Once you do that, consider embellishing them with more illustrative shapes.

Most diagrams describing qualitative relationships between objects are some form of the conceptual model. They may not look like standard "boxes connected with lines" pictures, but you could quite easily boil them down into one.

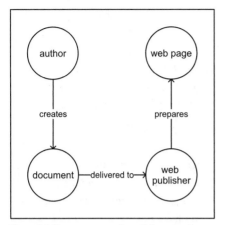 

Figure 6.6 Here are two versions of the same diagram—one standard and one using embellished nodes and connections.

Embellished nodes

A node doesn't have to be a circle or a square. It can be any shape that represents the concept. This is effective when there are already icons that represent ideas—clocks and calendars to stand for time, stick figures for people, dog-eared pages for documents and other content.

Figure 6.7 Nodes can be just about any shape, and the more abstract the concept, the more it will benefit from having some sort of icon. This "nodes gallery" shows icons for a range of ideas—time, people, events, systems, processes.

You can also embellish nodes by playing with size and color. Don't go nuts, but you can use colors to group related nodes where you're not otherwise connecting them. For example, the various nodes in Figure 6.2 can be visually distinguished by whether they come before or after publication on the web. In Figure 6.4, the more important ideas are bigger, because it's these central ideas (the type of musical instrument) that set the context for the entire diagram.

Embellished connections

Sometimes what's interesting about one connection is interesting about other connections as well. For example, in part–whole relationships—in which one object in the concept map belongs to another object—the connections are uni-directional. Navigational relationships—in which users access one object in a concept model from another—are usually bidirectional. Some connections are optional. Some connections are of a specific type, like procedural or semantic. If two or more connections are of the same type, they should be represented using the same embellished line, which takes the simple line to the next level.

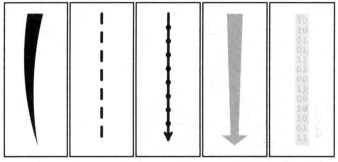

Figure 6.8 If you thought a line was the shortest distance between two points, you need to get out more. These lines can be used to indicate all kinds of connections between concepts—part-whole, chronology, semantic, parent-child, romantic, platonic, optional. Varying line weight and color can also show importance or directionality. Because it can be difficult for people to remember what shapes mean what, you should limit the number of lines you use. Remember that the purpose of a connection is to illustrate the relationships between concepts and compare relationships between concepts. In **Figure 6.3**, the relevant comparison is whether the connections are optional or whether they're mutual, and the line patterns are used to illustrate these meanings only.

Layer 3: The Complete Picture

By using more elaborate nodes and connections, you may create something that's hardly recognizable as a concept model. This is an important evolution: What starts out as simple diagram of circles and lines can end up something much more elaborate, even if the purpose remains simple—to show how different ideas relate to each other.

Once you embellish your nodes and connections, there's little left you can do to the concept model to add depth or detail, except use background elements to represent further abstract groupings.

Backdrops

A backdrop is a subtle change in color or contrast to indicate that certain nodes are grouped together. With a backdrop, the nodes and connections themselves are unaffected. Backdrops should be labeled to make their purpose clear.

It's important to be subtle in your backdrops because there's already a lot going on in your diagram. Too much of a visual change can be distracting. You should also consider whether the backdrop is necessary to communicate the ideas. A backdrop is just noise when it doesn't contribute any additional information to the model.

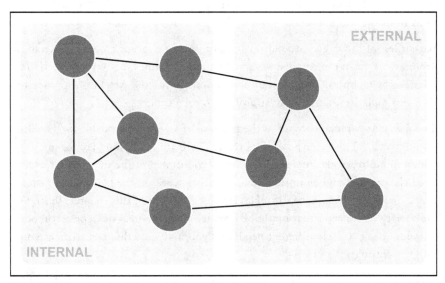

Figure 6.9 Backgrounds should be as subtle as possible. Don't hit your readers over the head with the difference between one area and another. In general, the average eye is good at picking up these visual distinctions. Before throwing a background in there, consider whether it truly adds anything interesting to the drawing. In this concept model, the background helps distinguish between internal and external processes. This information may be self-evident after carefully reading the diagram, but backgrounds help establish the gist of a diagram at a macro level before the reader digs into the details.

Modeling Concepts: The Basics

Like any good document, the successful concept model is a product of its situation. In order to work well, the document must address the particular needs of a given audience at a specific time in the project. Concept models are versatile enough that you can use them to address any number of situations, but they must be tailored appropriately. Therefore, before starting a concept model, make sure you understand the situation.

Finding purpose for your concept models

The line is fuzzy, but concept models aren't necessarily design tools—or, they certainly don't start out that way. Although concept models may be built into a project plan, they work best when the project team realizes either (a) they're having trouble communicating with each other because the terminology is inconsistent, or (b) they've stumbled upon a real mess of interconnecting ideas that they need to sort out before moving forward. The concept model is, initially, a tool for getting stories straight. Once the ducks are aligned, however, the concept model can become a tool for getting others to buy into the foundations of further design work.

Regardless of the trigger, the ultimate purpose of a concept model is to establish groundwork for more detailed design. The model frames the web site's requirements—the technical documentation describing what the system is supposed to do—in simpler terms and in relationships to each other.

The previous paragraph says that the purpose of a concept model is to "establish groundwork." This is purposefully broad: There are many foundations upon which to build a web site design. It's up to you to determine the concepts that need clarification and definition before starting work on the hard part. (That was tongue-in-cheek.) The examples at the beginning of this chapter illustrate the variety of concepts that might be clarified with the help of a concept model. Different projects have different needs and you may only discover them as you progress through the project.

When to model concepts

Concept maps, the forerunner of conceptual models, were designed as teaching tools—that is, tools to be developed after the fact, when a set of ideas is already fully realized. When incorporated into a design methodology, however, concept models are usually used to facilitate development, before anything is fully realized. Therefore, there's no specific time to do a concept model.

Imagine a design team is working on a web site to sell musical instruments. They develop a site map that accommodates every instrument in the client's inventory. Mandolins are sorted under stringed —> fretted —> mandolin family; violins under stringed —> orchestral —> violins and violas. As development of the site progresses, however, the designers realize that some of their customers may look for violins and mandolins closer to each other in the hierarchy, since they are frequently used together in a variety of folk and world music styles. The team realizes it needs to step back and reassess the classification schemes, and so creates a concept model like the one in Figure 6.4.

The main trigger for creating a concept model is when the project stalls and the team needs to step back to better understand the ideas that are causing the disruption. The symptoms can vary from project to project, but usually include miscommunication because of inconsistent labeling, or working with a business that hasn't taken a hard look at its essential components. Consider Figure 6.4, where a store selling musical instruments might never have tried to break its business down into discrete categories, or identify the essential attributes of each product. These categories might have grown organically, because the store's owners never considered the need to impose some order on their inventory.

Consumers of conceptual models

Initially a concept model might be for the person creating the model: Someone employs a concept model to get the ideas straight in his or her own head. (I frequently use concept models at the very beginning of a new project to understand office politics, weird business processes, or business relationships that stakeholders take for granted.) Ultimately, the concept model will be crucial in putting the design in place because it sorts out some of the fundamental assumptions behind a design. Therefore, it may be a prerequisite for others working on the project to understand the evolution of the design.

For concept models, one size fits all. The simplicity of presentation and detail suggest little wiggle room based on audience. Since the point of a concept model is to give everyone a common understanding of the fundamentals, it wouldn't help to give everyone a different model.

Nodes and connections

The situation analysis (the when, who, and why discussed earlier in this chapter) for a concept model may be quick, even unconscious, because of its function.

Unlike other documents in this book, which require considerable planning, you may be deciding what's important as you're creating the diagram.

The layout of a concept model is driven by the data: You'll need to show how certain concepts cluster together, or how certain concepts are more important than others, or how certain concepts occur chronologically. The layout plays an important role in communicating these differences between nodes.

FIGURE 6.10A

FIGURE 6.10B

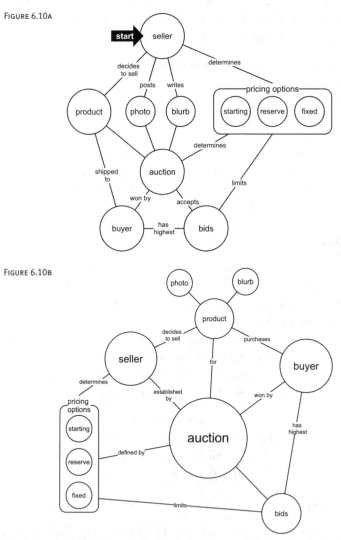

Figures 6.10a and 6.10b You may be tempted to scatter your nodes across the page, but the placement of a node says a lot about it. Nodes in the upper left are starting places. Nodes in the middle, especially coupled with size, show importance. These two drawings use the same nodes. The concept model above encourages readers to start at the top of the page and read down, while the bottom model emphasizes importance over direction by putting the central concepts in the middle of the page.

How to Be the Next Top Modeler

Working in the abstract can make it hard to know where to start. Unlike some of the other documents in this book, concept models often benefit from starting out with too much information. With other documents, you generally want to cut down the things you are trying to say or they become too complex and instead of communicating everything, you communicate nothing. Having at its heart only two kinds of elements—the node and the connection—the concept model is easier to cut down after the fact by simply lopping off nodes that don't contribute to the message. The following principles should limit any "writer's block" while keeping you in check. When in doubt, refer to your situation analysis: Does the information you want to include help you to meet your goals? Is the information essential to understanding the underlying foundation of the design? Use these questions as a litmus test for your development process.

Have a message

The hardest part with concept models is deciding what to leave out. Since the method of concept modeling has few rules, there's little to stop you from kitchen sinking your concept models. The best way to limit the enthusiastic concept modeler is to have a message: What is it you want the concept model to say? You can express this message as a question. Table 6.1 lists the messages for the concept models at the beginning of this chapter.

TABLE 6.1

The Messages Behind the Models

Concept Model	Message (expressed as either question or statement)
Figure 6.2, The Business Objects	From a business process perspective, what is the difference between a regulation and a policy?
Figure 6.3, The High School Web Site	Though there are a lot of different people and groups in this high school, we can boil the site down to a few main content types.
Figure 6.4, The Musical Instrument Model	What are the different ways people look for a musical instrument, and what criteria do they use to determine whether they'll buy it?

By developing a message or a problem statement, you have a simple means for eliminating unnecessary information from the diagram.

Start with nouns

Make a list of all the entities you need to represent in the concept model. Don't censor yourself, at least at this point. Once you have two handfuls of nouns, put them on the page and start connecting them, experimenting with different verbs for showing the relationships, if necessary.

Normalize your nodes

Once you have all your nodes down on paper, it's time to remove some of them. Hopefully you'll begin to see which ones help define the concept and which offer supporting information that's not essential.

One way to shear your concept model is to limit it to certain kinds of nodes, especially if it's a high-level model covering lots of ground. For example, in a model that has nodes for people, processes, documents, systems, and events, you might limit the model to just people and documents, using connections to illustrate the high points.

Another means for normalizing nodes in a high-level model is to seek out the part-whole connections. If the distinction between a whole and its parts is not immediately relevant to the design process, you can remove one or the other because they may just stand for each other. For example, a concept model of several related business processes may show how the publishing process includes authoring, reviewing and distributing. You could eliminate either the parts (authoring, etc.) or the whole (publishing) because including both might be redundant. This might be a good opportunity to use backdrops: The general processes (like "publishing") form backdrops for more specific processes. This can make for a more interesting model because it digs a little deeper into the unseen relationships.

Finally, the last telltale sign of nodes in need of elimination is a node growth— a cluster of nodes hanging off one side of the model with limited connections to the rest of the model. If there isn't much linking this set of nodes and the rest of the model, you could move them to a separate model, or roll them up under a single node.

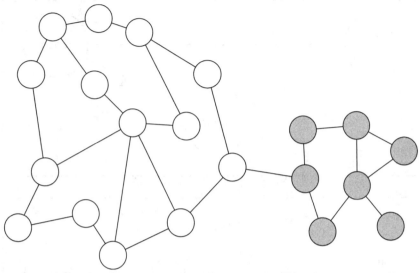

Figure 6.11 Here's a mocked-up concept model that shows what a "node growth" might look like. When one concept sits at the junction of two groups of concepts, it can yield a concept model like this one. If the purpose of the concept model is to show how two groups of concept relate, this might work for you. It could also show that the diagram is losing its focus. In this case, the question the author needs to ask is whether the diagram will lose its meaning if the gray circles are eliminated.

Economize your connections

Your first attempt at connecting the concepts will generate a real mishmash kind of network, and as you look closely you'll start to notice redundant connections. For example, you might have a subject matter expert, a report, and a review process. You can connect all three of these to each other, but you might find one of the connections is doing the job of the other two, and you can opt to remove one of the nodes or one of the connections between the nodes, as illustrated in Figure 6.12.

Once you spend a bit of time with concept models, you'll find that there are patterns to the connections that yield opportunities to consolidate. For each connection, ask yourself whether it's telling you something new or significant that contributes to the overall message of the diagram. If this is too hard, snip a few possibly redundant connections and ask yourself whether the stakeholders will be missing a crucial part of your message without it.

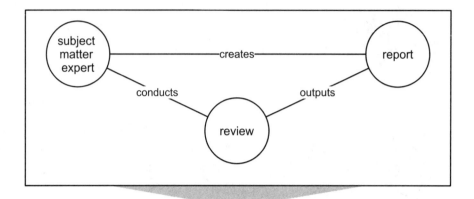

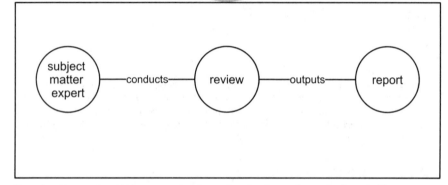

Figure 6.12 Three nodes with three connections is usually a sign that you have redundancy. In this case, you can simply connect subject matter expert to review process to report.

Potential Pitfalls in Concept Model Creation

In building concept models you may run into some issues, especially around utility and relevancy. Keep an eye out for these potential pitfalls as you push nodes and connections around the page.

Balance concept and design

Creating a concept model after you've begun design work, while helpful in clarifying the assumptions behind the design, may cause you to rethink your design altogether. Objectively speaking, this is not a bad thing, and under ideal circumstances this is a risk to be embraced. Your project manager might say otherwise.

The problems arise when you discover, for instance, that the way your design represents the underlying concepts is inadequate. In the design of a commercial site selling musical instruments, you might have accommodated only one way of navigating to a product while your concept model indicates there are three or four ways people categorize instruments.

When there is a discrepancy between the design and the concept model, you can make modifications either to the design or the concept model to bring them into closer alignment. These revisions, however, may spiral into a never-ending cycle of adjusting one document to accommodate another. A better approach is simply to indicate on the design (or the concept model, or both) where the discrepancies exist, and why.

Keep the concept in perspective

Web sites need to be simple, even if they represent complicated ideas. One risk in building a concept model is that you become too entrenched in the ideas to step back and consider the model's impact on the overall user experience. A concept model is supposed to help identify all the relevant concepts and their relationships in a given context, but some of the best designs explicitly conceal these complexities.

Imagine a site that allows users to attach notations to a document. Given the business process, there may be several different kinds of notations: those applied automatically by the system based on a series of business rules, those applied by other users to solicit questions about the documents, and those applied by management to render some kind of decision about the document. The concept model may account for these distinctions, but the ultimate impact on the interface can be overwhelming.

Build practical concept models

Undoubtedly the most common risk with a concept model is that you create a document that is useless. You'll stare at those circles and lines and wonder why you spent the time arranging them just so. Fear not, you're not the first person to line birdcages and recycling bins with documents that never make it out of version 0.1.

If you worry about the document's utility, however, you can ask yourself some questions before you get too far in the modeling process. As you put your initial list of nouns together, ask yourself about the potential impact on the design. You can score each noun on its exposure in the interface. For example, a concept model that includes nodes for people, processes, and documents might indicate the latter as being fully represented in the interface—for example, users must select a document type from a list. Processes may not get represented at all because we don't want to clutter the final design with business process names that may be meaningless to the users participating in them. Finally, people nodes may have some representation in the interface because the layout of the page may vary depending on the user's role, but the name of the role (e.g., "Author") might never show up explicitly on the page.

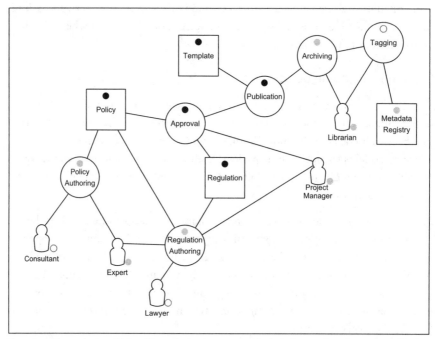

Figure 6.13 The concept model from **Figure 6.2** has been marked to show that certain nodes are immediately relevant to the interface (the dark dot) and others as not so relevant (the lighter colored dots). The darker the dot, the more likely the concept will explicitly appear in the interface. In this example, the interface will explicitly make reference to Policies and Regulations. That is, the world "Policy" will appear somewhere on the screen while the word "Expert" or "Archiving" may not appear on the screen at all but users will have to understand it to use the interface. Meanwhile, "Consultant" is not relevant to the use of the system at all. With this information, the designers can see how much of an impact the concept model has on the site's interface.

Presenting Concept Models

First things first: Ask yourself, "Do I need to present my concept model to stakeholders at all?" If you're using it as a tool to get things straight for your own purposes, or with a small team, this may not be a formal deliverable, meaning it may never see the light of the conference room. It may be more responsible to shield your stakeholders and other team members from this kind of document if it won't help them understand the overall design.

If you decide that the concept model includes ideas that are essential for understanding the overall approach, think about whether you need to show the entire model. Is there an abbreviated version you can put together that boils the ideas down to just what's needed as prerequisites for the rest of the design?

Ultimately, the key to presenting a concept model is telling a story, putting the concept model into a context that team members and stakeholders can relate to. Your story needs to be grounded in reality, and this section describes several ways to do this.

Meeting Purpose

The presentation should be driven by the purpose. With concept models, there are usually only two reasons why you'd present them: to prepare participants for more in-depth design discussions, or to hash out the model itself.

The prep meeting: Greasing the wheels

One reason for presenting a concept model is to lay a foundation for the design, prepping the meeting participants for a more detailed discussion about the user experience. These meetings usually start out with, "I know you're eager to dig into the design, but there are some basic concepts we need to clear up before we do." For example, if you're about to show wireframes for an online musical instrument store, you may lead with a concept model like the one in Figure 6.4 to help participants understand the different ways instruments may be classified.

The brainstorming meeting: Modeling together

The other reason to put a concept model in front of team members and stakeholders is to collaborate in its construction. In this case, rougher models are better because they lend themselves to feedback and discussion. It's important to come to a consensus about the underlying structure that supports a web site's design because it drives so much of the conversation.

As described previously, concept models can help at any point in the design process. Building them collaboratively does not change this. You may come to an impasse in the design process, a clue that there's disagreement about the underlying assumptions, and use that as an opportunity to take a step back and facilitate a brainstorming meeting to flesh out the basic concepts.

Meeting Structure

There are a few ways to structure a concept model meeting and you should select the agenda that suits your purpose best. The more complex your concept model is, the more you'll lean toward a meeting structure where you can present the model in pieces, or gradually.

Problems solved approach

In this type of meeting structure, you identify the obstacles you are running into and show how the concept model helps you work through them. Usually, these obstacles are related to the design itself. For example, you might realize you don't know how "regulations" and "policies," two different types of documents produced by your client, are related to each other or to the people who work on them. You can explain this to your client by saying something like this:

"Even though we talked to a lot of people in the organization about regulations and policies, we got some conflicting reports about how they fit into the overall process. Of course, we wanted to make sure that the design of the new document management system represented these documents appropriately. We put this concept model together to clarify the relationship between these documents and key players in the organization."

This approach tends to work best if participants have never seen a concept model before because it spells out the context and gives them a sense of the kinds of nodes they'll see. You can be explicit about this approach and include the problem(s) on the document itself.

The nodes and relationships approach

If your concept model is focused around a particular node or set of nodes, you can start at that focal point and work your way outward. From the focal point, there are a couple different ways to proceed. You might, for instance, address the next "level" of nodes—those immediately connected to your primary node. Alternatively, you could address each cluster of nodes attached to the focal point.

For example: In the musical instrument concept map (Figure 6.4), the central node is the instrument itself. Starting there, you can work around the "parent" nodes, describing each one. Alternatively, you can describe each trail leading to this central node—the instrument family, the musicians, the qualities of the instrument, and the maker.

When presenting a concept model with more than one focal point, start by describing the primary relationship between each of these key nodes.

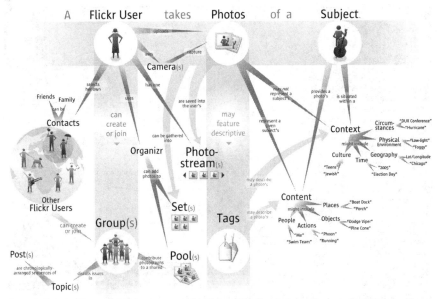

Figure 6.14 Bryce Glass put together a concept model describing the photo-sharing web site Flickr.com. His model has three main nodes—the user, the photo, and the subject matter—and nicely spells out the relationships between them. In presenting this model with the Nodes & Relationship Approach, you'd start with these three and expand from there. (Flickr User Model diagram by Bryce Glass, http://mApplogic.com. Used with permission.)

The whiteboard approach

This approach takes two different forms, depending on the purpose of your meeting. If you need to prep meeting participants for a design discussion, you might build the concept model progressively on the whiteboard. In other words, with this method you would describe the concept model by drawing it on the board as you talk through it. The advantage is that you can focus the conversation on one node and relationship at a time and avoid overwhelming the participants with a complex set of ideas.

For the brainstorming meeting, you'll just need a few nodes to start with. Put these up on the board and let the participants come up with others. Like any brainstorming meeting, the challenge here is keeping things focused, but concept modeling has the added risk of being somewhat abstract and subjective. There are, after all, lots of ways to classify musical instruments. To preserve the focus without stifling creativity, write a purpose statement or two on the board before you begin.

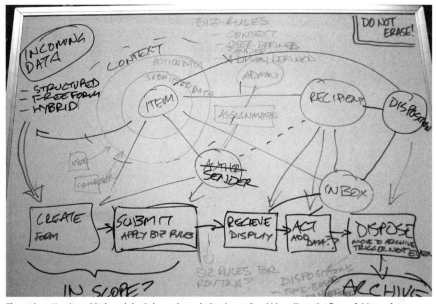

Figure 6.15 Here's a whiteboard that's been through the ringer. Good ideas litter the floor of this conference room, and the stench of dry erase hangs in the air. Brainstorming is messy, smelly business, but someone has to do it. In the brainstorming process, the team clearly revisited some ideas again and again, identifying and creating new relationships. Additionally, they added new types of information as the model grew. Note the-ever important "DO NOT ERASE!" Including a name, phone extension, and date in this message can help preserve your brilliant ideas. Presumably, this mess will be turning into something clean and legible in a drawing program like Adobe Illustrator or Microsoft Visio.

The beauty of this approach is that you can show up at your presentation meeting without an actual deliverable. Instead, you just bring a list of possible nodes. On the other hand, if you want to guide the conversation in a particular direction, you may want to have a concept model in your back pocket (literally).

Presentation Risks

Even the more concrete concept models may confuse participants. Unless they can draw a parallel to something in the real world, they may not understand exactly what they're looking at. And even if they do get it, they may not care.

Potential response 1: What am I looking at here?

Some people may just not get it, especially if the concept model dabbles in the really abstract. Models can represent categories of categories or tiny little blocks of data or information about metadata (which is information about information). They can use slight variations in visual conventions to represent different abstract ideas (arrows for navigation, arrows for transporting data, arrows for indicating semantic relationships). For people who are used to looking at spreadsheets, or the simple infographics in *USA Today,* these diagrams can be exhausting.

Before going into a presentation where you think you might get this response, boil the concept down into three sentences. If you're not getting anywhere with the diagram, whip out those bullet points. As you watch your meeting circling the drain, these three sentences can be a lifesaver, giving participants the essential message without belaboring the diagram.

The key here is to not make them feel dumber than they already do. To that end, you might say something like: "Why don't you take some time to digest this and give me feedback in a couple days. This model is important because it creates the overall foundation for our design work. While you're looking at it, keep the following three things in mind. (Insert your summary sentences here.)"

Potential response 2: So what?

Even if the meeting participants get it, they may not realize why it matters. You have two possible strategies in this situation: Try to show the connections between the model and the design, or simply cut the meeting short.

Cutting the meeting short is always an embarrassing and difficult tactic, but sometimes you have more to gain by avoiding conversation than forcing it. Since concept models tend to be highly abstract tools for designers to get their thoughts in order, the stakeholders may have little to gain by going through it.

Again, the key here is to not make them feel stupid. Try saying something like: "I think I've gotten everything I need. I appreciate your time. We'll take this feedback and incorporate it into the design. If you have further thoughts, let me know. Otherwise, the next time we talk we'll start to show you some of our design work."

Ending the meeting is a last-ditch tactic, and you should only use it if it's clear the stakeholders or other team members aren't interested in engaging at an abstract level.

Concept Models in Context

Like any other deliverable, concept models are a stepping-stone to the final product. Concept models, as abstractions, may seem very far removed from that goal, which is why it's crucial to draw connections to other documents in order to show how the ideas in the model support subsequent design activities. Concept models will become more important over time as technologies evolve to allow more complex interactions. In other words, as technologies evolve and our interactions with the web become more complex, it will be more difficult to plan the precise categorizations established in a site map. Instead, we will need to think more abstractly about the relationships inherent in a web site. Bryce Glass's Flickr example is a good one. Though it was developed after the fact, it could have been built as part of the planning process and would have been more useful to the developers than a site map because of Flickr's dynamic user experience.

Using Concept Models with Other Documents

Concept models in this book are categorized as strategy and planning documents because they support design activities. The line, however, is fuzzier than that: Concept models may also be a good way to document design ideas.

Concept models and user-needs documentation

After researching the web site's target audience, you may have a sense of how it thinks about the information presented on the site. The audience may have particular ideas about organization or navigation that you could represent in a concept model.

A concept model can help bridge the gap between a user's understanding of a business and the business's understanding of itself. In other words, user research can reveal that users employ a certain vocabulary or have a certain notion of what the organization does and how it operates. You could use a concept model to translate the user's notion into terms the stakeholders in the organization understand.

If you've organized your user research into personas, you can use persona names as nodes in your concept models. Your model might illustrate the relationships between the different types of users. A concept model can be useful to show how different types of users relate to the overall business, where nodes represent not only users, but business processes and outputs of those processes as well.

This can help stakeholders incorporate a new way of thinking about users into their existing framework for thinking about their business.

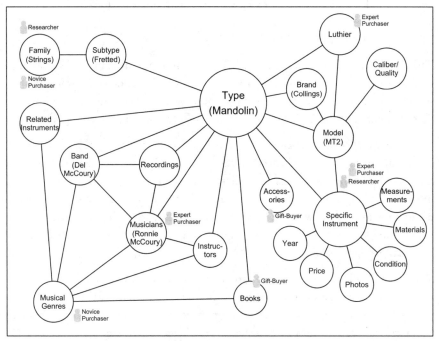

Figure 6.16 The musical instrument concept model has been modified to include persona names. In this case, the personas describe different ways people will navigate musical instruments. The advantage here is that in constructing the site, the designers can prioritize which categorization schemes are more important to the business goals. If a user group is important to the business, the categories important to the user group will have more prominence in the design. Of course, you should use concept models to emphasize conclusions from actual user research, showing how what users want overlaps with the underlying structure of the web site.

Concept models and other strategy documents

The other strategy and planning documents this book discusses are the content model (a systematic inventory of a web site's content) and a competitive analysis (a comparison of the site to others like it). The concept model is more flexible than these documents, since it's a method for representing a wide range of ideas, rather than a specific set. Depending on how you're using the concept model, there are a few opportunities to link it to these strategy documents.

If the concept model establishes different types of content (as Figure 6.3 does), you can include content types in the content inventory. For the high school web site, the concept model defines nine different content types, which you can use to label the different pieces of content in the inventory.

Since the concept model format is so simple, it affords an easy way of drawing comparisons, and so is ideal for a competitive analysis. You can show how different sites model similar content, or how competitive organizations do business.

Concept models and design documents

The concept model has a funny relationship with design documents because in many ways the concept model is part of the design. This book lumps it into the strategy documents because the main purpose of the concept model is not to describe what the user will see, but instead help the designer to that point.

The extent of a formal relationship between the concept model and your flow-charts, site maps, and wireframes should depend on how entrenched the model has become during the process. In other words, if you made heavy use of the model and the rest of the team is familiar with it, try to include it in the other documents to show how they all tie to a single model. On the other hand, if the concept model was just a personal tool to iron out some of the more difficult assumptions, leave it out.

The easiest (and most reliable) way to create a relationship between a concept model and the design documents is to reuse the conventions in the model. If you used a particular icon to represent a node in a concept model, use that icon again in a site map or flowchart, or use it to label a wireframe. This approach creates continuity between your documents.

Concepts Matter

Imagine a concept model, designed for a news publishing service, that describes the anatomy of a news story. It shows how the news story is composed of different kinds of information, the metadata attached to a news story, and the different types of news stories displayed on the site.

The concept model establishes a vocabulary for talking about the structure of these stories, and how they might be formatted in different ways on different parts of the site. The front page will have short teasers. Subject category pages might have longer teasers and a couple of features with longer introductions. The design team gives all these data points distinct names so they can talk about them easily: short summaries, headlines, subheads, long summaries, main body, extended body, and many others.

For all the effort put into this terminology, it may never be exposed to the end user. Its purpose is simply to facilitate the design process, to come to a common understanding of how the underlying concepts relate to each other. It is through the final design that the people using the site are supposed to understand these concepts. Ironically, the design needs to be more effective than the concept model in communicating them.

And yet, many designs couldn't get off the ground without some kind of conceptual model. This won't change anytime soon, and with web-based systems becoming more complex and richer in their interactions with users, concept models will be more critical than ever to the planning process. Web sites whose navigation systems rely more on searching than browsing, or that depend on organic growth with content contributed from users, or that simplify information delivery through syndication, will require more conceptual designing up front. The concept model may become a more central tool in the process of designing web sites.

CHAPTER SEVEN

Content Inventory

kän'-těnt in'-věn-tŏr'-ē (n.)

A list of all the information contained in a web site, along with data that describes the information from several points of view, like target audience or location. Also known as a content analysis or content audit.

If any part of a designer's job is the most painstaking or most difficult, it is the content inventory. On the other hand, it is hardly the most thankless. By unpacking a web site, unearthing every (or nearly every) piece of content and documenting these discoveries, the designer creates a tool that many different people will find useful. Despite the mind-numbing work required to inventory a site's content, the designer can become the hero of the project team, creating a document that supports many different activities in constructing a site.

This chapter will use two terms—content inventory and content audit—to describe documents that come from processes of the same names. The main distinction between these two documents and processes is the level of granularity. In essence, the distinction is how much of the site you describe. With an inventory, the intent is to capture and describe every piece of content on the site. A content audit captures and describes less, focusing perhaps on the main content areas of the site or the top two levels of navigation after the home page. An audit establishes a boundary around the scope of the investigation.

A significantly smaller endeavor is the content analysis, which is meant to provide an overview of the site's content for a particular purpose. Imagine an intranet that has grown organically over the last several years. The project team might do an analysis to determine just how out of hand the growth of content has been. Even though the analysis presents less information, usually a content audit or inventory is required in order to acquire the necessary data for it.

Like all the other documents in this book, the exact nature of your content inventory depends entirely on its purpose and how you intend to use it. You may have your own reasons for doing a content inventory, but the main reason is in anticipation of some kind of redesign. In some cases, the project may entail installing a new system to store and publish the content. In other cases, the site may be overdue for a spring cleaning and an inventory is the best way to get a handle on the agenda. In still other cases, you've just conducted some user research and you need to understand how the content you have matches up with the needs of your audience.

Content Inventories at a Glance

Any content inventory worth its salt will be a spreadsheet, and a substantial one at that. Typically, the list of pages on the site runs down one of the first columns on the spreadsheet. Subsequent columns show a variety of data elements related to the content.

	A	B	C	D	E
1	ID	Page Name	Page Type	Location	Owner
2	1.0	Our Programs	News Gallery	/pgm	Alexis
3	1.1	Wells for Sudan	Program Profile	/pgm/sudan	Alexis
4	1.1.1	Program History & Timeline	Program History	/pgm/sudan/history.html	Alexis
5	1.1.2	Program Financials	Financial Profile	/pgm/sudan/finance.html	Alexis
6	1.2	Wells for Chad	Program Profile	/pgm/chad	Alexis
7	1.2.1	Program History & Timeline	Program History	/pgm/chad/history.html	Alexis
8	1.2.2	Program Financials	Financial Profile	/pgm/chad/finance.html	Alexis
9	1.3	AgriAid	Program Profile	/pgm/agriaid	Mary
10	1.3.1	Technical Specifications	General Content	/pgm/agriaid/spec.html	Mary
11	1.3.2	Program Financials	Financial Profile	/pgm/agriaid/finance.html	Mary
12	1.4	Tech for Change	Program Profile	/tech	Mary
13	1.4.1	Aid Management Software	General Content	/tech/aidmgmt	Mary
14	1.4.2	Development Project Management Software	General Content	/tech/devpm	Mary
15	2.0	About Us	News Gallery	/about	Morgan
16	2.1	Board of Directors	Gallery	/about/board.html	Morgan
17	2.1.x	Dr. Sarah Jones	Personal Profile	/about/profiles/sjones.html	Morgan
18	2.1.x	Adam Williams	Personal Profile	/about/profiles/awilliams.html	Morgan
19	2.1.x	Rebecca Smith	Personal Profile	/about/profiles/rsmith.html	Morgan
20	2.1.x	James Parker	Personal Profile	/about/profiles/jparker.html	Morgan
21	2.1.x	Lisa Reed	Personal Profile	/about/profiles/lreed.html	Morgan
22	2.2	Staff	Gallery	/about/staff.html	Morgan
23	2.2.x	Alexis Evans	Personal Profile	/about/profiles/aevans.html	Morgan
24	2.2.x	Mary Richards	Personal Profile	/about/profiles/mrichards.html	Morgan
25	2.2.x	Morgan Black	Personal Profile	/about/profiles/mblack.html	Morgan
26	3.0	Volunteers	Gallery	/volunteers	Alexis
27	3.1.x	[Volunteer Profile]	Volunteer Profile	/volunteers/profile/[name]	Alexis
28	3.2	How to volunteer	How-to/Form	/volunteers/howto.html	Alexis
29	2.3	Major Donors	Gallery	/donors	Mary
30	2.3.x	Microsoft	Corporate Profile	/donors/msft.html	Mary
31	2.3.x	Google	Corporate Profile	/donors/goog.html	Mary
32	2.3.x	General Electric	Corporate Profile	/donors/ge.html	Mary
33	2.3.1	How to Donate	How-to/Form	/donate.html	Mary

Figure 7.1 This screenshot of a typical content inventory is thick with data and the number of pages seems never ending.

Content Inventories Overview

Purpose—What are content inventories for?

A content inventory is a precursor to some kind of redesign. It is the only tool that can give the design team any sense of the scope of content on the site. Regardless of how tight a rein the content managers keep, sites tend to grow organically, and content springs up like fungus. With a content inventory, design teams about to embark on a major site reorganization or migration to a new system can get their arms around the level of effort necessary for their project.

Audience—Who uses them?

Content inventories are invaluable both to people directly involved in the planning of a major redesign and to the grunts who will do the actual execution. For the project planners, inventories help make sure all the details are covered. The last thing you need in a major redesign is a slew of important content orphaned. For those doing the legwork in migrating content to a new system, the content inventory is a tool for planning and tracking progress.

Scale—How much work are they?

Unless you're just doing a cursory review of the content on your site—a high-level audit, for example—putting together a full-fledged inventory can be days or weeks of work, depending on the size of your site. The good news is that this is easy work to cut up—Mary takes section A of the site, John takes section B, etc. Occasionally among web design blogs you'll come across a first-person account of creating a content inventory. Although these intrepid web designers have clearly jumped the couch after cataloging 2,000 pieces of content, by the end they've found their rationality and appreciate the process.

Context—Where do they fall in the process?

Like other strategic documents, a content inventory is most useful at the beginning of a project, when the project team is still establishing scope. Waiting until later in the project may cause unnecessary delays if the team hasn't allotted enough time to do the inventory.

Format—What do they look like?

Ninety-five percent of all content inventories are spreadsheets. Although you'd be hard-pressed to find an inventory in another format, they must be out there—hence, the 5 percent. If you can devise an alternate format that's useful to you, more power to you. This chapter assumes you're building a content inventory in a spreadsheet application like Microsoft Excel. (Though the bane of most designers, Excel does have some nice features to help in this endeavor.) Though the specific data collected about each piece of content may vary from project to project, the basic spreadsheet always includes a long list of content in one of the left-hand columns.

Challenges

Content inventories come with two main challenges. Unlike some other documents in this book, the community hasn't zeroed in on a standard format, and the literature in the community is slim at best (except for those few first-person accounts mentioned earlier). Your format will be driven by your purpose. The second challenge is that there are no good tools for creating content inventories or even managing the process of cataloging content. Unfortunately, this is still very much a manual process.

Creating Content Inventories

There are only a couple essential elements for a content inventory, but on their own they don't make for a particularly useful document. The information you can use to supplement the basic inventory, on the other hand, is nearly infinite. Anything you might say about content—who authored it, where to find it, how old it is—is fair game. You are limited only by what you need. The third layer of information isn't much more than nice-to-haves, items that can add some context to the inventory but are not essential for using it day to day.

Layer 1: Quick and Dirty Inventories

Really, the bare-bones content inventory is just a list of content, though the value of such a list is questionable. Inevitably, you'll need to know something else about each piece of content in order to make the inventory worthwhile. In the realm of web design, the one constant piece of information that is useful regardless of the project is the content's location. But the basic element for a content inventory is the name of each piece of content.

Content name

The name of the content in the content inventory should be self-evident. There are a couple nuances, but for the most part, every piece of content on your site should have a title or unique human-readable identifier. On a nonprofit's web site, this might be something like "Building Wells in Sudan Program Overview," for example, as opposed to "wells1.html."

Even pages that don't represent discrete documents should have meaningful names, and perhaps something in their title that distinguishes them from "regular" documents. The nonprofit may have a page listing all of its charitable programs, called "List of Our Programs." Including "list of" distinguishes it from a document that provides, for example, an overview of all its programs.

Layer 3 describes content inventories that document the content at a higher level than the individual page—in other words, navigation categories—or at lower levels, the smaller elements—often called "chunks"—that make up a single piece of content. The nonprofit's program page may have content chunks for program name, synopsis, accomplishments, donors, and the program director.

Content location

On the web, the two main ways to describe the location of a piece of content are through its technical address—the URL—and where it sits in the hierarchy of your web site. The first is more technical and the second is grounded in the web site's navigation scheme. Your content inventory may include both of these pieces of information because they are useful to different users of the inventory. People who have editorial responsibilities, for example, may find it more useful to know where the content sits relative to other content on the site. The content's location in hierarchy provides context within the user experience, and therefore would be more useful to the editorial people. On the other hand, the technical people on your team may be looking at the site through the underlying directory structure—from the back-end, so to speak—in which case, URLs will be more useful.

Suppose content lives in more than one place. Imagine that on this nonprofit web site, biographies for the organization's officers are linked both from a central officers' gallery page in the "About Us" section and from program pages, which appear in the "Our Programs" section. From the user's point of view, the officer bios live in more than one place, but really the same piece of content is just linked twice. Successful content migrations may depend on knowing where to link all the different content. Therefore, your inventory may need to list two or more locations for each piece of content. The content inventory for the nonprofit would list both About Us and Our Programs as locations for the officer bios, though the inventory may designate About Us as the primary location.

Layer 2: Inventories with Purpose

As useful as the bare-bones content inventory can be, every project will demand other kinds of information as well. For a migration—where you're moving content from an existing system to a new system, a task that's nearly as mind numbing as creating an inventory—knowing the destination for the content is important. If you're doing a purge of your content management system, information about the original author, the person who last edited the content, and when it was last edited can support this endeavor.

One thing that distinguishes layer 2 elements from those on layer 1 is that the information described below may not be available as you're building the inventory. In other words, at some point you will click through every page on the site, recording what you see. (I shiver at the thought, dear reader, that you should be subjected to such indignity, but it is the nature of the beast.) As you do this, you may not be able to capture every data point on your inventory—for example, traffic data, which may be stored in some report outside the site. Your inventory may attempt to capture something like a "Relevant Strategic Goal"—the strategic objective from the site's business plan that provides rationale for the content. Such judgments require a background knowledge that may not be available to everyone working on the content inventory.

And this is perhaps one of the defining features of a content inventory: It has a long shelf life. Your initial foray into building the inventory should not be your last. As you learn more about the content on your site, you'll revisit the inventory to flesh it out, adding some of the elements, perhaps, from layers 2 and 3.

Even if you can't fill in this information at the time of taking the inventory, it's important to carve a space for it in your inventory document. When your team members see the kinds of information you intend to include in your inventory, they will understand its purpose and context.

This list of possible additional data elements is neither mutually exclusive nor comprehensively exhaustive. It is a sample of the kinds of information web designers have included in their inventories over the years.

Known people

Different people may be associated with each piece of content. Usually, these people have some responsibility for creating or maintaining the content. In the best case, these people are "known"—that is, you can name them explicitly in your content inventory.

Naming names is not something to be taken lightly. A person's name in a spreadsheet, seemingly innocuous, can put them on the hook for responsibilities they don't necessarily have or want. Still, when you know the go-to person for a piece of content, there is some sense of relief: Orphaned content can be scary. Leave it, and it's another file that needs to be migrated, another page that needs to be redesigned, another document that needs to be rewritten. Cut it, and there's bound to be an angry email—or thousands—from the people who depend on that information. But when a piece of content has an owner, you can leave these sorts of tough decisions to him or her.

The decision you need to make is whether to include this information and what kinds of information you need. A content owner—a single person responsible for the content—may be sufficient. You may want to break it down further and identify the original author, the people who have edited the content, and the person who ultimately pushed the publish button.

Groups of people

Although naming groups of people doesn't put a single person on the hook for content ownership, it does give you a place to start. Obviously, when it comes to the people responsible for content, the more specific you can be, the better. So "HR" is not as good as "HR—Benefits," which isn't as good as "Sam Washington."

In addition to content ownership, you can use a group to indicate target audience. For example, the nonprofit may have five target audiences: members, potential members, volunteers, donors, and politicians. For each piece of content, the inventory may indicate which audience it's meant to serve. This exercise can help the design team identify potential imbalances in content, especially if the business strategy calls for supporting one type of audience more than another. If the nonprofit has created personas to describe each of these target audiences, so much the better. The content inventory can reference these personas by name.

Traffic

It's often helpful to indicate how much traffic each piece of content gets. Those numbers can support subsequent analytical activities for skimming the fat from your site. On the other hand, web analytics is a complex topic in and of itself. Few software packages offer statistics that are reliably accurate and comprehensive. Those that do may be difficult to use. Even as the technology for measuring our web traffic catches up to our needs, our needs shift as well as we develop different kinds of content and different ways to serve it up. Either way, it is unlikely you'll be able to add this information at the time of taking the inventory because traffic data is usually captured by a piece of software outside the web site and traffic information is not usually embedded in the web pages themselves. Instead, you'll need to supply it after the inventory is complete.

Often, an accurate count of traffic is not necessary. You may simply decide to indicate how often a piece of content has appeared in the top 10, top 50, or top 100 pages. Before going through the potential hassle of running traffic reports on every page in the site, consider how you'll use this information for your purposes.

Destination

If your team plans to move the content, you can indicate each item's destination in the inventory. This information may serve the people who are doing the legwork for the content migration. In the case of the nonprofit, the profile of each officer may be consolidated and moved to a section called "The Board of Directors."

Template

If your content is served out of a content management system, it probably has been assigned to a template, a guide for the system on how to render the content. In some content management systems, templates are specific to a type of content. Press releases, for example, are all published in the same template. Sometimes, you can select the template independent of the content type, or a single content type has several templates to choose from.

Including this information in your content inventory can help you identify how often different templates are being used. It may help you anticipate how your content has been chunked—broken up into subsections—which might be important during the content migration.

Purpose

As you're building the content inventory, you might assign a purpose to each piece of content that would describe how the content is meeting the site's objectives. The nonprofit's site might include profiles of its officers to demonstrate commitment to its cause. (Whether the content actually achieves its purpose is another story.)

Purpose is another data point to help in content purges. You may see through subsequent analysis that most of your content supports only a portion of your overall objectives.

Source

Another tool to help with purges is a column listing the source of each piece of content—for example, indicating that a piece of content originally appeared in a print publication. By identifying where information comes from, you can assess the value of including it on the site. Lots of content from print publications may indicate, for example, that the organization is migrating everything to a digital medium, but that you'll need to make some effort to check that the content has been updated to be appropriate for the web. The content inventory for an intranet may show that most of the content is from the organization's public-facing site, in which case you may decide to forgo including it in an intranet redesign.

Milestones

Content is, in many ways, like a living entity. It is born when the author first enters it into the web site. It may go through many changes, and eventually it goes to the great content management system in the sky. Your process may have specific names for different stages in the lifecycle—authored, edited, expired. Though this information may be hard to come by, it can provide a good sense of how old some content is.

Format

Long gone are the days when every piece of content on the web appeared in HTML. Though content must be in HTML to be rendered in the browser, it doesn't have to be stored that way. Lots of content is spit out of databases, or comes as a PDF or some other file type. Knowing the content's format can help the team scope content migration efforts.

Accessibility

One of the columns in your spreadsheet may indicate whether the content requires a password for access. On intranets, access privileges may be more complex: Different people may have access to different kinds of content. Though it may be difficult to map out the entire security model on the content inventory, you can give some indication of whether content is accessible to everyone or only certain groups.

Compliance

The web works because a variety of technologies follow an established set of standards. In the emerging web space, standards are more important than ever because they determine whether your content is portable, available to multiple channels (like cell phones), available to people with disabilities (as in Section 508 standards), or whether it's machine-readable. Compliance can also refer to internal policies and procedures established by the organization. If you find that content compliance is relevant to your project, be sure that the column in the content inventory reflects exactly what the content is compliant to, and what it would take to make it meet the standard.

And on and on...

The list can keep going. There are an almost infinite number of things you can say about any given piece of content, and your choices will depend entirely on your project and your team's needs.

Layer 3: Inventories with a Twist

Not every inventory is a straight list of pages or documents. Your inventory may be limited to the containers that hold the content—navigation categories, for example—or it may inventory the content at an even deeper level, such as the individual "chunks" of content on a single page, like title, author, and body.

Content inventory at the chunk level

If a content inventory at the page level isn't deep enough, you will need to include entries for individual content elements—often called "chunks." For example, on the Officers' Gallery page, your content inventory could go so far as to list the components of the page, like the header, the list of officers, the navigation, and the footer. Each of these components may be divided into further components. This approach allows the design team to account for consistent content elements across the site. The nonprofit may inventory the chunks for every gallery page on its site and may find that some are missing the footer, or some include multiple lists. If you don't need to go into such detail, you may opt to include this kind of information as an additional column of data in your spreadsheet.

	ID	Page Title/Content Area	Type	Location/Source	Update Strategy
3	1.2	Wells for Chad	Program Profile	/pgm/chad	1 mo: Owner checks with program manager
4		Program Name	Title	N/A	N/A
5		Program Overview	Short Text	Program Fact Sheet	6 mos: Owner checks with program manager
6		History Overview	Short Text	Program Fact Sheet	6 mos: Owner checks with program manager
7		Financial Overview	Short Text	Program Fact Sheet	3 mos: Owner checks with program manager
8		Volunteer Highlight	Short Profile	Volunteer Database	Selects new profile at random each week
9	1.2.1	Program History & Timeline	Program History	/pgm/chad/history.html	6 mos: Owner checks with program manager
10		Page Title	Title	N/A	N/A
11		Table of Dates	Table: Date/Short Text	Program Project Plan	6 mos: Owner checks with program manager
12	1.2.2	Program Financials	Financial Profile	/pgm/chad/finance.html	3 mos: Owner checks with program manager
13		Page Title	Title	N/A	N/A
14		Financial Overview	Short Text	Program Fact Sheet	3 mos: Owner checks with program manager
15		Table of Expenses	Table: Expense/Description	Program Project Plan	3 mos: Owner checks with program manager

Figure 7.2 This content inventory offers a more granular view of the web site by showing every "chunk" of content on every page. In this case, each chunk has its own row in the spreadsheet and is differentiated from pages by its position centered within the cell. This spreadsheet also uses a nice feature called "grouping" in Excel. The lines on the far left show that some rows are grouped together. Clicking the little minus sign at the top of the line collapses the group, so you can just show the page names without showing the content areas.

	ID	Page Name	Page Type	Location	Owner	Contents
15	2.0	About Us	News Gallery	/about	Morgan	Page Title Sub-Navigation News Lead News Headlines
16	2.1	Board of Directors	Gallery	/about/board.html	Morgan	Page Title About Us Sub-Navigation List of Profiles
17	2.1.x	Dr. Sarah Jones	Personal Profile	/about/profiles/sjones.html	Morgan	Person Name Photo Bio Links to Programs Links to Resume and Publications
18	2.1.x	Adam Williams	Personal Profile	/about/profiles/awilliams.html	Morgan	Person Name Photo Bio Links to Programs Links to Resume and Publications
19	2.1.x	Rebecca Smith	Personal Profile	/about/profiles/rsmith.html	Morgan	Person Name Photo Bio Links to Programs Links to Resume and Publications
20	2.1.x	James Parker	Personal Profile	/about/profiles/jparker.html	Morgan	Person Name Photo Bio Links to Programs Links to Resume and Publications
21	2.1.x	Lisa Reed	Personal Profile	/about/profiles/lreed.html	Morgan	Person Name Photo Bio Links to Programs Links to Resume and Publications
22	2.2	Staff	Gallery	/about/staff.html	Morgan	Page Title About Us Sub-Navigation List of Profiles
23	2.2.x	Alexis Evans	Personal Profile	/about/profiles/aevans.html	Morgan	Person Name Photo Bio
24	2.2.x	Mary Richards	Personal Profile	/about/profiles/mrichards.html	Morgan	Person Name Photo

Figure 7.3 In this alternate approach, the emphasis is still at the page level, but the chunking information has been incorporated as data points for each page.

Container information

If you're not going very deep in your analysis, your inventory may include information on the content containers, not the content itself. A container can be a directory on the file server, a content type, or—most likely—a navigation category. The nonprofit site we've been using as an example may have six main categories of navigation—About Us, Our Programs, Volunteers, Donors, Media, and Annual Report. For each container, you might indicate how many pages it holds or the number of subcategories or how "deep" the category goes, based on the number of additional navigation levels. You could also take any of the information described in layer 2 and use it to give a general sense of the content in that category. The nonprofit, for example, may give general traffic numbers for each category, showing which areas of the site get the most visitors.

Suppose a design team is doing a simple content inventory for this nonprofit web site, and, instead of going page-by-page, the team just looks at the main navigation categories. If they're doing a migration without purging any content, they can just count the number of pieces of content in each category, and perhaps break that number down by format.

	A	B	C	D	E	F	G
1	ID	Content Area	Sub-Categories	Orphaned Pages	HTML Pages	Non-HTML Files	Dynamic Content?
2	1.0	Our Programs	4	3	24	8	No
3	2.0	About Us	3	7	19	5	No
4	3.0	Volunteers	1	1	4	2	Yes
5	4.0	Donors	2	1	8	1	Yes
6	5.0	Media	3	8	11	120	Yes
7	6.0	Annual Report	0	0	1	12	No
8							

Figure 7.4 This content inventory—more of an audit, really—doesn't inventory the content at all, but instead gives the team an overview of the site by providing some statistics about the major content areas. The audit describes only the top levels of navigation categories, but the design team could easily have gone down another layer, providing stats for the subcategories.

Introductory material

If you use a spreadsheet program like Excel, you can divide your content inventory across multiple pages, or "worksheets." Though it's not absolutely essential, it's a good idea to make the first page an introductory page to set some context. There are a handful of things you can include on this page.

Scope: Use the introductory page to define the scope of the content inventory, setting reader expectations about how much of the web site the inventory covers. For example, if an organization has multiple web sites, you can indicate which of those sites you inventoried. If the site has many external links, you can indicate that you focused on content hosted on the site itself.

Column Descriptions: Since you'll be capturing more than just the name and location of the page, you'll need to provide a description of all the information in the inventory. Columns like "destination" or "template" may not require much explanation, but should provide references to the relevant site map or wireframes so that people using the inventory will know how it fits it with other documents.

Summary of Findings: After having gone through every piece of content on the site, you may notice some patterns or have some interesting observations. Perhaps most of the content from one area of the site has been sourced from a different part of the site, or the vast majority of content appears in a particular template, or some templates go unused entirely. These observations may seem small at this point, but they can have an enormous impact later in the project, and they're the kinds of things you can only learn by doing a content inventory.

Version Information: Like any document described in this book, a content inventory will grow and change over time. Preserving those changes with version control can help keep track of progress and provide justification for various design decisions.

Author Information: Always give credit. Attaching a person's name to a document is more than just ego. It demonstrates a willingness to stand behind observations and conclusions, and provides accountability.

Getting Started on the Massive Project

The prospect of sitting for days or weeks clicking through a site's links is, in a word, daunting. The pressure to collect information about each and every page—if that's the scope of your content analysis—doesn't help. Doing a situation analysis prior to embarking on this tedious process is crucial because it can help establish some boundaries. If you know who will be using the content inventory and what role the inventory will play in the project, you'll know how big it needs to be.

The necessity of numbing neurons

Few people go willingly into conducting a content inventory, so it is likely to be the best-justified document in your catalog of deliverables. Still, just because you haven't thought of a reason not to do a content inventory doesn't mean you have zeroed in on a reason to do one.

A content inventory helps the design team get its arms around content, and the main reason to do this is that the project calls for touching each piece of content in some way. Most likely, the content is being moved, either from an existing infrastructure or design template into a new one. Anticipating the level of effort required for that move means knowing what you're dealing with. Migrating a 100-page site is different from migrating a 10,000-page site, and various other factors play a role, too.

Beyond simply calculating the level of effort, a content inventory is essential for other planning activities as well. For example, you may decide to do a content inventory before you develop a new structure for the site. Your navigation system needs to accommodate every piece of content, so it helps to know all the content there is. Only a content inventory will help you make sure your system is sufficiently comprehensive. In fact, a content inventory can be empowering: Knowing every piece of content on the site may inspire designers to see patterns they couldn't see otherwise. Even if you've already decided upon the navigation structure, you'll need to know where each piece of content goes. In this case, however, a full content inventory may be overkill; it may be enough to simply identify groups of content to move whole hog into the new navigation scheme.

It's never too soon

The only thing that should delay your inventory efforts is the situation analysis. Once you know why you're doing a content inventory and who will be using it, you should get started immediately. Sure, if you're migrating the content from one system or design to another, you might benefit from knowing something about that new design or system. But, really now, aren't you just making excuses? If you know that you need an inventory, you pretty much know what you need it for, which means you can get started. If you want some more information about where the content is going before throwing yourself completely into this task, at least you can lay the groundwork by cataloging the higher levels of the site. Besides getting the process under way, this also can give you a good sense of how much effort the inventory will take.

Spreadsheet gazers

The last piece in the puzzle for your situation analysis is the audience, the people who will be using the content inventory. The value of this tool, however, makes it useful for a variety of people. The workers responsible for your content migration may be the inventory's primary audience, but information architects, content strategists, usability analysts, and many others will find a use for it, too. People outside the design team will also be able to use it in their work. Be sure to talk to everyone on your extended team to understand which tasks they have related to content, and what information they need to support those tasks. Even if you're not 100 percent sure how you'll get this information, make space for it on the inventory. You never know when you'll be able to include it.

Building the inventory one cell at a time

Say what you will about the aesthetic elegance of spreadsheets, they offer just enough text formatting capabilities to add some depth to the content inventory. That said, use color sparingly. Otherwise, the content inventory will get lost in a jumble of colors. Here are some ideas on how to use color most effectively in the context of your content inventory:

Separating Content from Container: Each row in your content inventory may not represent a specific piece of content. Some rows may represent containers or categories of content. You can distinguish these from the actual content by changing the font color or background color. A distinct background color across the whole row can help visually separate long documents.

	A	B	C	D	E
1	ID	Page Name	Page Type	Location	Owner
2	Programs				
3	1.0	Our Programs	News Gallery	/pgm	Alexis
4	1.1	Wells for Sudan	Program Profile	/pgm/sudan	Alexis
5	1.1.1	Program History & Timeline	Program History	/pgm/sudan/history.html	Alexis
6	1.1.2	Program Financials	Financial Profile	/pgm/sudan/finance.html	Alexis
7	1.2	Wells for Chad	Program Profile	/pgm/chad	Alexis
8	1.2.1	Program History & Timeline	Program History	/pgm/chad/history.html	Alexis
9	1.2.2	Program Financials	Financial Profile	/pgm/chad/finance.html	Alexis
10	1.3	AgriAid	Program Profile	/pgm/agriaid	Mary
11	1.3.1	Technical Specifications	General Content	/pgm/agriaid/spec.html	Mary
12	1.3.2	Program Financials	Financial Profile	/pgm/agriaid/finance.html	Mary
13	1.4	Tech for Change	Program Profile	/tech	Mary
14	1.4.1	Aid Management Software	General Content	/tech/aidmgmt	Mary
15	1.4.2	Development Project Management Software	General Content	/tech/devpm	Mary
16	Organization Information				
17	2.0	About Us	News Gallery	/about	Morgan
18	2.1	Board of Directors	Gallery	/about/board.html	Morgan
19	2.1.x	Dr. Sarah Jones	Personal Profile	/about/profiles/sjones.html	Morgan
20	2.1.x	Adam Williams	Personal Profile	/about/profiles/awilliams.html	Morgan
21	2.1.x	Rebecca Smith	Personal Profile	/about/profiles/rsmith.html	Morgan
22	2.1.x	James Parker	Personal Profile	/about/profiles/jparker.html	Morgan

Figure 7.5 In this excerpt from a content inventory, the content areas act as headers throughout the document, visually distinguishing one group of content from the next. The content inventory in Figure 7.1 shows both, using indentation to represent pages that belong "inside" a category. You may be building an inventory where this isn't as relevant as simply showing all the content and providing the high-level categories is just for convenience. This approach also allows you to separate pages that represent categories—like a gallery page that shows the list of everything in the category—from the category itself.

Highlighting Important Information: Suppose your project has very distinct boundaries describing the overall scope—certain areas are in and certain areas are out. Perhaps you need to inventory everything on the site, but ultimately, you are only restructuring the areas that are not, for example, password protected. This is a crucial piece of information for your project. Instead of relegating that information to a single column on the spreadsheet, you can color-code the content to emphasize this distinction.

	A	B	C	D	E
1	2.3	Major Donors	Gallery	/donors	Mary
2	2.3.x	Microsoft	Corporate Profile	/donors/msft.html	Mary
3		Microsoft African Project	External Content	EXTERNAL	(Mary)
4	2.3.x	Google	Corporate Profile	/donors/goog.html	Mary
5	N/A	Google Foundation	External Content	EXTERNAL	(Mary)
6	2.3.x	General Electric	Corporate Profile	/donors/ge.html	Mary
7	2.3.1	How to Donate	How-To	/donate.html	Mary
8	N/A	Donation Form	Form	EXTERNAL	(Mary)

Figure 7.6 This content inventory uses color to show that some content is hosted outside the site, and thus outside the scope of the project. Really, it is in color. You just can't see it because the book isn't printed in color. These rows have also been marked with "EXTERNAL."

Prioritizing Questions: When you need to call attention to one of your rows, a high-contrast color is your best bet.

	A	B	C
1	3.0	Volunteers	Currently lives under "About Us" -- keep style of that section?
2	3.1.x	[Volunteer Profile]	Need details of volunteer profile template. How is this information captured.
3	3.2	How to volunteer	Volunteer form hosted elsewhere.
4	2.3	Major Donors	Given new grassroots fundraising, how does this section change?
5	2.3.x	Microsoft	Keep this page?
6	2.3.x	Google	Keep this page?
7	2.3.x	General Electric	Keep this page?
8	2.3.1	How to Donate	Escalate? Move out of About Us?

Figure 7.7 There's no doubt about it, the person who put together this content inventory has some outstanding questions about some of the content.

Content Inventories in Small Bites

Though this book is tool-agnostic—you should be able to use any software you feel comfortable with to make any of these documents—the content inventory is very much married to Microsoft Excel. The vast majority of inventory work is done in a spreadsheet and no spreadsheet program is as widespread as Excel. This isn't to say that other spreadsheet programs aren't available, or that there aren't other tools you can use to create a content inventory. Unlike the other documents in this book, however, content inventories appear overwhelmingly as Microsoft Excel spreadsheets. These tips assume this is your approach as well.

Separate categories into different worksheets

One advantage to Microsoft Excel is that a single Excel file (also called an XLS file after the three-letter extension to the filename) can have multiple worksheets, represented by tabs across the bottom of the window. Many designers use worksheets to create separate lists for each web property—if an organization has multiple regions, for example—or even different categories on the same site. Cataloging every page on the site can quickly add up and any one category may have hundreds of pages.

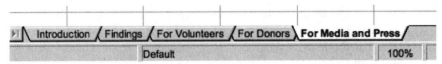

Figure 7.8 These tabs show that the spreadsheet has five worksheets: an introduction, a summary of findings, and three worksheets for the main content areas on the web site.

Worksheets can also keep contextual information separate. Many designers will put general information (see layer 3, above) on the first worksheet to establish conventions, define the scope, or capture version information.

Multiple sweeps

Even if you decide to capture ten different pieces of information, trying to do that all in one sitting will make you pull your hair out. Instead, try building up the content inventory as if you're applying successive layers of paint. You might assign different pieces of information to different subject-matter experts. For example, after creating the basic list of content with primary locations, you might pass the inventory to a developer who can query the database to pull out other identifying information. Your interface design team may have the best handle on the kinds of templates being used, and your information architect can help with the purpose of each piece of content. Each successive sweep of the site adds more information to the inventory, dividing the responsibilities among everyone on the team and limiting the tasks of any one person.

If you can easily consolidate versions, you might have the team use a staggered approach on the inventory where the first group creates a basic inventory for the first category of content and then passes it to the second group. While the second group does their thing, the first group is inventorying the next category of content.

Establish classification strategy up front

As you inventory content, you'll be assigning it to different categories based on the columns in your spreadsheet. If your inventory calls for identifying content by its template, for example, you'll need to know the names of all the possible templates. Some pieces of information, like template, are known quantities—there are a limited number of templates and most likely they've already been established. There may be other pieces of information—like the purpose of the content—which are not known quantities and where you do not have a list of predetermined categories.

In these cases, you have two options. You can brainstorm a list of all the possible options for the category—in our example, the purpose of the content—and then keep that list handy as you take inventory of the site. The advantage to this approach is that you have all your options determined up front. The disadvantage is that your categories, in retrospect, may not be perfect fits. As you create the inventory, you may realize that the categorization scheme you came up with does not suit your purpose.

The second approach is to classify content on the fly as you're building the inventory. The advantage to this approach is that it's easy to respond to changes in strategy or need. For example, an organization's intranet may draw content from a variety of sources, one of these being the organization's main public site. You might classify the source for content drawn from the public site as "public site." As you progress, however, you might discover that the organization actually maintains several public-facing web sites and that it's worthwhile to distinguish these in your content inventory. You can now change your classification strategy midstream by adding a new category to accommodate this situation.

If you use this approach, you may worry that you won't use your categories consistently, especially if the content inventory is a multiday affair. It might be difficult to remember from one day to the next what category labels you selected. In some cases, for example, you might say "public site" and in others you might say "public web site" or just "public." You're worried because you'll end up with a real mess of categories at the end. Here's another advantage to using Microsoft Excel: The list-processing capabilities of the spreadsheet allow you to smooth out the wrinkles of your classification scheme after the fact. Excel has some pretty simple functions for extracting the list of values, identifying which ones are used most often, and replacing unique values with ones that you select. So, besides being able to respond to new needs quickly, this approach also takes the stress out of having to select from a predetermined list of values and getting the categories right. Excel makes it easy to correct this at the end.

Two screens

Donna Maurer, a user experience professional from Australia, went through a grueling content inventory and provided a blow-by-blow on her blog at maadmob.com.au/donna/blog. The blog indicates that she used two screens. Not everyone has the luxury of working with two displays, but if you can, this setup can speed up the process considerably. One screen shows the web browser and the other shows the spreadsheet. Some screens have a high enough resolution such that you might be able to easily accommodate both windows, but you'll find that having multiple browser windows open can also facilitate the process. Your high-res display can fill up quickly. With multiple browser windows, you can keep a category's main page open all the time, showing sub-pages in separate windows.

Avoiding the Pitfalls of Content Inventories

The picture is not a pretty one. A talented, senior-level web designer sits at her desk all day clicking through page after page on the web site. With each click, she dutifully records the page in a spreadsheet. As the list of pages grows, her sanity diminishes. This is, by all accounts, a mind-numbing process, though many wear the experience as a badge of honor. In some circles, you can't call yourself a web designer until you've done a content inventory. But the slow decent into madness is hardly the greatest challenge in preparing a content inventory, at least as far as creating the document is concerned.

Find a format

There are a few related decisions to make in this regard. First, you need to decide if you're going to do any analysis beyond the content inventory. In creating the spreadsheet you are merely collecting the raw data—the bare-bones information about the content on the site. But if you need to say more, if there are other messages you want to give, you may need to prepare a different document. For example, in looking at a company's intranet, you may realize that most of the content is drawn from the organization's public site, the content merely duplicated on each site. This may be an important message, but would be more effectively communicated with a graph or some other visual representation, not a long spreadsheet.

The other decision you need to make about the format of your inventory is its granularity and scope. That is, how deep are you going to go in the site (granularity) and how much are you going to report on for each page (scope). Content inventories can describe the content at a high level, identifying only the main content areas without describing each page in the site. (If you can get away with this, you'll make your project team very happy.) At the other extreme, your content inventory can describe every element on the page. Each row in the spreadsheet, then, will describe a different "chunk" of content.

Establishing a purpose for the content inventory before beginning the process will help define a format, but, inevitably, the process itself unearths problems with the format. You need to be prepared to make changes to the spreadsheet midway through the content inventory as new needs arise.

Develop your own set of tools

There is no good tool for doing content inventories. Although most web designers resort to a spreadsheet, it presents some problems because it's difficult to maintain and does not format easily. For the most part, creating a content inventory is still a manual process. Although there are automated spidering tools for running through each page on a web site, the web design community has yet to discover (or build) the silver bullet. As late as 2005, renowned information architect Lou Rosenfeld solicited the IA community for the best inventory tools, to no avail. The biggest problem with the available tools is that the assessment of any given page depends on a person to evaluate it in the context of a project. Only a person can recognize what's important about a page and collect certain kinds of data about it. Unless this metadata is built into the page somehow, computers cannot generate the necessary output.

Keep an open mind

As you build the content inventory, you'll learn more about the content on the site. Perhaps new sources of content will emerge, or you'll find a connection between two different sections of the site that you didn't think existed before. (Unfortunately, framing the content inventory as a fantastic voyage of discovery somehow does not make it more pleasant to bear.) The main risk with a content inventory is that the information you need to capture outgrows the original structure you established in the spreadsheet.

Imagine you're conducting a content inventory for an intranet and one of the pieces of information you're capturing is whether the intranet simply points to the public site. You have a column in your spreadsheet called "Target URL" where you can indicate the original web address for content from the public site. So far, so good. But suppose you run across a series of pages where the content has actually been cut-and-pasted from PDF documents appearing on the public site. You have the URL or the original PDF, but technically this doesn't match the original purpose of the column.

There are two directions to go to accommodate this unanticipated growth, and the choice is entirely up to you. The first approach is to add another column, which will allow you to preserve the purpose of the original column. The downside is that every time a new situation arises, you'll be adding another column and by the end you won't be sure which column to use for what.

The other approach is the opposite direction: Boil everything down to one or two columns and use annotations to clarify the information in the cells. For example, you might change the original column "Target URL" to "Content Source." Then, instead of just using a URL, you can include "linked to:" or "copied from:" in front of the web address to indicate the relationship to the source. Although this approach provides more flexibility, it can be more difficult to maintain and read with everything in one column.

Presenting Content Inventories

The spreadsheet meeting is the worst kind of meeting. This is when each person in the room gets a copy of the spreadsheet, or it's projected up on a screen, and the group goes through it row-by-row. (This approach is typical of meetings involving content inventories, but is not limited to it. If you've ever gone through a list of system requirements, you've sat through one of these meetings.) This is neither the time nor the place to rail against meetings of this type and structure, because everyone knows how horrible and unproductive they can be. Instead, let's explore alternative approaches so we can stamp out these meetings once and for all.

Meeting Purpose

One problem with the spreadsheet meeting is that it allows the organizer to avoid declaring a real purpose for the meeting. Inevitably, the purpose of the meeting is to "go through the spreadsheet." This isn't a purpose. This is just a bad way to spend everyone's time. (So much for not railing against spreadsheet meetings.)

Instead of resorting to a row-by-row extravaganza, think about what you need to get out of going through the content inventory. The most likely reason to bring people together is to discuss content that is out of the ordinary. Perhaps it was difficult to classify because it did not have a primary location, for example, or the purpose was unclear.

Another reason to meet about content inventories is to help people understand them. This kind of meeting is instructional, so you're not going through each row of content, though you may go through each column to explain the kind of information it captures about the content. A twist on this meeting is to review the spreadsheet before you've captured any content in it. In this kind of meeting, you're not only instructing people on the use of the spreadsheet, but you're also soliciting feedback on the kinds of information you'll be capturing. These meetings can help you identify how people will use the document and show you how you might alter the format to support the variety of needs.

Finally, do not mistake a content inventory conversation with a content strategy conversation. A content inventory describes what is there, while content strategy focuses on what should be there.

Clearing up content questions

As you put the inventory together you'll find that you have some questions about the content. Maybe you're not sure how to classify certain kinds of content or whether it should be included in the inventory at all. Content might live in multiple places in the site and you're not sure what is the most appropriate place to put it in the inventory. A meeting might be the best way to clear these questions up.

Prepping the troops

If you've got a team of people helping you put together the content inventory, you'll need a meeting to establish the ground rules. In addition to explaining the structure of the content inventory, you'll want to divide up the responsibilities. You may also want periodic meetings to check on progress and ensure that the team doesn't have questions as they move through the content.

Planning the inventory

Prior to digging into the site, you can bring the team together to review the structure of the inventory document. In this meeting you can identify additional information to capture about each piece of content.

Explaining the inventory

Once the inventory is complete, different people may use it for different purposes. Unfortunately, it's not as simple a tool as a hammer, and you may need to walk people through it, explaining how content is represented in the document, and the different kinds of information captured.

Reviewing analysis

If the clients have totally lost track of the content on their site, you may need to do a bit of analysis with the data in order to help them understand what they're dealing with. A content analysis can boil an inventory down to its essentials: how much content, where it comes from, what it's for, how old it is, etc. In this meeting, you don't run through the inventory per se, but focus instead on the conclusions that you draw from the inventory.

Strategy planning

Like the analysis review meeting, a strategy planning meeting isn't about the content inventory, it's about the conclusions you draw from the inventory. Instead of going through your analysis, however, you make decisions about how to evolve the content on the site. Many factors go into these decisions, and a content inventory is but one of them. Besides looking at what's already on the site and the possible holes, you also need to know what your users' needs are and what your organization is capable of producing and supporting.

Meeting Structure

Once you have a purpose for your meeting, you can determine the appropriate structure. The meeting agenda should be designed to get at exactly what you need and minimize distractions. In a so-called "spreadsheet meeting" the spreadsheet becomes the structure of the meeting, completely overshadowing the original purpose. Using this approach, you are dooming yourself to long, unproductive hours and unhappy colleagues.

Set up the problem

The key to avoiding the spreadsheet meeting is to establish the purpose of the meeting at the outset. While this is true for pretty much any meeting you schedule, it is especially helpful in content inventory meetings because the content inventory can appear so overwhelming as to be paralyzing.

To prevent this kind of organizational response, keep your content inventory meetings tightly focused. People tend to prefer short, 15-minute meetings in greater quantities than two-hour meetings that happen less often. The 15-minute meeting is focused and productive: It answers a handful of questions and keeps the process moving. By the end of the two-hour meeting, people have no idea if they actually accomplished anything.

Using examples

Instead of going through the spreadsheet line by line, you can pick out salient examples that illustrate your points. For example, suppose you're holding a meeting to clear up some questions about the content inventory. Rather than ask a question about each piece of content, generalize the questions as much as possible. You might realize that your questions about the site content come down to two main issues: where the content comes from and what to do about redundant content. Instead of going through every instance of these issues, you can pick out one or two examples that best demonstrate them.

Doing a demo

If you're teaching people how to use the spreadsheet, you will need to do a little demonstration. Although this borders on the "spreadsheet meeting," it will help people understand how to get the most value out of the content inventory. In the case of training people to help with the content inventory, a demonstration is necessary because a small investment in training now means avoiding potential errors later in the process.

The difference between this and a row-by-row meeting is that you're going through the spreadsheet's columns, explaining the purpose of each one and the possible values it can hold. Treat this meeting as a training session as much as possible because it will set expectations appropriately.

Presentation Risks

Like any meeting, presenting a content inventory comes with a few risks— opportunities for participants to derail your meeting. Here are a couple things to watch out for.

Explain the value of the inventory

Before actually doing the content inventory you may hold a meeting to describe the purpose, train people to do it, or simply show the stakeholders an example of what the final product will look like. You may bump up against people who do not think the effort is worthwhile. Although you should zero in on why they think they do not need a content inventory (hey, we all could use a good excuse not to do one) your best defense here is the project plan.

A project plan lists all the tasks you need to do in a project, the steps to get from your starting point to your ending point. Any given task may be understood in terms of its inputs and outputs, in other words, what you need in order to complete the task and what the task will give you. You see where I'm going here. Most big projects need a content inventory as an input to many of the tasks. By showing your naysayers the tasks that require a content inventory as input, you can quash the objection.

A more productive conversation, however, covers the scope of the content inventory. Looking carefully at the tasks, you should try to anticipate how much information you need—how deep your content inventory needs to go and how much detail you'll want about each piece of content. You may be able to trim your activities if you only need a general sense of how much content the site has.

Support your team

Perhaps you've seen it before. The glassy-eyed stare of a team member's first content inventory. He starts to lose it, going on about never having enough time to do what needs doing, about tight schedules and tight budgets, about the client never letting them do anything the right way. Hopefully, the client isn't in the room during his tirade.

The content inventory can make people feel consumed by data. It's a spreadsheet of thousands of cells and it gets into minute detail. The best pep talk you can give your team members is to help them understand that they are taming the beast. The real enemy here, if we need to use those kinds of terms, is not the client or the content inventory—it's the unknown. It's the vast web server with thousands of files that no one person has conquered. The spreadsheet is the primary weapon, the means for exerting some control over the chaotic mess.

Do not deny that creating the content inventory will be difficult. Even after the content inventory is complete, do not deny that the tasks ahead will be challenging. Instead, you can safely admit that despite the difficulties, the content inventory will prepare you for what you face. It is by far the best tool yet for defeating the unknown. The content inventory gives you what you didn't have before: an understanding of the range and scope of content on the site. It is not something to be worried about, but something that can give the project team great power.

Content Inventories in Context

Unlike some of the other documents described in this book, a content inventory is not a document you produce on every project. When it does occur, however, it is a major piece of the project. Content inventories take lots of time, and when they're done, they serve as a major springboard for other activities. This section describes their role in the overall project.

Using a Content Inventory with Other Documents

In this book, the content inventory is categorized as a "strategy document," which means it does not directly contribute to the design itself, but contains essential information for creating a design. Even though it contains minute levels of detail, it can still play well with other kinds of documents, which might deal with different kinds of issues.

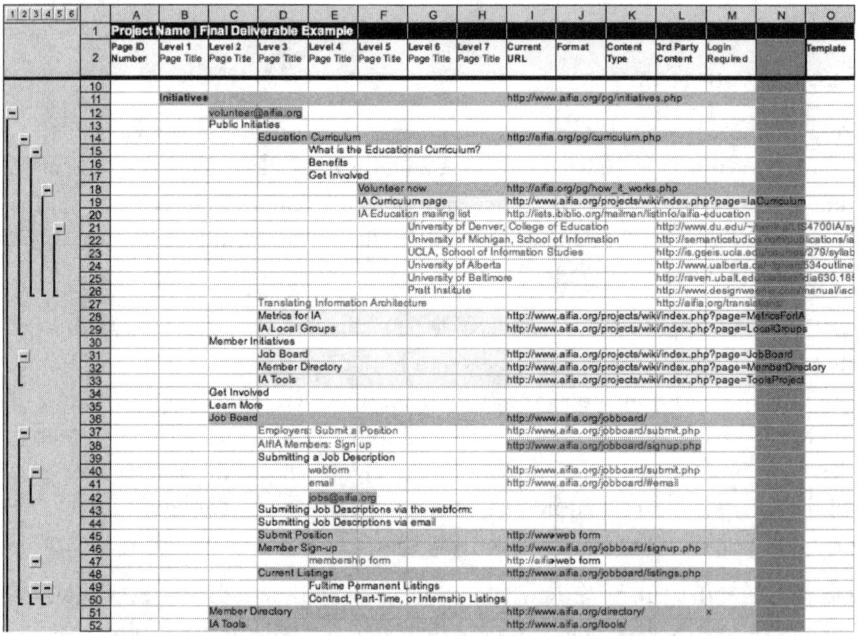

Figure 7.9 Sarah Rice prepared this content inventory for the Information Architecture Institute's web site. You can download it from there or from Sarah's site at www.seneb.com/example_content_inventory.xls. Sarah's example is rich with detail and has lots of tips for preparing your own content inventory. She uses three worksheets in the spreadsheet: one for introduction, one for gathering the data, and one for presenting the content inventory in a final format. (Used courtesy of Sarah A. Rice, Seneb Consulting, www.seneb.com)

Content inventories and user-needs documents

User-needs documents—like personas and usability test reports—offer the design team some perspective on the web site's users, and there may be some connections between them and the content inventory. Perhaps the main connection is indicating the target audience for each piece of content. If you've prepared a set of personas for your project, you can reference the personas by name in the content inventory.

Your content inventory may also identify information like the template used for the content or the amount of traffic it gets. Usability testing may shed some more light on this information. For example, you may find that pages using a certain template do not test well, in which case you'll want to find out how widespread that template is on the site.

Content inventories and other strategy documents

There are two other strategy documents described in this book: the concept model and the competitive analysis. Whether there's any value in drawing a relationship between the content inventory and these documents really depends on the project, but there are a couple of opportunities you can consider.

Your content inventory can include an account of the competitors by indicating whether their sites have equivalent content or that content's relative position in their navigation scheme. Including this information potentially means adding substantial work because you'll need to gather the information not only for your own site, but for any number of competitors' sites as well. An audit of your competitors tends to happen at a higher level anyway, not at the detailed level of each piece of content. It may be more valuable to indicate which pieces of content give your site a competitive advantage. Use color in the spreadsheet to indicate whether certain content is unique to your site or whether you've added some value to the content in some way that the competitors have not.

Concept models represent an abstract structure underlying the web site. They may describe different types of content or the relationships between elements of the web site and the organization. In many cases, the concept model is used by the design team alone to build an understanding of the business and to lay groundwork for the main design work. For that reason, referencing it in the content inventory may not be relevant for the intended audience. At the same time, if a concept model is meant to identify all the different types of content on the site, the design team can use the content inventory to validate it.

Content inventories and design documents

Design documents describe how the web site looks and behaves. Flowcharts, site maps, wireframes, and screen designs show how the user will experience the site. The content inventory, of course, describes what the user will see on the site, so there are clear connections between these documents. Since all of these documents describe how the content will appear on the web site, you might reference them by name in the content inventory to show how the existing content fits into the new site.

For example, wireframes or screen comps may describe the design templates that you'll use throughout the site. Giving these names like "bio with photograph" or "article" allows you to reference them in the content inventory, showing how the content will appear on the site.

A content inventory can also facilitate moving content around on the site from one category of navigation to another. A content inventory can reference a well-labeled site map or flowchart to document the final destination for existing content on the site.

The Future of Taking Inventory

Any designer will tell you that content inventories are difficult and time consuming but usually worth the investment. There's no other way to have a complete understanding of the content issues facing a web site. Right now, two factors make content inventories as important as they are.

First, there is no single piece of software that can do this for us. Although there is content inventorying software, none is particularly effective. If there were such software, people would no longer have to put the inventory together themselves. What's more, every content inventory is different, varying by the nature of the project, the expertise of the team, or the needs of the underlying technology.

Second, the web still operates—for the most part—on a centralized publishing model. Most web sites are set up to give their organizations a voice in the digital world. Their message goes more or less unhampered into the public space. Even intranets—private networks to support the internal workings of an organization—operate on this model, with some centralized authority in an organization controlling the distribution of content. In this environment, drawing a boundary around content and creating a list of everything owned by an organization seems realistic and plausible.

Though both these factors are changing, the need for content inventories will not diminish. The web is becoming less about a centralized publishing platform and more about a collaborative commons. New web sites create space for people to contribute their own content, building an ever-changing landscape of information. As these sites become more pervasive, the need to maintain a big-picture view of the content will become more essential. That they change constantly and quickly means that humans alone will not be able to inventory the content.

The content inventory, as a tool, will become increasingly important as the amount of content on the web grows exponentially. Clearly, designing for the web and offering services that make content accessible and usable will always depend on having a clear understanding of the scope of content.

PART III

Design Documents

Design documents
▶ Site Maps
▶ Flow Charts
▶ Wireframes
▶ Screen Designs

Once you've accumulated information about the users and established further context through strategy deliverables, you will document the design itself. Each of these documents shows a different aspect of the design. Screen designs, for example, generally show what the web site looks like, but are short on how the web site behaves or interacts with users. Flow charts show behavior, and wireframes generally focus on how to structure each page on the site. Site maps document how the whole thing fits together.

Ultimately, each document is a view of the final product from a different angle, much like a set of blueprints for a building, where each one captures a different aspect of the construction—structure, materials, electrical, plumbing, ventilation, and others. Each of your site's design documents should contain enough information for the project team to build a fully functioning web site, nothing more, and definitely nothing less.

CHAPTER EIGHT

Site Maps

sīt' măp (n.)

A visual representation of a web site's structure. Also known as a structural model, taxonomy, hierarchy, navigation model, or site structure.

Designers and information architects use site maps to represent the structure of information on a web site. Site maps generally illustrate part-whole relationships, where an item lower on the map belongs to an item higher on the map. It's a hierarchy. And while site maps generally show how a user will experience the information—in other words, the hierarchy matches the steps a user will take to get through the site—this is becoming less and less of a concern. The dynamic nature of sites and the prevalence of search functions embedded into sites make the user's path to the lower levels of the site much less obvious.

By the way, just to be clear, the site maps we're talking about here are not the kinds of site maps you'll find on the web site itself. Some sites include a "site map" which is meant to act as an index of everything on the site. Though some implementations of the online site map may look like the deliverable discussed in this chapter, it is a very different animal.

Site Maps at a Glance

Site maps have become commonplace, and even those who have never before seen one in the flesh recognize their purpose. This is perhaps less a function of site maps having a common visual language (though many of them do look alike) and more about how people experience the web.

The first of the examples (Figure 8.1) shows a typical site map, rendered in "org-chart format," so called because it looks like one of those charts describing an office hierarchy. The second (Figure 8.2) is a site map for a manufacturing company, showing many more layers of information, including which pages appear in the site's global navigation and which template is used to render each page. Though the second site map contains much more information, it still shows the hierarchy explicit in the first.

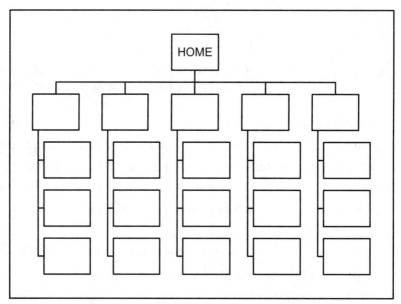

Figure 8.1 The most basic site map looks a bit like an org-chart, a system of boxes representing pages, connected by lines representing links. The placement and connections imply a hierarchy between the pages, such that the site's home page is at the top and the categories and content descend from there.

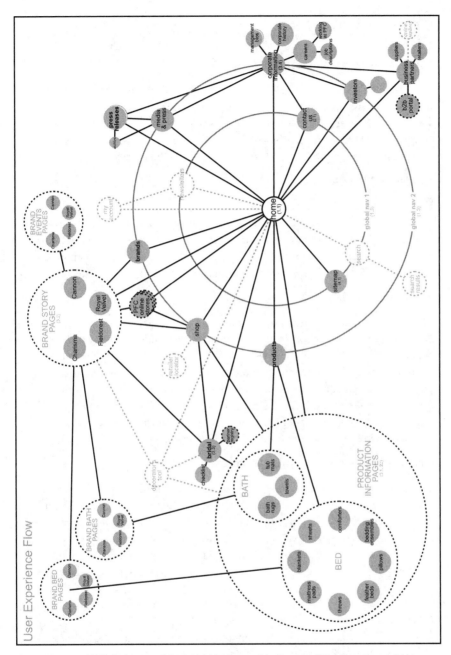

Figure 8.2 Even without the boxes and the rigid grid structure, this site map still implies a purposeful hierarchy. This site map was created for a manufacturer's web site and shows lots of information embedded in the representations of the pages, including page templates, project management information, and page groupings.

Site Maps Overview

Purpose—What are site maps for?

A web site, in its simplest form, is a collection of information. A site map shows how all that information fits together. It provides the project team with one view of how the site will be constructed. Navigation, which may be a major component of site maps, can be fraught with political and design controversy, and site maps allow project teams to work through these issues.

Audience—Who uses them?

Designers and developers will be interested in how the site fits together and how the site map handles content that can live in multiple categories. Depending on your site design and maintenance methodology, a site map can play a crucial role in determining project schedules. During the design process, site maps help design teams hammer out navigation issues.

Scale—How much work are they?

As with most documentation, the amount of work it takes to make a site map depends on how much you've thought through the underlying ideas. If you've planned the site structure from soup to nuts, pulling it all together into the form of a site map shouldn't take more than a couple days. On the other hand, there's something about the process of turning ideas into formal documents that reveals holes in the ideas. A site structure is never final after a first draft. You may need several revisions to make sure user priorities are adequately represented and every piece of content is sufficiently categorized.

Context—Where do they fall in the process?

While occasionally used as a diagnostic tool to help designers get their arms around the scope of the existing site, site maps are used more often to define a new structure for the web site. If your methodology has a specific design phase, the site map will appear toward the beginning of this step in the process. A site structure cannot be created in a vacuum, and it depends on a complete understanding of the content on the site, the business goals, and what the users need.

Format—What do they look like?

Generally speaking, a site map is a paper document consisting of boxes representing different areas of the site, connected by lines. The lines show the semantic relationships between the areas of the site and may also represent navigation, but don't have to.

Challenges

Of all the documents in this book, the site map ranks at least in the top three for stability. Most designers and information architects are not only familiar with site maps, but have used them extensively. The challenges with site maps lie not in creating or using them, but instead in their ability to scale to accommodate larger and more dynamic sites. This challenge boils down to answering the question, "Should I be doing a site map at all?"

For sites that consist of information that people will consume in some way, a site map is indispensable because it allows the design team to create a model for the structures that hold that information. It facilitates the rest of the design process because it allows the project team to deal with broad categories consisting of multiple pieces of content rather than every individual piece of content.

For web sites that do not rest on highly structured relationships between content, the site map may be of questionable value. Instead of specific content, however, a site map can show how functions relate to each other. A web site that allows people to share media with each other may exclude specific navigation categories, and instead have a series of functions that allow people to manage their media collections. The site map could show how the site stitches all these different functions together.

These two cases illustrate another important distinction facing designers building site maps. In some instances, the site map accurately reflects the user experience of the site—each rectangle on the site map represents a page on the site and each line between the rectangles represents a physical link. Other site maps may simply represent relationships between content without explicitly suggesting navigation.

This latter case is important because it also covers situations where each piece of content has multiple locations, where the user can reach a single piece of content through any one of many different pathways. The site map may suit content in a particular set of relationships, but the dynamic nature of the web means that these relationships are not exclusive. It can be important to establish a set of primary categories for the content on the site, but the major risk is that other team members will think that the navigation is static.

Creating Site Maps

Depending on how you want to use your site map, you may decide not to invest a lot of time in its preparation—there may be no need to include so much information. At its most stripped down, a site map is a collection of web pages with their connections highlighted. The additional layers of a site map can help create a more specific understanding of these pages and the links between them. Layer 2 includes information on different types of pages and links, while layer 3 includes further context—the basis for structuring the site as shown in the map.

Layer 1: Boxes, Arrows, and Little Else

At its essence, a site map is a collection of shapes representing different areas of the site connected by lines. As discussed above, the lines can be structural, showing how users navigate through the information hierarchy, or semantic, showing how different pieces of content relate to each other without implying navigation.

Pages and more

The basic unit of currency in a site map is the page. Pages are typically represented by a square or rectangle, and sometimes by a circle, and they are always labeled with the name of the page.

Your site map may focus on a higher level of the site, describing relationships between groups of pages, such that a node on the map represents a set of pages that share some function or purpose. Of course, your site map can include both individual pages and groups of pages, in which case it should clearly distinguish between them.

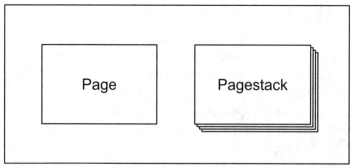

Figure 8.3 Jesse James Garrett created a set of shapes for use in site maps and flowcharts called the Visual Vocabulary. In his stencil, web pages are represented by rectangles and pages that have dynamic content are represented by stacks of rectangles. Courtesy of Jesse James Garrett. For more information visit http://www.jjg.net/ia/visvocab.

Your site map may include things other than HTML pages, specifically downloads of other file types. If you're keeping your site map basic, you can differentiate these kinds of downloads from regular pages by including the file type in the label—for example, "Company Overview (PDF)." If you decide to make your site map more elaborate, as described in layer 2, you can differentiate between these different formats visually.

Finally, a node may represent an entire area of the site. More than just a group of pages, a node on your site map can represent an entire section consisting of many, many pages. This works well when you just want to present a general structure for the entire site at a very high level. A site map using areas, rather than groups or individual pages, can act as an introduction to a much more complex site map or set of maps.

Frankly, the distinction between a group and an area is somewhat arbitrary—there's no specific number—but, generally speaking, a group of pages can be represented by a singular purpose, like "book a flight," whereas a site area is more general, like "customer service."

Links

There's not a lot to say about the links between pages and other areas of the site. They are usually represented by a line between nodes, although you may find situations where a line is unnecessary and adds visual noise. In the excerpt pictured here, these pages all belong to the same group, and the links between them are implied by the visual grouping.

This excerpt also demonstrates that the links don't have to occur between specific pages. In this case, the site map shows a link to the group of pages, indicating that every page in the group is linked, without showing multiple lines.

There is one other consideration for the links on a site map: The physical links can easily outnumber the semantic links. In other words, there may be many hyperlinks on the site between a variety of pages that are not represented explicitly on the site map because there are just too many of them. Instead, the site map focuses on the hierarchical relationships. If you want to show both hierarchical relationships and physical links, be sure to visually distinguish between the two.

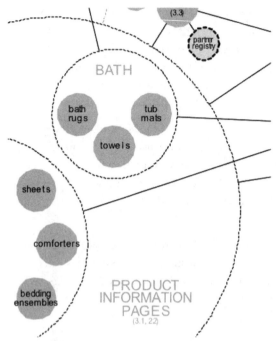

Figure 8.4 Because this site map has so many connections between different areas of the site, the links between individual pages in a group are not represented explicitly.

Hierarchy

The nodes and links on your site map combine to form a hierarchy, a set of relationships implying that some things belong to other things. A hierarchy is comfortable for people because part-whole relationships are easy to understand, even if reality suggests that the actual relationships are more complex. Your site map should be as clear as possible about the hierarchy in your web site's structure.

The most obvious way to imply hierarchy is through the layout of the site map. Higher-level pages usually appear at the top or the left side of the page, especially if you use the "org-chart" approach. Using the connected bubbles approach, higher-level pages might appear in the middle of the page.

You can use other visual cues to indicate hierarchy, but be careful not to be redundant. The size of the node or formatting, like the use of heavier line weights, can show that some nodes are higher in the hierarchy, but with a good layout, this formatting may be unnecessary. In fact, you might reserve special formatting for showing other kinds of information about the node, as described in the next layer.

Layer 2: Elaborating on Pages and Links

Rectangles connected by lines can say a lot about the structure of a site, but your situation may call for more detail. Layer 2 builds on the basic structure created by the boxes and lines to elaborate on each.

Page types and priorities

There are many details you can describe for each page on the site map, though you may find it difficult to pack them all into one small rectangle. Before trying to come up with a visual convention for any of these properties of a page, you should consider whether it's immediately relevant to your need.

Static vs. Dynamic Pages: Even though most web pages these days are generated by a database, there are still many static pages—stand-alone HTML files that do not rely on programming or scripting to show information. If your web site is like most, it will contain a mix of static and dynamic pages, and it may be worthwhile to visually distinguish them. A site map that highlights these differences can tell people at a glance how many pages require more than the attention of an HTML jockey. On the other hand, your site may be built on a system of entirely dynamic pages, which changes the focus of your site map anyway, as shown in Figure 8.5.

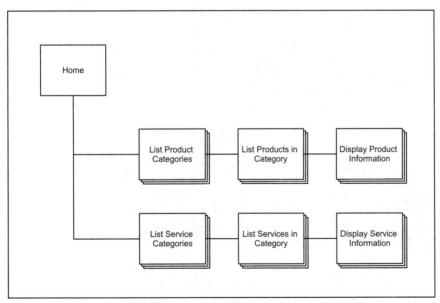

Figure 8.5 This site map describes a web site that has mostly dynamic pages, in which content is pulled from a database. The page names, therefore, represent functions rather than content, and the dynamic pages are portrayed as stacks of pages.

Content vs. Interactive Pages: While the static/dynamic distinction indicates the differences between what goes on behind the scenes for each particular page, pages also vary in what the user sees. The basic distinction is between pages that contain information to be consumed and pages that contain forms for the user to submit information. This distinction may be important for maintenance planning, or for keeping an eye on the different ways users can interact with your site.

HTML vs. Downloads: As described in layer 1, your web site may include non-HTML content, like a PDF or Microsoft Word document. You can use visual formatting to distinguish HTML from other types of files, or be even more specific and distinguish between file types. Some site maps use conventional logos—the icons for the files that appear on your desktop—to represent these files in the site map.

Project Management: Your site map can also include information specific to the project itself, like when pages will be deployed or whether a page contains new content, repurposed content, or old content. Another useful distinction for project managers and team members is whether some pages are out of scope for the current project.

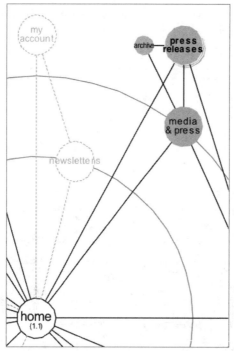

Figure 8.6 The site map for the manufacturing site reflects two broad phases of development—what will be built now, represented by the solid circles and lines, and what will be built later, represented by dotted lines.

Page Ownership: In addition to the technical properties of the page, you might also show organizational properties, like which group or person owns each page. By coloring each node on the site map differently, according to the group that owns the content, for example, you can create a startling picture showing the number of groups responsible for maintaining the site.

Editorial Properties: Finally, a site map can show information about the content of the page, like how often the page needs updating. A related property is the template used for the page. The site map in Figure 8.2 has three main templates, not including the home page and off-site pages, and uses color to distinguish between them.

Groups of pages

Plain site maps make no attempt to show relationships between pages or nodes other than the links between them. But relationships between pages are much more complex, and while they may not be immediately relevant to the user, they can help the organization make sense of how the site works.

Functional groups are collections of pages that relate to a particular purpose or task, like logging in or booking a flight. Contextual groups are collections of pages that relate because of some external context, like being intended for a particular set of users.

There are any number of ways to group pages visually, but the key concern from a design perspective is to avoid confusing groupings with links. The visual conventions you use to group pages, therefore, should be subordinate to the links between them.

Link details

Since a link can represent a semantic relationship—one page "belongs" to another page—or a physical relationship—one page may be accessed from another page—you may need to distinguish between them visually. Links, of course, can represent so many different things, and you could devise a unique visual convention for each of them. For example, the movement between a search page and the results page is conceptually different from the movement between a category page and a page for an item in that category. The question becomes whether there's value in representing all these distinctions, and that's up to you and the project. Most site maps do well to focus on differences between pages, and not on the links between them.

In Figure 8.2, the site map does not vary the formatting of the lines between pages, but through subtle differences in how the lines connect to the pages indicates the variety of links on the site.

Layer 3: Providing Further Context

The information in the last layer takes readers outside the user experience and provides context for the site's structural information. With regard to user experience, there are two types of context: user needs and business strategy. To put a page in context, the site map can show how important that page is to users or to the business, or how it relates to a particular aspect of the business strategy or user profile.

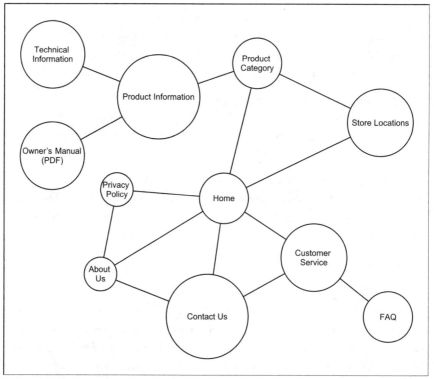

Figure 8.7 This site map varies the size of the nodes to show their relative importance. The larger the circle, the more directly it supports the overall needs of the user or business.

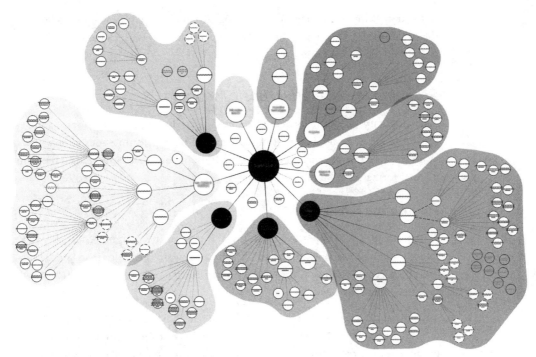

Figure 8.8 Color-coding can show which aspect of a user profile or a business strategy a page supports. If there are five different elements to the business strategy, for example, the site map can show how different pages support those elements. Courtesy of James Melzer. For more information, visit http://www.jamesmelzer.com.

User needs

Incorporating what users need into the site map can provide a rationale for the site's structure. Some site maps show the relative importance of different pages based on how well they address the needs of the user. If your site supports a variety of users, it may be difficult to show that some pages are more important to some groups of users.

Business strategy

Like user needs, business strategy can show the rationale for certain structural decisions. It provides further context by showing how the site map supports all aspects of the business and demonstrates continuity in the process—the work you did establishing or capturing the business strategy feeds directly into the design work.

If you're making a site map of an existing site, these devices can show where the organization falls short, supporting one aspect of the user needs or business strategy in abundance and others not enough.

Scanning the Skeleton: Basic Mapping

The simplicity of site maps makes it tempting to dive right in without careful planning. Like any documentation, however, a little planning goes a long way. Who will use the site map and how they'll use it can make a huge difference in its final format.

Purpose and timing

The site map is probably the first step you'll take in the design process. If you've done, say, a content inventory and lots of user research, the site map is the logical next piece of the story, showing how the content on the site will be organized to meet user needs.

You might also use the site map as a diagnostic tool, and build it to show the current structure of the site. This can help point out inconsistencies or simply nonsensical navigation pathways. Line this kind of site map up with user research and you have a very compelling argument to change the structure of the site.

Audience

The message behind a site map is relatively simple, which means there isn't much nuance based on who you're building it for. Designers, developers, and project stakeholders all expect the same thing: a document that establishes site structure, site navigation, and page priorities.

Some elements included in your site map may be more relevant to the project team than to the client—for instance, the templates for the content—but this isn't a reason to leave the information out. Generally, this information can be layered into the site map unobtrusively, without obscuring the parts of the site map that are important to the client.

The document's audience may affect the overall format of your site map. If the people who need to use the site map have never used one before, or are used to a certain approach, you may not want to deviate too much from their comfort zone.

Content development

Before committing the site map to paper, you may find it useful to create a list of all the pages you want to capture in the document. This approach allows you to think through each data point you might want to capture for each area of the site—how important it is, what type of page it is, or any of the other distinctions mentioned in layers 2 and 3. If you've done a content inventory (described in Chapter 7) you've already done most of the legwork for this exercise, although you might be mapping new structures where the inventory shows existing structures.

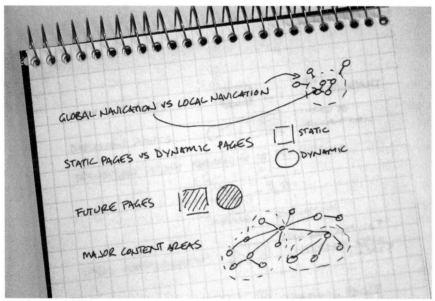

Figure 8.9 In planning a site map, this information architect made a list of all the elements he wanted to show and identified how they will be represented in the site map. The use of graph paper by an information architect is inevitable.

Improving Your Mapping Skills

There's nothing wrong with the basic org-chart format for a site map. If you're new to this process, that may be the easiest approach. After having done a few site maps, however, you might begin to see some inadequacies with this format. These tips can help you move beyond the rigid presentation of site maps as boxes and lines.

Play with layout

Typical site maps look like organization charts—similarly-sized rectangles connected with right-angle connectors. These maps are easy to understand because they follow a prototype of sorts. On the other hand, they don't show a lot of detail, and this format can take up a lot of space on the page. There are many different ways to show relationships between two shapes, and experimenting with different techniques might help you create a more refined document that allows you to show more.

The risk here is that you'll build something too difficult for your stakeholders to understand. The org-chart approach, while somewhat inelegant, is perfectly clear and very familiar. The flip side is that you may find yourself boxed in—nearly literally—and unable to effectively capture all the necessary information. In these situations you must judge whether you can hold your client's hand to help them understand your approach to site maps. The site maps shown in Figures 8.1 and 8.2 illustrate the difference between the traditional "org-chart" approach and something a little more far out.

It's also important to consider the placement on the page. Convention says that people start in the upper-left corner of the page and read down and to the right. But visual depictions operate differently, and the center of the page may be an appropriate starting point. Putting the main page in the middle, for example, gives you much more room to work with for laying out the site map.

Use a consistent visual language

If you find that you need to show a lot of different kinds of information—importance to the user, where content is hosted, template types, etc.—you can adopt a visual language that makes these distinctions so you don't have to specify them explicitly. The most effective way to develop a visual language for your site maps is to make a list of everything you need to describe for each content area represented in the map. After prioritizing this list, you can identify how to represent each kind of information.

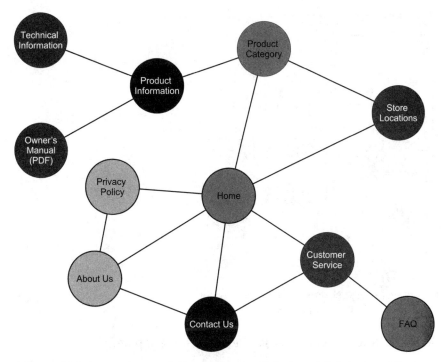

Figure 8.10 This is the same site map as in **Figure 8.7,** but uses shading instead of size to show relative importance. Each approach has implications for the overall look of the site map, and can compete with other information you're trying to convey. Consider all approaches carefully before settling on one convention or another.

Most illustration tools—like Microsoft Visio or OmniGroup's OmniGraffle— allow you to save individual shapes in a template or stencil so that you can reuse them. Once you have a visual language that works, there's no point in reinventing the wheel.

Many designers and information architects have made their visual languages available publicly and for a variety of tools. If you're short on time, you can download one of these stencils and go from there. You'll find links to these resources on www.communicatingdesign.com.

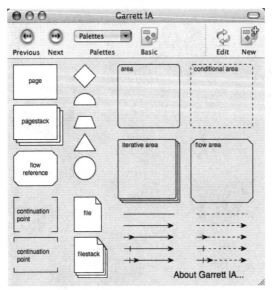

Figure 8.11 OmniGroup's OmniGraffle for Macintosh comes with Jesse James Garrett's site mapping shapes.

Separate different parts of the site onto different pages

One way to tame the site map beast is to break it up across several different pages. Separating each logical section of content onto a different page makes the map easy to understand because each page is more or less self-contained. A cover page can show how all the smaller site maps fit together.

Avoiding Missteps in Mapping Sites

As web sites become more complex and dense with information, it will be more difficult to capture all that information. This risk appears in several different ways.

Describing links between pages

With even the simplest web sites, it can be difficult to show the extensive linking in site map form. It's easy to get carried away, showing every possible link between one piece of content and another. Avoid this problem by deciding what links you want to represent, whether they are semantic/hierarchical relationships or physical links. In the case of physical links, you should focus only on those links that are most meaningful or most likely. Even though there may be links between pages at the lower levels, you can simplify your site map by only showing how someone would browse to each page from the home page.

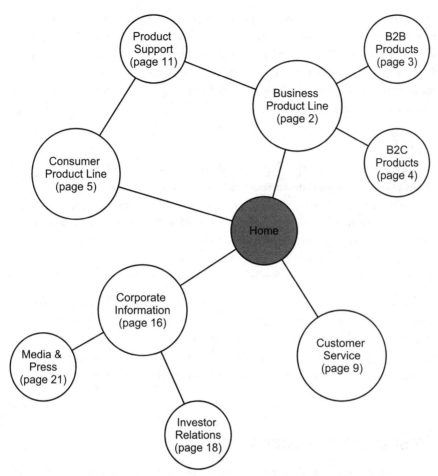

Figure 8.12 This cover page ties together a site map that spans several different pages. It indicates page numbers for the supporting site maps—acting, in effect, as a table of contents.

Defining types of pages

Web pages come in all shapes and sizes, despite your best efforts to put them in nice little buckets. As described in layer 2, there are all kinds of properties your site map might illustrate, from the behind-the-scenes technology to project management issues. You may be tempted to pack as much information in as possible—after all, it's a special feat to communicate lots of detail in a little space. On the other hand, this can make your site map dense and clumsy.

One way to show additional information about the pages is to create multiple versions of the site map. Before you groan about the difficulty of maintaining several different versions, consider the tools you're using to map the site—some may offer features to make this easy. Microsoft Visio, for example, has a layering function that allows you to hide or show different parts of your drawing. Regardless of how you make it happen, you can create different versions that show different aspects, so one version might focus on the technical issues and another on the editorial issues.

Oversimplifying

You can also go in the other direction, showing too little information. You might not show enough detail about the site itself, missing categories of information or failing to account for pieces of content. Site maps play a role in this failure because they hide an underlying chaos of web sites. Seeing sites represented cleanly as boxes and lines makes it easy to forget the spaghetti-like structure that's really there. Your urge to make the site look clean on paper may overwhelm the need to capture the details accurately.

The best way to avoid oversimplification is to capture the data outside a site map first. A site map is a visual tool for representing data, nothing more. Before building a site map, perform a content audit or content inventory, creating a list of what you need to document. Even if your site map oversimplifies the site, you can always go back to the raw data to validate the visualization.

Presenting Site Maps

At some point you'll need to gather the project team together to discuss the site structure. A site map can be an effective document, but it contains complex and sometimes controversial information. The only way to work through these issues is through a meeting. Or two.

Setting the Agenda

With any design deliverable, there are three reasons to gather the troops together. At one extreme, you're simply providing an introduction to the document, expecting nothing in return. At the other extreme, you're expecting stakeholders or team members to apply their seal of approval. In the middle of the road, you are working with an incomplete document and seeking feedback.

Regardless of purpose, your meeting should include an account of the project context—where you are and where you're going. A site map, while providing some concrete information, can feel very abstract to participants and it can be easy to lose the thread of your design process. By telling a quick story at the beginning of the meeting, you can help project participants locate the site map in the overall project. You might say something like this:

```
OK, we finished our content inventory—remember we went
through the high points last week—and we've been looking at
all the content and have come up with a site structure. We'll
look at that today. This site structure is just a draft, and
we intend to test it in the next few weeks. We're working on
devising the test mechanism and we can discuss that at the
end of this meeting or run through it at our status meeting
on Wednesday.
```

Introduction and overview

What distinguishes an introduction meeting from the others is that you're not digging into the details of the site structure. The purpose of the meeting is to get the team on board with the document, educating them enough so they can look at it themselves. There are three key pieces of information you need to communicate.

First, you need to help them understand the document itself, especially the visual conventions you may be using. You don't need to walk them through the entire document, but you should point out major concepts and explain the visual system—what each of the shapes mean, how you've grouped things together, and other elements that might contain meaning. You might use a key, a box off to the side of the page that describes each symbol. Good visual design, they say, shouldn't require a key. But, frankly, I don't know who "they" are, and they're certainly not the ones in the room presenting the site map to your stakeholders.

Once you've given the participants an overview of how the document works, the next information to cover are the major design highlights. The intent of the meeting is not to run through every detail, but you still want to give meeting participants a sense of the key design decisions. To decide what counts as "key" or "major," think about which content areas will be the most surprising to stakeholders, and which represent important areas for customers. Working on a site for a major airline a few years ago, my team consolidated disparate customer service information under a single heading. This was one of the things pointed out in the presentation because it represented a new direction for the site.

Finally, you'll need to provide meeting participants with some background information, in other words, the key inputs that went into building the site map. This can include an overview of the user personas or results from user research. If you've done some analysis of content types and are distinguishing between them in the site map itself, your meeting participants will benefit from an overview of the different types. It never hurts to recap project goals. Any bit of information you used as part of the design process for creating the structure is fair game.

Feedback and brainstorming

The structure of a web site generates lots of conversation, but spend enough time in this business and you'll realize that every design decision is charged with ego and politics. In a meeting where the purpose is to solicit feedback on a site map, the challenge is to make the feedback constructive. This means, of course, distinguishing legitimate structural feedback from feedback that comes from outside the business requirements and objectives. (Unless the business objectives of your site include satisfying stakeholder ego.)

If this is the first time the team has seen the site map, you may need to cover some of the introductory stuff from the overview meeting. Otherwise, there are two kinds of information you need to dig into for a feedback meeting.

First, you need to be clear about the kind of feedback you're looking for. A free-for-all doesn't help anybody. If you haven't finalized the labeling scheme, be clear that you welcome suggestions, but that the focus of the meeting is the site structure. If you are seeking feedback on labeling, you might want to give the meeting participants a handful of choices—two or three—and have them select one. Leaving it completely open will lead to circular, unproductive conversations.

If you're seeking structural feedback, you need to be clear about the structural issues that require input. For example, the lower levels of a site may be well squared away, and you need to focus on the priorities of the main sections of the site. Or perhaps you've got a piece of content that could fit in several different places on the site and you need to know where its primary home is.

The other kind of information you need to address in a feedback meeting is the motivation for the design decisions your team has made, either structural or labeling. That will help the participants understand that the site map wasn't created in a vacuum. Walking through the site map and offering explanations for decisions shows that there's a reason for everything on the map. Team members and stakeholders will be less likely to offer unsubstantiated feedback.

Buy-in and approval

If you need approval on a site map, the buy-in meeting shouldn't be the first time the stakeholders or team members see the site map. The buy-in meeting should be, to a great extent, nominal—that is, you should already know the outcome. The best way to ensure a smooth acceptance of your work is to keep the stakeholders and other team members involved with it from the very beginning. You're not only getting their input as you go, but you've also given them a sense of ownership, such that rejecting the site map would be rejecting their own work.

Structuring Meetings

Site maps can be very elaborate and complex. Merely splaying one in front of your project team and "talking about it" does not make for successful meetings. Think about how you want to structure the conversation and the best way to discuss the ideas represented by the site map. Two possible approaches are narrative—using the site map to structure a story where the users are the main characters—or by content areas—where you simply move from category to category and describe each one.

Narrative

The narrative approach starts with users. To structure your meeting in this way, begin by reminding the project team who the users are and why they're coming to the site. Each "chapter" in this story is a different user or a different collection of user needs. For each type of user, show how the site structure supports their needs. If your client has prioritized the user groups, start with the highest priority group. If not, you can start with the user profile that represents the most common tasks or scenarios.

For example, most government web sites need to support two broad groups of users: some users are "in the business," so to speak, and follow the government's regulatory and policy activities, while other users are simply citizens who need to understand how to interact with their government on specific issues. Using the narrative approach to describe a .gov site for a particular agency, the team would start with the Policy Wonk and show how that user can follow the inner workings of the government organization. The team would next turn to the Disinterested Citizen, who has a specific concern for a specific topic, and show how the site structure supports a highly targeted scenario.

Content areas

It can be challenging to organize your meeting around how people use the site. In the ideal world, every piece of content on your site matches up perfectly with every possible scenario, but reality shows that this isn't always the case. (This isn't to say that it's OK for your site to include useless content, just that structuring your meeting around usage scenarios may not be the most efficient use of time.) A more practical approach, especially if you want to be sure to cover every part of the site, is to walk through each content area, one at a time. Start at the first level and dig down through each one.

To create a meaningful organization scheme for the meeting, you can prioritize the content areas by risk. More "risky" content areas are those that perhaps represent the greatest shift from the existing site structure, or those that will require the most investment of time and resources from the client and project team.

Of course, this kind of meeting can be very tedious. Sifting through every layer of detail in the site can be mind numbing, and is definitely not the best use of everyone's time. Instead, point out the highlights and describe what kinds of content ended up in each section. Instead of reading every label on every box, ask participants if you've used labels that they don't understand.

Imagine you're working on a .gov site for the Office of Meaningless Bureaucracy. (Any resemblance between this fictional agency's initials and those of an actual government agency is purely coincidental.) Your client for OMB is its Director of Communications, and you're sitting down with her to walk her through the proposed site structure. OMB, inherent to its mission, has lots of information on its site, but you don't want to waste the whole meeting hitting every piece of information. Instead, you say something like:

```
The current site divides content up by type, giving each one
its own category, like "Policies" and "Regulations" and "Direc-
tives." We've re-categorized the information based on issue.
This approach will help the web site scale to accommodate new
information, as well as easily archive old information as
issues become less relevant over time. We're proposing you
launch with the following broad categories of information…
```

After listing the categories, you would continue:

```
You'll find that we've reshuffled the content so that poli-
cies and regulations and other types of content are not dis-
tinguished explicitly in the hierarchy. These distinctions
would happen at the page level. Instead, each category is
further categorized. For example, under "homeland security,"
we have the following sub-categories…
```

The meeting would not require you to walk through all the subcategories. Instead, you've provided a set of guidelines for how they can review the categorization on their own time. If there are categories of content that you think will be controversial, you should point them out, giving stakeholders an opportunity to make suggestions right then and there.

When Maps Steer You Wrong

The challenges of site maps really come out when you're discussing them with other people, especially those who have different ideas of how the site can be structured. Unlike other areas of the design process, creating a site structure can seem like a somewhat arbitrary process to the untrained eye, and therefore easy to modify without considering the consequences.

Getting stuck on labels

One of the hardest things to get meeting participants to do is divorce structure from labels. A label on your site map refers to a category, but it may not be the exact wording you use on the site. Thinking of the structure before you hash out the categories is a perfectly legitimate approach and process. But to meeting participants, the labels can be a distraction. Still, if this is the worst thing that happens during your meeting, consider yourself lucky (see the next section).

To mitigate this risk, you might build the site map to make the labels look like placeholders. Parentheses or brackets can help with this. You can also include several alternatives, in order to show that you're considering several possibilities for the label of a section. Ultimately, the goal is to diffuse escalating tension that comes from purposeless conflict. When people argue about labels without any real foundation for validating their choices, meetings lose steam and take on a competitive atmosphere rather than a collaborative one.

On the other hand, perhaps your agenda includes exploring labels. In this case, you want to make sure the conversation with meeting participants generates meaningful feedback. Going round and round on different names for categories wastes time and makes everyone frustrated. Ideally, your users will validate label names, but you can use your meeting to brainstorm suggestions.

The politics of hierarchy

Creating a structure for a web site brings out the worst in organizational politics, which is why so many web sites—especially in the early days—were organized around corporate structure. To validate the site structure, you may need to bring all the different players to the table, and these people won't want to see "their" content buried deep in the site while someone else's content is at the surface.

Even if you're not facing such bald-faced political discussions any more—at least a few people learned their lessons from the proliferation of poorly designed sites—competing agendas or misconceptions about user priorities can still skew the feedback you receive.

Deflating arguments about categorization based on office politics is no easy task. As in most tough situations, it can be useful to rely on user research or business goals to redirect conversation. If you haven't agreed on a common understanding of users or on the purpose of the site, it can be difficult to argue about which content is most important. This scenario presents a good opportunity for you to discuss the importance of setting business goals or criteria for judging priority, but your stakeholders might at this point just think you're being pedantic. (No one likes to hear "I told you so...")

If you can't steer the stakeholders in the right direction, your next line of defense is to show examples of well-designed and poorly designed site structures. Ideally, your examples will fall into a realm well outside the expertise of your stakeholders. This way, they can see how obscure a site can be to users not well versed in the lingo. For example, you might take your government client to the site of a high-tech manufacturer—the more obscure the technology the better. Instead of making your client walk through this site—which can be embarrassing and perhaps backfire if they're as geeky as you are—do some role-playing, pretending to be an average consumer looking for a new camcorder. Draw parallels between the high-tech site's jargony language and that of the government agency.

Your last line of defense is to generate two prototypes, one based on the political compromise and another based on user-centered design principles. Even if you can't do full-fledged user testing, you can walk your stakeholders through each approach and show how one supports user goals better than the other.

Site Maps in Context

One of the nice things about site maps is that they've very familiar. More than ten years into the web business, site maps are among the documents that have the longest history and most exposure. Because of this, they are useful tools in various circumstances, providing a backdrop for other ideas in the design process, or serving as a basis for comparison.

Using Site Maps with Other Documents

As you read this section, think of a site map as more than just a representation of a specific site. Think of it as a convention for representing structures of information. In this sense, site mapping is a tool you can use in a variety of documents to draw attention to relevant structures.

Site maps and user needs documentation

Creating a new site structure obviously depends on having an understanding of users, but site maps can be used in user needs documents like usability test results to provide further context. In usability test results, for example, a site map can show users' preferred path through a web site. Chapter 4 includes an example of this.

Site maps and strategy documents

Strategy documents provide background information necessary for doing design work. By integrating a site map into these documents, you show how the strategic groundwork relates specifically to the site structure.

For example, instead of presenting a site map on its own, you can present it next to a concept model. The concept model describes the different types of content on the site and the site map shows how those content types work together.

A site map can be a useful tool for comparing the structures of competitive sites. Color coding can show how the same information is positioned differently on different sites.

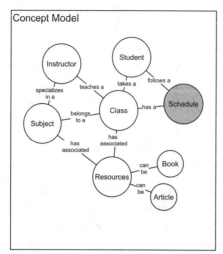

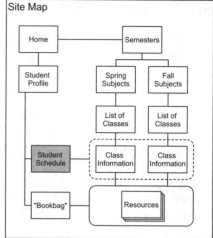

Figure 8.13 In this very simple example, the concept model shows the basic relationships between different "objects" for an educational institution. Without color, it's difficult to show how all those concepts translate to a site map, so in this case, the site map just shows how a schedule appears on the site. More sophisticated sites and concept models may need more elaborate ways of drawing connections between them.

Site maps and other design documents

Since site maps are among the first documents created in the design process, they can provide context for the rest of your design work. Lined up with wireframes or screen designs, site maps can help the project team see where a particular screen fits into the overall user experience.

Figure 8.15 Stephen Anderson of Geniant has an elegant way of referencing wireframes with site maps. This example shows how he includes an excerpt and then highlights the relevant page. Image courtesy of Stephen Anderson.

The Web's Cartographic Conundrum

Of all the documents in this book, the site map has the least hopeful future. Site maps are products of a time when web sites were more static, and when a site's content was more easily quantifiable. Site maps suggest a view of web sites as simple information environments created and maintained by a centralized authority. Most people think of moving about a web site as moving through physical space. A site map is appealing because it corroborates this metaphor, representing the connections between different areas on the site.

While sites like these probably won't go away any time soon, newer technologies permit a looser relationship between a site and its content. Some web sites have little predictable structure—this it true, for example, of sites that act as repositories for user-contributed content. Some sites, like weblogs, have predictable structures but no hierarchy of information. Site maps, therefore, have the difficult challenge of representing more and more complex information spaces—ones that don't resemble physical space.

Is the site map up to the challenge? It's doubtful. Conceptual models and user flows are better positioned to address this need. A structure of discrete and definable pages may still have value for simple web sites that don't push the boundaries of technology and our interactions with it. But as more web sites move away from strict repositories of centralized information, the site map will be replaced with more meaningful conventions. Still, while this progression seems inevitable, it is also difficult to imagine that—in our lifetime—we'll see the complete extinction of this kind of site.

CHAPTER NINE

Flow Charts

flō' chärt (n.)

Flow charts attempt to visualize a process, usually centered around a specific task or function. For web-based processes, flow charts often represent a series of screens that collect and display information to the users. Also known as flows, user flows, process charts.

Even the simplest explanations of the web acknowledge that it is far from a static medium. The relationship between users and web sites is one of movement and interaction. To a greater or lesser extent, the paths through web space must be planned, and flow charts are the designers' tool for defining those paths.

What separates a flow from a site map is that in the former, time is the defining factor. The relationships between the steps are sequential, not structural or hierarchical. While site maps capture an information structure that may or may not match the user's experience of the site, a flow chart defines a process from beginning to end. They come in all shapes and sizes, and while several conventions have emerged, there is still no single right way to do a flow chart. One reason for this is that a process may be defined at different levels—from the high-level business process to the detailed step-by-step specification of how a user creates an account on a web site.

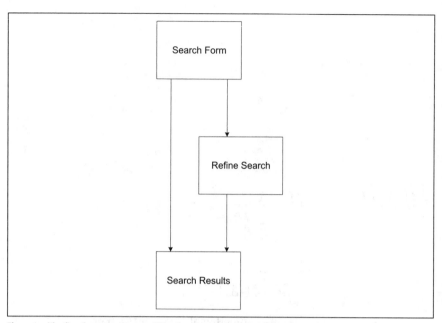

Figure 9.1 The flow for a search exemplifies the simplest flows possible—the computer requests input and provides output. This flow also shows an option to go to an advanced search screen.

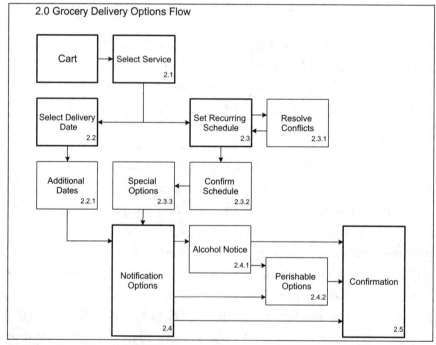

Figure 9.2 This flow is for a fictional online grocer. It shows more complexity in branching logic and relative importance in various stages of the flow.

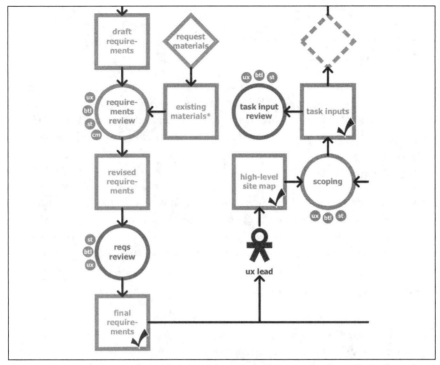

Figure 9.3 This is an excerpt from a flow describing a business process. Like a flow for a web site, it uses boxes and arrows to show different steps in the process. Instead of web pages, however, the boxes, circles, and other shapes represent actions participants take.

Flow Charts at a Glance

There are two main uses for a flow chart: One is to show a business process and the other is to show a user experience. Business process flows describe how people interact with each other, while a user experience flow describes how people interact with a web site. This chapter will explore both kinds of flow charts because they're very similar. One thing to note about flow charts for user experience is that unless combined with wireframes, they don't do a good job of showing every aspect of the user's interaction with the site.

Stripped-down flow charts can look like site maps or concept models—shapes connected by lines. Like those other two documents, a flow chart can represent reality— how people go through an existing process—or it can be prescriptive, describing what a web site or organization should do. On the other hand, the unique layout of a flow chart is designed to communicate movement through time rather than movement through space. A site map may have a clear starting point, but not a clear ending point, and no specific path through the structure. A flow chart, however, is specific about where the user begins and ends, and has a clearly marked path.

Flow Charts Overview

Purpose—What are flow charts for?

Flow charts give team members a picture of how users complete specific tasks. A flow chart may not reveal all the details of the interactions, but it does offer a comprehensive view of the user experience for a particular objective. The objective can be high-level, like researching cars, or more specific like establishing a user account.

Audience—Who uses them?

Every member of the project team will use the flow. For developers, the flow is an overview of the logic in the system, documenting each step in the process and the business rules linking them. Designers will use flow charts to plan screen designs. User flows are also a good way to give stakeholders an early glimpse into the final product.

Scale—How much work are they?

These documents can be used at a broad level, painting an entire picture of how an organization interacts, or a microscopic level, describing how a single person accomplishes a specific task. As with any other document, the amount of work depends on the level of detail and the amount of research or planning required. Even the simplest tasks can require a complex series of business rules to accommodate every situation, which must be documented for the flow chart to have any value.

Context—Where do they fall in the process?

User flows are flexible tools that can be used throughout the project to document different aspects of it. Business processes may constitute requirements for the system, and can be documented using a flow chart. Further into the project, the design team can use a flow chart to define how a particular function works on the site.

Format—What do they look like?

There are many different ways to illustrate a flow. The typical approach involves using a variety of symbols to indicate different steps in the process, but some designers create a series of rough HTML pages. Linking these pages together, the designer shows—at a high level—how the flow will work. Other technologies, like Flash, offer additional approaches to describing flows. Of course, none may be more effective than a simple written narrative.

Challenges

Site maps represent structures and wireframes represent screens, but flow charts represent what people do. In this way, they have a unique position in the deliverables pantheon. Sure, a flow chart can represent a series of screens, but there is generally an enormous dependency on user action to move the process along. Behind the scenes, the web site needs to make decisions about what to display based on what information the user supplies. Compared to all the other documents, flow charts most represent a conversation between user and web site. (If you're using flow charts to represent business processes, the conversation is even more complex.)

Embedded in the document is the assumption that this is an effective way to represent reality, that our processes really do look like boxes connected by arrows. And it's easy to get caught up in this assumption. At our worst, we may even become indignant when reality doesn't fit so nicely.

The sad truth is that we have little better way of talking about process, and so we'll have to settle for boxes and arrows. (Even those among us who can make the flows look especially sexy know that under the hood, every process chart is nothing more than boxes linked by arrows.) Acquiring the information to represent a process effectively and sorting out all the business rules that might dictate the various paths through the process may be the hard part day to day, but the real challenge comes from what we lose when we resort to boxes and arrows to represent reality.

In short, everyone is different and brings something different to the table. The point of a flow chart is to normalize users, smooth them out, and force them to have the same conversation with our web site every time: Every flight booking should look the same, every online gift purchase, every bill payment, and every hotel reservation. But behind every one of these actions is a person whose circumstances differ from the user who came before. As much as we'd like every process to be executed the same way every time, this just doesn't happen in the real world. Slightly varying circumstances introduce complex processes, and what appears simple on paper is in reality much more involved.

The problem with a flow chart is that these circumstances are invariably, inevitably lost. There's no way we can tell a complete story because the situations that bring people to the flow are infinite and inherently unpredictable. As designers and developers, our job is to keep the user's best interest in mind. A flow chart—as useful as it can be—can get in the way because it represents this crazy mix of user needs as a singular, unified whole. The greatest challenge for us working on flow charts is to take a step back, look at them critically, and ask ourselves "What's really going on here?"

Creating User Flows

Despite the challenges, a flow chart must tell a story with the user as protagonist, and therefore must include a beginning, middle, and end. The middle is the meaty part, showing all the places the user may go before reaching the end.

Like all the deliverables in this book, flow charts are defined by three layers. The first layer includes all the essentials: Leaving one of these things out would fundamentally change the deliverable. Even the simplest flow charts have everything in the first layer. The second and third layers contain additional information providing additional levels of detail for your audiences. Whether to include them depends on your audience, your project, and your team.

Layer 1: Must-Haves

Flows have a few more minimum requirements than site maps. Site maps show structure, but there's no prescription for the type of structure, whereas flow charts have more direction. The essential elements of flow charts include more than just the steps in the process. You need to indicate starting and ending points, as well as any rules that guide the direction of the process.

Anchors

Every flow has a starting point and an ending point—that is, where users enter the process and where they conclude the process. The flow documentation should show this. There are several different ways to distinguish endpoints from the rest of the flow.

If the flow represents a modular process, the starting and ending points can be distinguished with unique symbols that represent users entering the flow from somewhere else. This matches traditional flowcharting notation, which uses a circle to indicate beginning and ending. Typically, this circle will include a unique identifier for the flow and where it returns upon conclusion.

Self-contained flows that represent a main process in the application may start on one of the site's main pages. In this case, you can use the same symbol for this page as other pages, with slight variation to distinguish it, thickening the line weight or changing the background color.

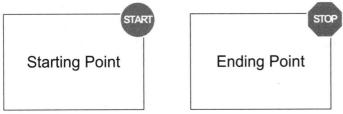

Figure 9.4 One way to represent starting and ending points is to use "go" and "stop" symbols. It's glib, but effective.

Steps

The shortest processes consist of two steps: collect input, show output. Online search applications are the best examples of this: They ask for a keyword and display results matching the keyword.

In some cases it may be useful to distinguish the importance of various steps. Some processes, for example, have a set of required steps. Every user must move through these steps in order to complete the process. Depending on options they select, though, there may be secondary steps.

These days, a shopping cart is a shopping cart. You've seen one, you've seen them all. From the main shopping cart page, you are asked for shipping information, billing information, and a confirmation. On the other hand, users choosing international shipping, gift options, or gift certificate payment options may need to provide additional information that temporarily takes them "outside" the main flow.

If necessary, you can distinguish between the flow's primary steps and other parts of the process by changing the size of the symbol representing a step. Larger symbols represent main steps while smaller versions represent secondary processes. I do not recommend changing the shape entirely since a step is a step, regardless of its importance in the flow.

Paths

No doubt most stakeholders are used to the convention of lines between shapes representing paths between steps. Although it may be tempting to change the style of the line to show whether paths are required or important, use caution here. Too much variation—thickness of lines, color of lines, dotted lines, dashed lines, double lines—can create visual noise, making it difficult to read the flow. Err on the side of simplicity and use notation rather than style to show differences in paths.

Like the space between panels in comic books, there is a lot happening in the "space" between steps, and the little lines between boxes are burdened by communicating this information. If there are conditions for moving from one step to the next, the document should reflect these conditions.

One simple way to do this is to include a special symbol on the line to show that it must meet a condition. You can have a callout to describe the condition right next to the path, or you can label the line with a number or letter and describe the condition in the margin.

Decision points

Complex conditions may be represented by their own nodes. In other words, a decision point in a process may be represented by its own shape. Traditional flow charts use a diamond. Typically, decision points are expressed as yes-or-no questions, with yes responses taking the user in one direction and no responses in another direction.

Examples of binary decision points:

- Is the user logged in?

- Is the user placing an international order?

- Is the data supplied by the user valid?

Don't feel constrained by this binary approach. Not every decision point should be documented this way. For example, to show a logged-in state, simply include two lines coming from the starting point with one labeled "logged in" and one labeled "anonymous." Or, you may want to reserve decision points for more complex logic and express them as system imperatives:

- Determine required taxes

- Determine access privileges

- Filter results

Try to design your flow such that path lines do not cross. Some paths make this difficult, but ultimately the diagram will be easier to read if you keep line-crossing at a minimum.

Process name and identifiers

Every process should have a name, if for no other reason than to make it easy to talk about. The name should be meaningful and related to the process' purpose, task, or function. Here are some good names: new user registration, log-in, edit account settings, establish new wish list.

You may want to give the process some other identifier, such as a series of letters or numbers, like A1 or 6.2. Your numbering scheme should be sophisticated enough to distinguish the different steps in the flow, so that 5.1 and 5.2 refer to the first two steps in flow 5.

Project and bookkeeping information

Besides the name of the process, there are several other pieces of information that can help identify your document. This information may seem extraneous, even if you're not using a lot of documentation, but it can help stakeholders and team members—who have a lot more on their minds than your flow chart—keep things straight. Your flow chart should make room for the name of the project, the names of contributors, date and version number, and perhaps the client's name. You may also want to leave room for a version history—a description of how the document has changed over time. There are more details on this in a few pages, but I wanted to tell you now so you won't be caught by surprise later.

Layer 2: Further Details

What distinguishes the second layer from the first is level of detail. Layer 1 should contain enough information to build the application, but the second layer of information can provide further detail to prevent confusion later in the process. By thinking about these distinctions now, you and your team will save time later.

Step distinctions

In the first layer of a flow chart you might distinguish between major steps in the process and minor steps. There are, however, further distinctions you might want to show by varying the look of the symbol for steps. For example, many web-based processes are a combination of give and take—the web site requests some information and provides a response, and the user offers additional information based on the response. Your flow can visually distinguish these different kinds of screens to show how this "conversation" between user and site emerges over time.

Step details: Who, what, where, when, why

The bare essentials of a step include a rectangle and a label, but there's much more to a step in a process than its name. There are any number of questions you might answer about a step in the process: Who performs it? What are the inputs and outputs? When does the step occur? And why is the step important?

In some cases, this information is part of the design, perhaps because the process is new. For example, a complex process might include error-checking routines, subprocesses that communicate to users whether they've provided incorrect information or committed some other error. Since these kinds of diversions from the normal process can be confusing and very detailed, you might include the error messages themselves in the flow.

Even if you do not need to specify this information as part of the design, it can provide contextual cues to stakeholders, helping them understand how the step fits in with their understanding of the organization. By relating specific people in the organization with steps in the process, you make the steps more meaningful by associating them with something recognizable.

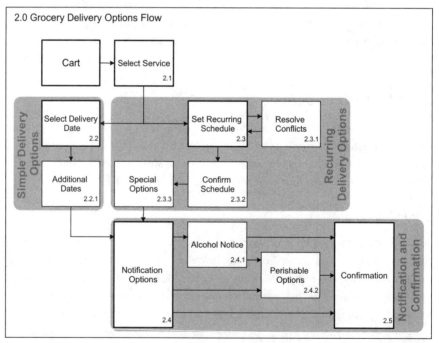

Figure 9.5 This complex process has been grouped into related functional areas, shown by the labeled, shaded backgrounds. The groupings make it easy to talk about different parts of the process.

Step groupings

Your process may consist of related groups of steps. These relationships may or may not be evident from the paths between them. Even if the paths do clearly show groups of related steps, an additional visual device may help clarify those relationships. Grouping related steps allows you to apply a name, which can make talking about the process easier.

In one type of grouping typically associated with flow charts, steps are organized not only in sequence but also by who is responsible for them. The template for this type of process includes "swim lanes" where each person or role is assigned a different lane, and the steps owned by that person appear in his or her lane. For web-based processes, one swim lane might represent the system itself, showing how the computer, in effect, contributes to the process.

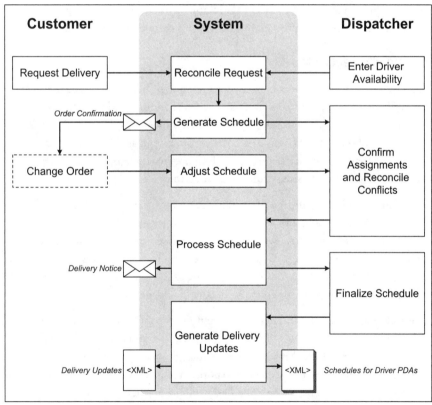

Figure 9.6 This mock-up shows how a process might be organized around "swim lanes" which represent different people responsible for different parts of the process. In this case, the system—represented by the shaded swim lane—also takes some of the responsibilities in the process. Shapes overlapping two swim lanes can show joint responsibilities or, in this case, how the system communicates with the humans involved in the process.

Error paths

Error scenarios describe what happens to users when they commit an error—neglecting to enter information in a required field, for example, or supplying inconsistent information. In some cases it is worthwhile to document these on the main flow and in others to separate it.

Documenting error scenarios is difficult because some interactions with users present many opportunities for users to commit errors—requesting payment information, for example. Illustrating all these possible errors requires a lot of detail. In complex processes, it may be difficult to capture all this information in one place and makes more sense to document each scenario separately.

Flows may not be a good place to document error scenarios at all. Wireframes, for example, are a better place to capture error scenarios because you can associate them with specific areas of the page. Some error scenarios are repetitive, and illustrating those paths on the main flow may make it difficult to read.

Variations on each step

Early web-based applications were easy to document because the "page model" was well entrenched; that is, web sites were built and programmed as if they were a series of pages. As technologies advance, however, it is more difficult to conceive of web applications as a series of discrete pages. Instead, a single "page" may have many variations depending on the mode or state, which could change depending on business rules or user actions.

For example, the landing page of an application may vary depending on whether the user is logged in or not. If the user is logged in, the landing page may contain different fields, even though it is conceptually the first page of the application. The increasing complexity of web applications creates new challenges for documentation. Representing these page variations in a flow can be difficult where conventions generally dictate "one page, one rectangle."

One technique would be to create separate flows for different scenarios. One flow would address the user's "logged in" experience, and another the "anonymous" experience. With this technique, you might want to also show which pages are "shared" between scenarios. Another technique is to represent each page variation separately on the same flow, and group them visually. This can demonstrate that conceptually this group of variations is the same page—the user will never see more than one at a time—but its display varies depending on state or mode. Whatever technique you use to show page variations, it is important to document the scenarios, the circumstances in which one page variation will appear over another.

Layer 3: Further Context

Layers 1 and 2 focus on the flow itself and details about the steps. If you decide to include additional information, you might focus on the context behind the entire process.

Triggers

For the purposes of web design, processes are typically conceived as self-contained mechanisms that accept inputs and produce an output. The steps in the process account for the transformations to the input necessary for achieving the output, but none of this addresses how the process happens in the first place. In some cases, the triggers are obvious—a user clicks "checkout," a system receives a search query, or some such distinct action—but in other cases, the trigger requires some explanation. Near the starting point of the process, you can put a description of what conditions are necessary to start the process. By the same token, just because a process concludes does not mean that everything stops. The process may in turn trigger another process, or set of processes. The flow chart's stopping point can include a description of what happens when the process ends.

Scenarios

Like triggers, scenarios provide context and background for the process. Scenarios are broader than triggers, telling a story about the overall process, not just where it begins or how it ends. Sometimes the title of the process is enough to provide context—"new user flow," for example—but it may not be clear in cases where the flow depends on a number of outside factors, or includes many different functions. For example, imagine an online banking site that allows users to sign up for a variety of accounts. Due to the complexity of the account information, each type of account has a slightly different flow. What's more, the process is essentially the same for a completely new customer and an existing customer who just wants to add a new type of account. You can just call this the "new accounts" flow, but you may need to spell out some of these nuances on the document itself.

Going with the Flow: The Basics

On the surface, flow charts show the user's progress from one end of the system to the other, but, like every deliverable, they serve a deeper purpose in the project as well. The purpose of a flow chart is tied to its situation and audience. Since flow charts represent an abstract stage of the design and can appear just about anywhere in the process, they can serve a variety of purposes.

Purpose

As a design document, a flow chart's main purpose is to capture part of the user experience. But you can also create a flow chart to capture your understanding of a client's business process, separate from the user experience. For example, the checkout process on a commercial site is different from the internal business process for fulfilling a customer's order. As with any deliverable, the purpose of your flow chart will dictate, to some extent, the kind of information it includes.

When documenting the user experience, flow charts generally show a series of screens. Each step in the process is one screen, which is generally a form for entering information or a response based on user input. The arrows represent different paths depending on users' responses to the questions on the screens. A flow chart describing user experience should also include technical information for the developers describing the rules applied to the information supplied by the user. A simple example would be displaying different screens to users in a checkout process depending on whether they've selected the gift option. These are rules that operate behind the scenes, but have an important impact on the user experience.

Alternatively, you can create flow charts to represent business processes, which show the steps employees must follow to accomplish a task. This kind of flow chart can be useful for understanding how the web site should support the tasks performed by people in the organization. For example, you might use a flow chart to document an internal fulfillment process, where different workers have responsibilities for capturing orders, preparing the orders, packaging the orders, labeling them, and sending them off. Understanding this process will help you design the flow for the online system because you will know what kind of information you need to collect from users in the checkout process of a commercial web site.

Documenting business processes is even more important when you're working on an internal web site, which might support these internal processes. For example, you might capture the editorial process for creating and publishing a specific type of document in order to build a content management system to support it. In this kind of flow chart, technical rules might not be as relevant immediately. Instead, you'll focus on ensuring you've captured all the key decisions in a process, and the important participants.

Timing

Early in the process, the flow chart may have less functional detail and show more business context. Flow charts developed later in the design process will emphasize functional decisions.

One way to make sure your flow chart is appropriate to its position in the project is to make a list of all the inputs it will include. By identifying what you have to work with—specific requirements, results from usability tests, direction gleaned from personas—you can be sure you've accounted for existing work on the project. This list should also indicate what will come after the document. A detailed flow chart could lead right into development, or into further design activities, or prototyping. Understanding what comes next can help shape the document.

Early in the design process, you may not have all the functional details decided, in which case the flow chart serves as a method for encouraging discussion and brainstorming. Alongside the flow, you can include any questions you might have about the process or the functionality as points of discussion.

Later in the process, when you've got most of the functional issues ironed out, the flow chart must capture all the details that define the flow. With this kind of document, there must be strong connections to other design deliverables, like wireframes, to pull all the functional details together. References to earlier documents will help ground design decisions. At late stages in the design process, this deliverable serves as documentation for the system, and the details must be fully realized to support development efforts.

Audience

There are three primary audiences for any design document, and knowing the primary audience will help you decide what kind of information to include as well as how to spin that information.

For stakeholders, offer a basic description of the flow:

- Users move from the shopping cart page to the shipping information page. The shopping cart page will allow them to make changes to the quantities of products. The shipping information page will ask them for a location to ship their product.

For developers, emphasize business rules because these will have to be coded:

- Moving from shopping cart to shipping information, the system needs to check whether the user has set any quantities to zero. In this case, the system should not confirm the deletion, just assume the user wants to delete the product from her cart. No other error checking happens between the cart and the shipping information.

For designers, highlight the trigger mechanism because this is what will likely get the most visual attention:

- To move along in the process, users will indicate they want to check out from the shopping cart page. This will load the shipping information page.

Note that while all these audiences may be most interested in the contents of the pages themselves, that conversation is premature and those statements are kept to an absolute minimum.

Because of their distinct perspectives, each audience will need something different out of the flow chart. It may be difficult to accommodate all this information or to create three different versions of the diagram. By identifying your main audience, you can overcome these difficulties by focusing on the key messages for that group.

Content development

In thinking through the situation and the audience, you may find that you still need to do a bit more planning before putting a flow down on paper. Creating an inventory of all the different kinds of information you want to include will ensure you do not forget anything in the flow. It may also help you think through some of the issues in documenting a process or user experience. The document layers listed earlier capture these elements at a high level, but you'll need to create a more specific list, tailored to your specific situation, audience, and need. You may also find that it helps you identify those elements that you do not want to include.

You might prepare this list before determining the situation, audience, and need, and then use those other lists to prioritize the elements or even eliminate some of them. Alternatively, you could create the elements list after having established the situation, audience, and need. Either way, by creating a list of elements ahead of time, you can also think about how you want to represent them visually in the flow. (Sound familiar? This technique was also recommended for site maps.)

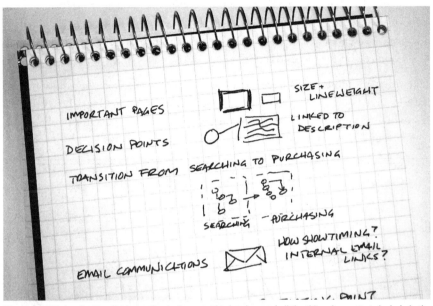

Figure 9.7 This handwritten list helps the designer get his head around all the things he wants to include in the flow. He's also started identifying how he'll represent each element visually.

Just because an element is on your list does not mean it must have a shape associated with it on the diagram. Good diagrams find ways to consolidate information, using a variety of visual formatting devices to communicate multiple dimensions.

For example, putting a lock icon inside a rectangle to represent pages requiring log-in adds a visual element to the page that might compete visually with other, more important elements. Compare the importance or relevance of a visual element to its visibility. In this case, making all logged-in pages a similar color may do a better job communicating this element because it easily distinguishes it from other pages and avoids adding clutter to the diagram.

Greasing the Wheels: Tips for Effective Flow Charts

Even if you've listed out all your content and anticipated the needs of your project and team, there are a couple more things you can do to make sure the creation of the flow chart goes smoothly.

Identify a visual language

As suggested earlier, you should determine a visual language—a consistent set of symbols—to represent the different aspects of the flow. Consistency is crucial: If a step is represented as a circle in one place and a square in another, there should be a good reason for the distinction.

Like site maps, flow charts have a long history before the web. Conventions have emerged and evolved to pace the development of technology. Links to shape libraries produced by information architects and available for public use can be found at www.communicatingdesign.com.

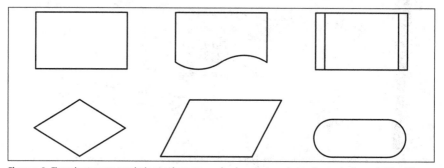

Figure 9.8 Flow charts were taught in my elementary school computer science classes in the early '80s. These symbols have been used for decades to represent the internal logic of computer systems, and have since evolved to describe user experience. Even back then, I was a stickler for good documentation.

Start with crucial landmarks

If you're struggling to represent the flow because there's too much going on, go back to the basics. Pull out the handful of steps representing the major junctions in the process and put them on paper. Once you have a shape for those, you can add additional important steps. Decide early on what's important to communicate. You may be more concerned, for example, about alternate paths or error scenarios than the details behind the main process. If this is the case, this is the kind of information you should start with, after establishing the crucial landmarks.

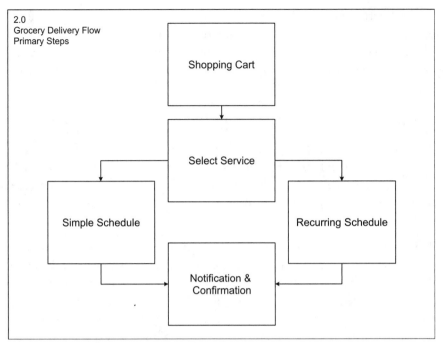

Figure 9.9 In this planning document, the designer has drawn out the main steps in the process, but has a lot more information to layer in. He's already started prioritizing his list of information to include.

Risks

Despite all your planning, you may still run into a few problems as you develop your flow chart. Here are some ideas about how to deal with them when they come up.

Express what's really happening

As described in the "Challenges" section, the biggest risk with flows is dehumanizing them. Flows have a tendency to smooth over the natural variations between circumstances, giving the impression that every user will go through the same experience. Getting caught up in the details of the flow, you might start to see your users as automated repositories of information who simply spit out data when it's requested, rather than individuals who bring unique scenarios along with them.

Perhaps the best way to avoid looking at the system as nothing more than inputs and outputs is to include personas right on the flow itself. You might even add further information for each persona, the circumstances in which they would be coming to the site, or the kinds of information they will and will not have in hand when they start the process. By superimposing information about your users over the flow itself, you stand a better chance of seeing the flow in more realistic circumstances.

Dot the i's and cross the t's

As conscientious as you are to capture every detail, you might still be missing something. The risk here is that you'll make it to the implementation stage and, in building the system, realize that you haven't accounted for a rule or potential scenario. You'll be scrambling to come up with a solution, but won't have time to design the right one.

The catch-22 is that the best way to identify whether you've missed a crucial detail is to use the system—and, of course, you can't use the system until you've designed it. Perhaps the best way around this conundrum is to recognize that there's no way to hash out every detail just by building a flow chart. A flow chart is a starting point for implementation, and it needs to cooperate with other design activities to ensure that every aspect of the user experience is documented. But the only way to find out if you've missed something is to build the web site and test it.

That said, there are still a few things you can do to make sure you've got as complete a flow as possible. First, develop a set of criteria for each step in the process, a litmus test to help you think through all the implications. This can vary from project to project, but it might include things like expressing in plain language the purpose or role of the step—for example, to gather shipping information from the end user. You can then ask yourself a series of questions about that task: What information is necessary for this task? When the system is done with this task, what will it do with each piece of information? Minute questions like these can uncover important details. With this technique, you're testing the comprehensiveness of the flow chart by imagining the actual system.

Another technique is to recruit another pair of eyes, even if they don't belong to a user. Tapping another designer or analyst or developer and walking him or her through the process will give you a different perspective, one that can shine light on details you might have missed.

Perhaps the best way to avoid losing sight of the nuances is to do a bit of role-playing. This technique is easier if you've already prepared personas and have some direction on who will be visiting the site. Stepping through the flow, put yourself in the shoes of one of your users and think about the kinds of information the site is requesting, and the kinds of information the user has on hand. Think about the order in which the site asks for information, and the likelihood of users being able to answer questions in that order. Putting yourself in the same position as the users will get you to experience the flow from their perspective, and perhaps allow you to envision the flow as they do.

As this book has said elsewhere, this problem of overgeneralizing your users is inevitable. It's just not possible for one person or a group of people to think through every circumstance and account for every detail. The best mitigation strategy is to build time into the schedule to account for these revelations. The second best mitigation strategy is to set the team's expectations: They need to try to get every aspect of the flow right, but the only way to identify all the potential issues with the system is to let actual people use it.

Keep the document up to date

Flow charts are hard to keep up to date because in the natural evolution of a design, flow charts may be quickly left in the dust. Before worrying about how you'll keep your flow chart up to date, you should decide whether it's essential to do so. If you're using a flow chart to kick-start the design process, but not necessarily as system documentation, you may decide that going back and keeping it up to date after changing the flow may not be worthwhile. If you decide there is some value to maintaining it, you should also decide how detailed your updates need to be. Do you need to capture every nuance? Can you just focus on the big changes? Answers to these questions will be determined by the role of the flow chart in your process, and how it relates to other documents.

Your ability to maintain a flow chart depends somewhat on the tool you've used to build it, but more on how you've constructed the document. A dense layout that makes use of every inch of the page can create problems when you need to add or change information.

One way to deal with this is to look through your list of elements (described above in "Content Development") and determine which ones will require updating. In constructing the document, you can make sure to leave room for these elements. Additionally, you can prioritize these elements, so that as you find the flow becoming too dense, you can eliminate information that you won't need to keep up to date. (Not to say this information isn't important, but perhaps you can capture it elsewhere, especially if maintenance is crucial to the document.)

Finally, always leave room for a version history. Generally, putting the version history on the same page as the flow itself is effective because it keeps the evolution of the document top of mind for other people on the team.

Presenting Flow Charts

Presenting flow charts to your audience can be challenging because although they represent something concrete—the interaction between system and user—they do so in an abstract way. Certain details like screen elements are necessarily absent because it is important to plan the interaction before tying down the interface. At the same time, it's much easier to talk about the user experience with an interface in front of you—people tend to provide better feedback on a wireframe or screen design. To help your audience understand the flow without having to resort to screen mock-ups, there are a few different presentation styles you can use.

Meeting Purposes

Your presentation style depends on the purpose of the meeting, and your agenda should be driven by what you want to get out of the meeting. For example, if you just want to provide a progress report, you may not need to go into great detail. On the other hand, if you're looking for buy-in, you may need to get your hands a little dirtier.

Introduction and overview

If you're not looking for any significant feedback on the flow chart, you can hold a short overview meeting. In this meeting, you might hit the high points of the flow chart, perhaps including the factors that drove the design decisions. In a short overview meeting, you may want to keep the deliverable itself simple. Too many details could lead to questions you are not ready to answer. (On the other hand, this is also a good opportunity to educate stakeholders and others about the complexity of these processes.)

In your overview, describe the important screens in the flow and the information the user must provide on those screens. Focus on the screens in the main process—the one that helps users complete the desired task. If there are any important supporting screens—those that appear when the user makes an error, for example—run through those next. You don't need to hit every screen and every nuance, just those that help meeting participants get a sense of the shape of the flow. To bookend the discussion of the flow chart, describe the triggers—what would cause users to get to this flow—and what happens when the user completes the flow, or how the system and user have "changed" as a result of it.

Your web site may include many different flows. You can follow the same structure for each of the flows. Keep in mind that in an overview meeting, the object is for the meeting participants to come away with a general understanding of the flows in a system, in other words, how the high-level requirements have been translated to features, not how the user will interact with the system at a detailed level.

Feedback and brainstorming

Going into this kind of meeting, it's useful to have a list of all the things you need help with—all the problems that need solving and unanswered questions. Brainstorming meetings are Petri dishes for tangents and distractions, so keep tabs on your progress by ensuring you're getting answers to all your outstanding questions.

A brainstorming meeting may require stimuli—inspiration to help generate ideas and provide boundaries. If you've documented requirements, these can be useful to include in the meeting, but not in the form of an enormous document. Boiling the requirements down to a handful of bullets for a particular function or feature gives meeting participants enough to go on for brainstorming.

When you need help fleshing out the basic design, the deliverable can serve as a springboard for discussion. In the case of flows, keeping the polish to a minimum can help: Participants may be unwilling to contribute if the deliverable looks like it contains fully realized ideas. You can also integrate your questions into the document itself, showing specifically where you need clarification. Figure 9.9 shows a high-level flow, with just the key areas, that can serve as a means for generating discussion.

You may also want to go in with nothing besides an agenda. You can spend the meeting capturing ideas on a whiteboard, then use the deliverable to document those ideas. Regardless of your approach, it is during this meeting that you dig into the details, and spell out the business rules for the flow. Talking through the flows of your site can help identify crucial functional details, and through brainstorming you can determine the most appropriate rules and behaviors for the site.

Buy-in and approval

You may need buy-in on the whole soup-to-nuts process, or just on the germ of an idea. In either case, you need to demonstrate that you've thought through all the implications of the design. Select a presentation style that's going to demonstrate that you've addressed all the different aspects of the process and have accounted for all exceptions. If you show up with a radical idea without having understood its impact on the rest of the system or the business, no doubt you'll be sent back to the drawing board.

Perhaps the one exception to this is when the meeting participants have been active contributors to the design process—they've followed the progress of the design all along the way. On the other hand, it may be irresponsible to assume that your stakeholders have the exact same ideas that you do: Even when you think your stakeholders are on board, they may have a different conception of the user experience, despite their continuous involvement.

In reality, your buy-in meeting can't stand alone. If you're seeking approval on a design or concept, your best bet is to have introduced and discussed the idea before asking for your stakeholders' blessing. The content of a buy-in meeting should be simple: You need to remind the meeting participants about the background and purpose of the flow, point out the highlights, show how you've addressed concerns that they've raised previously, and show how you're mitigating risks. (It sounds so easy when written out like that, doesn't it?) Like an overview meeting, you don't need to dig into the details, provided the rest of the meeting participants have been exposed to them before, or have been involved in the design.

Meeting Structures

Because flows are little stories in and of themselves, it's easy to structure a meeting around them. By far the most effective meeting structure is the narrative form, in which you walk participants through the flow as if you were a user of the web site. There are a number of other approaches you can use, however, and you should select the structure that best suits your purpose and audience.

Narrative meeting structure

In a narrative approach, you tell a story about someone actually using the site. Real-world scenarios can make the interaction come to life. This works even better if you've previously introduced user personas. By employing the user personas to tell the stories, you are relating a new deliverable to one the audience is already familiar with. This creates continuity and demonstrates that the flow was not created in a vacuum.

To use this style of presentation, you must identify the scenarios you will walk through. It may be tempting to walk through every scenario, but it's better to choose a number of scenarios based on your audience. If your primary audience is stakeholders and your goal is simply buy-in, use only a few scenarios that demonstrate the main features. For designers and developers, who will need other issues highlighted for them, select scenarios that have the greatest impact on their work.

Having selected the appropriate scenarios, you should elaborate on the details for each one. For each step in the process, make sure you're able to explain what information users must provide and the kinds of responses they will get. You'll want to describe what triggers each step in the process and what happens when the user has completed the process. At the same time, you need to avoid explicit references to screen elements—like "Joe clicks on Next"—because you don't want to create preconceived notions of what the screens will look like.

Your agenda for this kind of presentation will vary depending on the purpose of the meeting. For a simple overview, you can use this generic agenda:

- Introduction (includes project goal reminders, purpose of this meeting)
- Our Users (recap the user profiles)
- Flow Overview (identify three or four factors affecting the design of the flow)
- Scenario Overviews (before detailing each flow, give a two-sentence description of each one, ensuring you identify the user's goal for each one)
- Scenario 1: The basic scenario
- Scenario 2: An error scenario
- Scenario 3: An advanced scenario
- Other Possible Scenarios
- Next Steps

If you're holding a meeting to get approval on a draft flow, this agenda will work as well, though you may need to run through additional scenarios.

If you're doing a brainstorming meeting, the agenda should also include places to actually do the brainstorming. Narrative presentations are useful for brainstorming because you can indicate what parts of the scenario need fleshing out. First provide a quick overview of each scenario, indicating which parts require additional work, then go back to the beginning and work through it step by step, as a group.

Thematic meeting structure

Another way to structure your meeting is to select a theme and show how the flow supports it. Unlike the narrative structure, which attempts to imagine the user experience through pantomime, the thematic structure emphasizes design decisions centered around a key theme.

You can probably think of any number of themes for your flows, but here are a few to get you started.

- **The business objective:** By organizing your presentation around a set of business objectives, you describe how a flow supports particular goals. For example, if one of the goals of the web design project is to double new customer registrations, you can show how the flow has been designed with this objective in mind.

- **The user need:** In conducting user research, you may have identified broad needs from the users, like "make it easy to move from one function to the next" or "I need to share my information across different accounts." Whatever the need, you can show how the flow supports this. As with a business objective, making a user need the central theme of your presentation means you do not have to dig into every detail of the flow, but can instead simply point out the elements of the flow that support that need.

- **Technical requirements:** Far be it from me to advocate designing a system around technical requirements, but this message may be important to your stakeholders. In these cases, there is usually some overwhelming technical consideration that directly impacts the flow. Your theme might be something like, "The legacy system has a specific definition for a user account, so we designed the new flow to accommodate that definition." This isn't to say that the technical requirements *drove* the design. Instead, you're using the technical requirements to frame the conversation about the design.

- **Problem clarification:** Certain problems may seem intractable to clients or team members, and a flow can be an effective way to provide a solution or at least clarify the problem. For example, suppose your client says, "We have lots of disparate systems that all do the same kind of thing. Can we consolidate them?" Flow charts can be a useful tool for documenting each system, or documenting what the systems have in common, and then structuring the conversation to determine an answer to the question.

- **Organizational need:** Every online flow has some impact on the organization. As a new commercial channel, the flow impacts fulfillment and
  customer service. As a supplement to an internal business process—records
  management, for example—the online flow changes how people do business.
  You can use this impact as a central theme for educating people on the client
  side about how their jobs will be changing.

None of these meeting agendas advocate a non-user-centered approach to
design. The design process can be separate from the story you tell to describe
the final design, the outcome. The type of theme you select for your meeting
depends on the participants: They need you to put the flow into a context that
makes sense to them.

Inventory structure

A more straightforward approach is to simply create an inventory of the flows
and go through them in some hierarchical order. This order may be meaningless outside the context of your meeting, but it provides a structure for the 60
minutes you're sitting with other team members.

To plan this kind of meeting, simply make a list of all the flows, and identify if
any of them have subflows. You can put them in the order that users are likely
to experience them, or by risk—the flows that will require the most discussion
go first—or by any other criteria.

For each flow, identify the main things that users do over its course, and the
main screens they will hit. Once the inventory is in place, you can dig into the
details of each step in the process.

Losing the Flow: When Meetings Go Off Course

There are two main obstacles to a flow chart meeting that could derail it. On the
one hand, your participants may struggle to picture the user experience because
the flow chart is very abstract. The quality of feedback depends on participants'
ability to envision the process, and if they can't do that, your meeting could end
up being a waste of time. You want your flow to generate lots of feedback, shedding light in places you and the team hadn't considered before.

Make the abstract concrete

As concrete as the ideas in your flow chart may be, the document itself is an
abstraction. Your meeting participants may not be able to offer constructive

feedback because they can't picture the user experience. Knowing whether this is a risk or not depends on how well you know your clients. If you and your clients can comfortably have back-of-the-envelope kinds of brainstorming sessions, they may be prepared to deal with the abstraction of flow charts.

If you don't know your client well enough to know whether the flows will be meaningless to them, it will become painfully obvious in the meeting. They might complain that they want to see screen designs or that they can't picture it. Worse yet, they might sit there, nodding and smiling as if they understand everything about the flow.

If you're quick on your feet, you can change your approach in the meeting, presenting the ideas in a different way. For example, it might be best to put the documents aside and build the flows progressively on a whiteboard. This way, the client can focus on one thing at a time, and ask questions along the way without the distraction of the documentation.

On the other hand, you may realize that the clients' attitude suggests that you won't get anywhere in the current meeting. In that case, there's no harm in calling time out and ending the meeting. There's no point in belaboring a document if it's not getting you or the project team what you need. The lack of feedback may have an impact on the project schedule—the input you were supposed to get on the flows will have to wait until later in the process, creating some risk.

Knowing the disposition of your client may lead to you skip sharing the flows with them altogether—not a bad strategy if doing so would waste everyone's time. Whether you need to do flows at all is completely up to you and your team. Your development team may find value in seeing flows early in the process so they can begin planning the system architecture. Flows give designers a sense of the scope of the design, so they may be eager audiences as well.

Stay flexible

Like many other design documents, flow charts can open your team's eyes. Their exposure to the user experience, even in abstract form, can trigger ideas that did not occur to them earlier in the project process. Even though user flows are not very concrete, they may be more tangible and closer to the final product than anything that came before.

Imagine needing to design a checkout process for a commercial web site. The requirements called for some high-level functions, like a shopping cart, capturing shipping and billing information, calculating tax and shipping charges, confirming the order, and placing the order. Perhaps you and the team took the user experience for granted—after all, with more than ten years of e-commerce, the checkout process has been refined over time. You build out the flow, and when you show it to your clients they bring up the issue of back orders—products that are not in stock, but that they'll be getting soon. It wasn't something that came up during the requirements process, but it's something you need to accommodate.

These situations can be difficult because clients may not recognize why throwing new requirements into the mix at this stage can be risky. It can be difficult to see that a single new requirement can have a cascading effect, affecting other requirements and design efforts. The other issue is that the requirements document, for better or worse, drives project planning. Everyone on the project team uses requirements to estimate how long it will take them to do their part.

The best cure for this risk is to assume it will happen—that your requirement-gathering efforts do not end when you hand in the requirements document— and build extra time into the design process. This strategy isn't unique to user flows, of course. There are countless opportunities along the course of a design process for new requirements to arise. People in the computer business affectionately call this "scope creep"—when the boundaries around the project shift slightly, but perceptibly. Your project should have a general strategy for scope creep, one that allows your project manager (or whoever's running things) to push back or take the requirements away for further analysis. The key here is not to promise anything immediately because even the seemingly smallest change can have a profound affect on the scope of your project.

Flow Charts in Context

Like site maps, flow charts are flexible and can be used in a variety of circumstances and in conjunction with nearly every other kind of document.

Flow charts and user needs documents

Like other design documentation, flow charts can supplement user needs documentation to show how users fared in completing a process, or to contextualize user feedback from usability tests. In a usability report, you might show where the major stumbling blocks were for users. When planning a usability test, you can use a flow chart to identify the anticipated path through the web site.

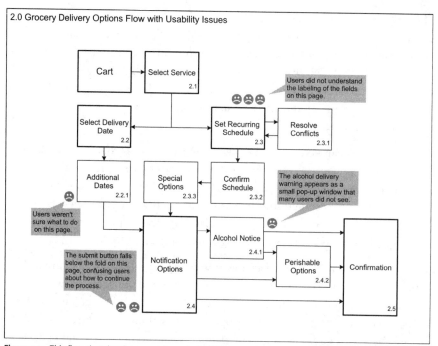

Figure 9.10 This flow chart has been supplemented with icons and callouts to show where users struggled most in completing a process.

In capturing user needs, personas can use flow charts to illustrate typical processes, outside the context of a particular system. These flow charts map user expectations, showing how target audiences are used to completing a task, or how they expect related tasks to work together.

Flow charts and strategy documents

In typical processes, flow charts documenting a web site's user experience come after strategy documents that establish a foundation for design. You may reference the competitive analysis or the concept model in the construction of the flow, but it's unlikely you'll draw any direct relationships between them.

On the other hand, flow charts can be useful in competitive analyses to show how different sites represent the same process. As entrenched as online shopping carts and checkout processes are, the user experience is slightly different on every commercial site. Lining up a series of flows that show the same task implemented in different ways can be a powerful way to draw attention to what your competitors do well.

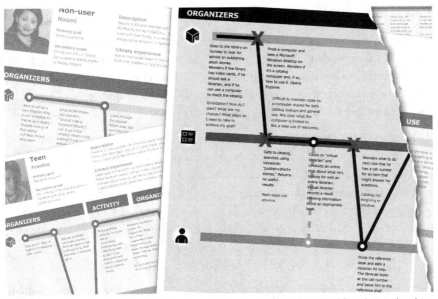

Figure 9.11 MAYA Design, in their work for the Carnegie Library system, used a stylized flow chart to show how users attempted to complete a task and where the library's user experience was "broken." Image courtesy of MAYA Design, www.maya.com.

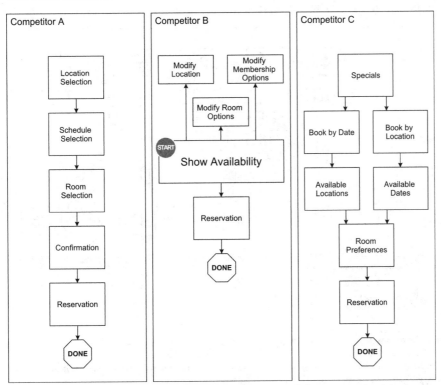

Figure 9.12 These three flows all illustrate the same task—booking a hotel room—but show how it has been implemented differently on different sites.

Flow charts and other design documents

Successful design documentation cooperates. That is, no design document should live independently of another. They build on each other and show different aspects of the same user experience. The flow chart is no different. It must cooperate with wireframes, site maps, and screen designs to provide a complete picture of the user experience.

Although you may opt to treat the structure of the site (the site map) differently from transactional processes (the flow chart), keep in mind that the user probably does not perceive a difference between them. To better illustrate the user experience, you might combine your structural/navigation documents with your process documents, showing how the user experience flows from one to the other. This transition is exemplified in commercial sites, which must transition users from a browsing mode (looking through the shop to find a desired item) to a transactional one (completing the purchase of the item).

Flow charts also provide good context for wireframes and screen designs, which show a slice of the overall user experience. Integrating a flow chart into a wireframe can help stakeholders recognize where they are in the process. (This is discussed thoroughly in Chapter 11.)

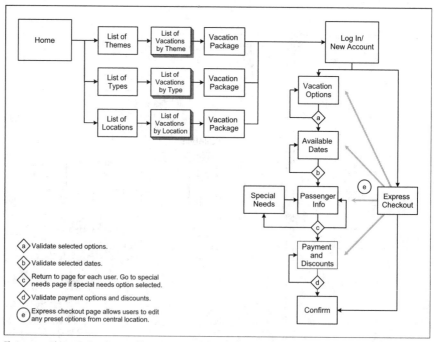

Figure 9.13 This complex site map/flow chart combination for a travel site shows how users move from browsing vacations to booking the trip.

If you have access to a large-format printer, you can create a document that combines wireframes and flow charts. Instead of connecting rectangles with arrows, you connect entire wireframes with arrows. This kind of document is very cool because it reduces the abstraction, creating something that's closer to a final product. People reading this hybrid flow won't lose the context that they might when looking at individual wireframes, nor will they have trouble understanding a flow chart that lacks user interface details.

The jumbo format gives you more room to include additional documentation and explain the business rules that dictate what users see. Putting a poster like this up on a wall is great for collaboration because it invites people to annotate. Of course, the size comes with several disadvantages: It's not as portable, physically or electronically; it's difficult to make without a large-format printer; and it can be difficult to maintain.

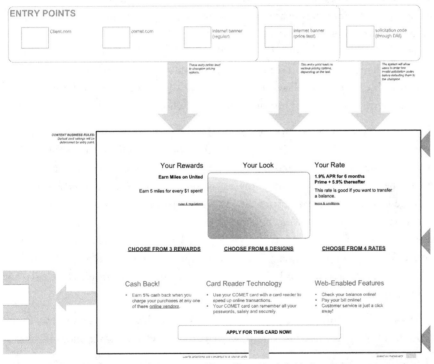

Figure 9.14 Freed from standard-sized paper, the wireframe/flow chart hybrid offers design teams countless opportunities to document every aspect of the user experience. This excerpt shows a couple of wireframes connected by arrows, elaborated business rules, and detailed behavior notes that aren't confined to a narrow column on one side of the page.

Weigh the disadvantages and decide if you can deal with them. You may need to create two documents from the same content—a large poster and a deck of wireframes. The poster may serve as a means for discussing the user experience, but the wireframe deck is the final word, and is the repository of the most up-to-date decisions.

The Many Levels of Process

In the early days of the web, sites were just repositories of information, where the structure of navigation was paramount. As the web evolves, permitting different types of interactions, designers and developers will need a means for planning and documenting these complex user experiences. Flow charts will become increasingly important as web sites become more interactive.

But there's another aspect of the flow chart that makes it important to the design process. Internet technologies are playing an increasingly strategic role in business, becoming an essential plank in the customer communications and internal business operations platforms. Process documentation is crucial because the web changes the nature of interactions with customers and between colleagues. The flow chart allows us to get our heads around not just how people interact with the web site, but operations as a whole.

This isn't anything new—management consultants have been using flow charts for decades to describe the internal operations of an organization. But with the web comes an unprecedented level of interaction between people and technology. The web does more than allow us to conduct business differently, it has changed the face of what business is. As work becomes increasingly focused on information, the kinds of interactions organizations have with their customers and the kinds of collaboration that takes place between workers change dramatically. Workers are no longer cogs in a machine with specific tasks to accomplish, and customers are no longer held at arm's length with minimal impact on the organization and the work.

The web, as a business tool, forces us to think about how information moves in and out of the organization. The flow chart illustrates this experience.

The web, as a catalyst for change, forces us to rethink the roles of workers and customers, and their contributions to conducting business. In this case, the flow chart needs to operate at a higher level, showing how organizations must take advantage of and participate in these kinds of interactions. To accommodate this change, our notion of a flow chart must also change. Flow and process will never go away, but our assumption that flows are linear and made of discrete steps must change to recognize the evolution of business.

Figure 9.15 The new face of work. As the web changes how we do business, we're going to see more scenes like this one, where process isn't linear and collaboration is more than just handing off documents from one person to the next. Photo © Bethany Del Lima.

CHAPTER TEN

Wireframes

wī-ər-frāmz′ (n.)

A simplified view of what content will appear on each screen of the final product, usually devoid of color, typographical styles, and images. Also known as schematics, blueprints, prototypes

Wireframes are rough illustrations that show, to a greater or lesser extent, the contents of each screen. They're called wireframes because they are typically rendered with simple lines, not elaborate designs. They illustrate, among other things, what kinds of information will be more prominent on which screen. It sounds simple, but wireframes are among the more controversial documents in the user experience library because they blur the line between underlying structure and visual design. In other words, wireframes cross the boundary between structure (how one kind of information relates to another kind) and display (how to represent information on the screen).

Wireframes at a Glance

Every team develops a coping mechanism to harmonize the responsibilities of various team members. But, since it would be impossible to address every nuance of every situation, this chapter captures the approach to wireframes that has worked best for me throughout my career, and makes these assumptions:

- The purpose of a wireframe is to communicate initial design ideas. Therefore, the team must have a solid understanding of the design problem.

- The scope of a wireframe is content and structure, not layout or visual design (though wireframes may be used in deliverables later in the process to document those issues). To a certain extent, wireframes illustrate how users will interact with the web site, but since they're typically presented on paper, they're not the ideal place to do that.

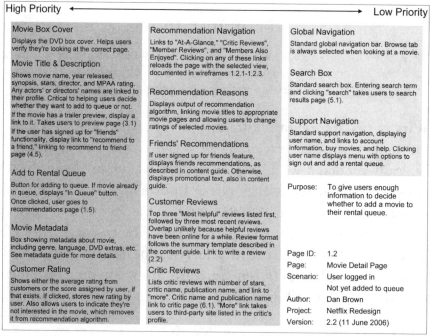

Figure 10.1 This is the simplest wireframe possible a description of the screen's content listed in priority order. To add some depth, this wireframe divides the information into three levels of priority high, medium, and low. Note how different areas of the page have been grouped together in discrete areas. Note also how the wireframe makes no claims about the design of the page, only the structure.

- The primary audience of a wireframe is the rest of the project team—designers and engineers. Wireframes contain information that is essential for the other team members to do their jobs.

- The wireframe must communicate what content the user expects to see on each screen and the relative priorities of the content on that screen. Wireframes are most effective when used in conjunction with other deliverables, since they tell only a partial story.

There are so many different techniques for creating wireframes and using them in a project. In the examples of wireframes below, I've supplemented my own work with some research from the web, in particular the excellent tutorials on the online magazine Boxes & Arrows (www.boxesandarrows.com). Where I've departed from my own experience, I refer to the source material in the text itself. A comprehensive list of sources cited appears at the end of the chapter.

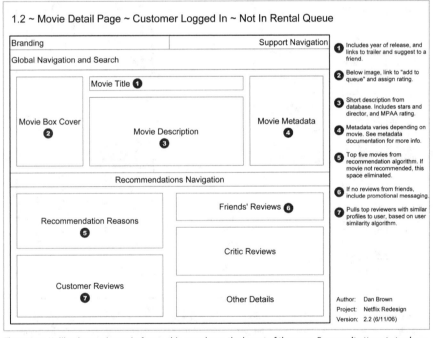

Figure 10.2 Unlike the previous wireframe, this one shows the layout of the page. Because it attempts to show what the page looks like, it would be a little weird to try to describe the content inside the rectangles—content descriptions may require more space than the content itself. The descriptions, therefore, are captured in annotations to the right of the page.

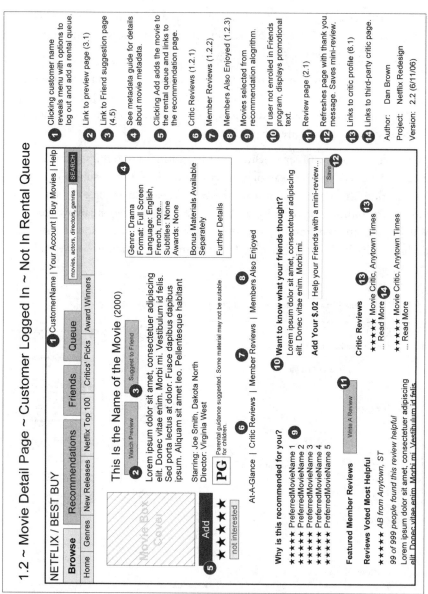

1.2 ~ Movie Detail Page ~ Customer Logged In ~ Not In Rental Queue

1. Clicking customer name reveals menu with options to log out and add a rental queue.
2. Link to preview page (3.1)
3. Link to Friend suggestion page (4.5)
4. See metadata guide for details about movie metadata.
5. Clicking Add adds the movie to the rental queue and links to the recommendation page.
6. Critic Reviews (1.2.1)
7. Member Reviews (1.2.2)
8. Members Also Enjoyed (1.2.3)
9. Movies selected from recommendation alogrithm.
10. If user not enrolled in Friends program, displays promotional text.
11. Review page (2.1)
12. Refreshes page with thank you message. Saves mini-review.
13. Links to critic profile (6.1)
14. Links to third-party critic page.

Author: Dan Brown
Project: Netflix Redesign
Version: 2.2 (6/11/06)

Figure 10.3 Finally, this version of the wireframe matches the screen layout and contents almost perfectly. It is a pared-down version of the final design, but does try to get the proportions correct. Note how the content varies. In some places, the content is exactly what it would be on the actual site (like labels and navigation). In those areas that are more dynamic, the wireframe shows placeholder text (like "The Name of the Movie Goes Here"). The annotations to the right describe links and functionality. This chapter will explore the pros and cons of creating a so-called "high-fidelity" wireframe.

Wireframes Overview

Purpose—What are wireframes for?

Wireframes may be used for a variety of purposes, from communicating structural decisions to the rest of the design team to serving as paper prototypes in usability testing. Whatever purpose wireframes serve in your process, make sure you don't depart from it. Wireframes fail when they try to do too much.

Audience—Who uses them?

If you're using wireframes as prototypes in usability testing, their audience will be the system's audience. If your wireframes are intended to document design and structure decisions, they will be used by the rest of the design team. Avoid making the stakeholders your primary audience since their expectations may be higher than appropriate for this stage in the project.

Scale—How much work are they?

The scale of wireframes may be measured on two dimensions: the level of detail in each wireframe and the number of screens represented in the set of wireframes. The level of detail is often referred to as "fidelity," where "high-fidelity" means lots of detail, or "low-level," and "low-fidelity" means less detail, or "high-level." Confused? This is just the beginning.

Context—Where do they fall in the process?

Ideally, wireframe creation begins somewhere between high-level structural work—like flow charts or site maps—and screen designs.

Format—What do they look like?

In the taxonomy of wireframes, there are two main species: paper and electronic. Of the paper-based wireframes, some are sparse, using only rectangles and labels to represent different areas of the screen. Some wireframes use more complex design elements, like color, shading, and typography. For the most part, wireframes are delivered as a set, with each page of the site described on one page of the wireframes. The tools to create wireframes for printing range from high-end illustration programs like Adobe Illustrator and Microsoft Visio to more mundane applications like Microsoft's PowerPoint. For electronic wireframes, some design teams use simple, unformatted HTML to represent the contents of each screen. Often, the experience of looking at these HTML screens may feel a lot like looking their paper-based cousins. Whether these simple HTML documents get integrated into the production system is up to the team's process, but anecdotal evidence shows it rarely saves any time.

Challenges

Even five paragraphs won't do justice to the challenges of wireframes, and ultimately you must weigh the benefit of wireframes—as a potentially useful initial representation of the user experience—with the costs, which I'll discuss below.

Web design teams see wireframes as a panacea—an opportunity to kill many birds with one massive boulder. With wireframes, you could legitimately document functionality, present initial screen design concepts, conduct user testing, experiment with different interaction models, elicit requirements, validate requirements, prioritize content, review draft copy in context, and much, much more! Plus, if you act now, we'll throw in strained team dynamics, stakeholder waffling, and scope creep absolutely free. (Make your checks payable to the author of this book.)

Good documents have singular purpose, and the closer they remain to that purpose, the more effective they are. With complex projects, the temptation is to stretch your documents to do more. But the more you try to do with wireframes—or any document or tool, for that matter—the less effective they will be in all those things.

For one government agency, a team created wireframes that attempted to show content priorities, production copy, links, and navigation—ultimately, the site itself rendered in Microsoft Visio. The document was a mess because it had to serve four different audiences: the client, the copywriters, the graphic design team, and the HTML jockeys. It was difficult to keep the wireframe up-to-date because there were so many people commenting on it. Although the wireframes were a central place for capturing all decisions, they did not do a great job, no doubt owing to the strain of competing priorities combined with the limitations of the medium.

This chapter on wireframes appears in the "what users see" section of the book because, based on the assumptions above, wireframes are best suited to capturing a design team's ideas on how a site should behave. That is, the design team already has an idea of what the site is supposed to accomplish and the wireframes offer a first stab at how it accomplishes its purpose. The challenge is that wireframes can be used for other aspects of the overall process, as well—not just to show design, but to better understand the problem at hand.

If you take nothing else from this chapter, take this: Decide upon a purpose for your wireframes and stick to your guns. Once you know what the wireframes on your project are for, you can design them to serve that purpose and set the project team's expectations, hopefully avoiding wireframes that ultimately do nothing for nobody.

Creating Wireframes

Typical wireframe documents have pages that are divided into two areas. The larger area on the page has the wireframe—the depiction of what's on a particular page—itself and the smaller area has supporting information that sets the context and describes the behaviors of the screen being displayed.

Like all the documents in this book, wireframes can be described in a series of three layers. The first layer contains the essential content, in other words, the elements of the document that make it what it is. The second and third layers add increasing levels of detail that are more or less optional, depending on your situation.

Layer 1: Wireframe Essentials

The first three elements described in the first layer appear in the wireframe itself—the visual representation of the page. The second two elements, the identifying information and the administrative information, appear in the area for supporting content.

Content areas

Most web pages can be divided into areas of content—discrete rectangles that hold different types of information. Sometimes a page has just one content area and sometimes it has many. The content area is the basic unit of currency for web pages.

A wireframe can represent these content areas literally, showing a large rectangle (the page) divided into smaller rectangles (the content areas). These content areas don't necessarily show actual content—they may only show a label or a sentence describing the content. (More on this shortly.) The wireframe could approximate the screen layout, so the rectangles reflect the actual screen real estate dedicated to each content area. While this may be useful to give project participants a sense of what the system will look like, it can stifle creativity in later phases of the project, when the team is working on the actual screen design.

Another approach is having the size and position of the rectangles reflect relative priority of different items, rather than the actual page layout. The value of this approach is that it provides direction to other members of the team without prescribing a particular layout.

One other possibility is to abandon any semblance of rectangles or screen layout and simply list content areas in order of priority. Such an approach significantly departs from the typical wireframe, but if your team is experiencing conflict due to the squishy nature of wireframes, this technique may help.

Content descriptions

It's not enough to simply indicate that a page is made up of different content areas. The wireframe must describe the content that will appear in each area. There are several techniques for doing so: using actual content, some form of sample content (described later), or a short description of the content. At a minimum, the description consists of a label like "list of articles" or "application form." The simplest wireframes are groups of rectangles with labels defining content areas. More complex wireframes include real content—everything from heading labels to navigation to actual prose.

Content priorities

One goal of any kind of visual design is to establish a hierarchy of importance among the content on the screen: On a good web page, for example, it's immediately clear that some pieces of information are more important or pertinent than others. More important content must be made salient in some way, either by giving it more screen real estate, contrast, or some other graphic design technique. Less important elements may find themselves on the periphery, represented with smaller typefaces, or rendered in some other way to avoid distracting people from the main purpose of the screen.

The purpose of the wireframe is to rank content in a simple, clear way, establishing guidelines for those who will design the site. Sometimes the relative priorities can be represented as a simple list, with the most important item at the top. In many cases, however, the relationships between content and functional elements are much more complex. To accommodate these complexities you can group related items in your priority list.

Wireframes are an intermediate step in the design process—they help designers understand all the information that each screen will need to accommodate.

Having this blueprint helps the design team ensure that they're not only meeting the needs of the users, but also the needs of the content.

Identifying information

Because wireframes tend to appear one to a page, and because they're generally presented on paper, each wireframe must include identifying information that answers some basic questions, like "what project is this for?" and "what's the name of this page?" In some cases, a single page may have multiple views—slight variations on the page depending on circumstances. Today's web sites are highly interactive—the user can accomplish a lot without appearing to leave the screen. In these more advanced applications, a single screen can have multiple views. For example, a site's log-in screen may have three different views depending on the scenario: default, username not found, and password error. From the user's perspective the screen remains pretty much the same, with only slight variations. The wireframe must show all three views. Even though these might be considered one "page" on the site, you might represent it with three different wireframes—one for each view.

The wireframe's supporting information, therefore, should indicate which page and which view of the page.

You may also have a system for enumerating your wireframes (e.g., 1.1, 2.4.1, etc.). Some project teams find these useful and others just find them difficult to follow. If your wireframes need to correspond with a site map or flow chart, a numbering system can help with the bookkeeping. On the other hand, if the site structure undergoes dramatic changes during the design process, you may find keeping these identifiers up to date more trouble than it's worth.

Administrative information

In addition to identifying the wireframe in the context of the system, the document must identify the wireframe in the context of the overall project. It's easy to forget to add the author's name, the page number, and the version number, but now you have this book and will never forget again. These elements should appear on every document described in this book.

Layer 2: Filling in the Story

Wireframes with just elements from layer 1 will get the job done, but they may benefit from some of the elements from layer 2, which provide additional details about how the screens function. Figure 10.3 at the beginning of this chapter contains some of the elements described here, like annotations.

Scenarios

Though it may not be essential in most cases, in some documents identifying a scenario for each screen may help explain its purpose. The scenario describes the situation that brings the user to this particular screen.

Scenarios, for example, may account for slight differences between otherwise similar screens. Some web sites—intranets in particular—may display different information depending on the user. Managers or administrators may have permission to view different kinds of information, for example, that regular employees don't have access to. Putting a scenario on your wireframe helps readers answer the question, "Why would I see this version of the screen vs. that version?"

This may sound a lot like a view, described above as "slight variations on the screen depending on circumstances." In some ways they are redundant: A single screen may have several different appearances, depending on some variables. The distinction, however, is in the source of the variation. The view gives a name to the variation and the scenario explains why the variation exists. A view is specific to a particular screen, and a scenario can affect any number of screens. In other words, the fact that a user forgot her password is relevant only to the log-in screen, but that she's a system administrator has implications across the entire site.

Links and form elements

To make your wireframes more detailed, you may elect to show how users interact with the site by indicating links and form elements—things the user can click on and type into. By including these, you are further illustrating the user experience, adding a dimension to explain the interaction between user and system. When they appear on your wireframes, functional elements raise the question: "What happens when the user...?" Consider coupling links and form elements on your wireframes with annotations to describe what happens when the user interacts with them.

Because a wireframe is like a screen without any stylistic information, links should appear in their default state: underlined and blue. Typically, blue is the only color used in the wireframe itself to indicate links. (Some purists believe that any color in a wireframe is deliverable treason.) Since underlined blue text is near-universal representation of actionable text, it effectively differentiates functional elements from nonfunctional.

As for form elements, these should also appear in their unstyled state: simple gray boxes.

Annotations

Showing the content of the screen is not enough, especially in modern web sites offering high degrees of interactivity. A highly interactive web site has depth—a conversation between user and system—which is difficult to represent in the two dimensions of a wireframe. Annotations remedy the inadequacies of paper by explaining the interactivity of a page in a short note. Some annotations describe the functionality of an element on the page, some explain the rationale behind it, and others provide further description or direction for content. With a dozen or more annotations on one screen, it's enough to give you a headache. You can format these different kinds of annotations differently to draw the attention of different audiences. Developers will be more interested in functional annotations, for example, so it is useful to have a way of distinguishing those from the others.

Functional annotations describe what happens when the user does something—clicks a link or a button, in most cases. The annotation can provide some description of the system's response to that action, like "The system validates the address information, comparing ZIP Code to City and State, and confirms that all required information was supplied. If not, the system returns the error screen (1.1). Otherwise, the next screen is displayed (2.0)." Of course, if your audience is familiar with how various screens work, you may get away with simply noting the reference number (as in the example above) or a URL.

Content annotations either provide direction to your team's copywriter or describe the source for the content. Since you're not providing the content itself in the wireframe, your team might benefit from further explanation of the kind of content you expect to appear in a particular area. If the content is dynamic, drawn from a database, you might explain the rules for pulling that content. If your team includes copywriters, these annotations save you from having to include sample copy. These annotations may simply indicate the gist of the content area, like "Describes the overall checkout process" or "Indicates the product's limitations."

Finally, the wireframe may capture the rationale for particular design decisions. Although you would no doubt cover these when you present the wireframes, documenting them can ensure that people who missed the presentation will understand the rationale. Don't underestimate the power of rationalizing your design decisions. Later in the project you may forget why you placed certain content on the page.

If an annotation refers to a specific element on the screen, place a numbered target next to that element. The annotation should appear with the same number in the sidebar. To distinguish different kinds of annotations, you can use different colored targets. But keep in mind that the target color should be something other than blue or red, which are generally used in the wireframe itself to indicate links and error messages.

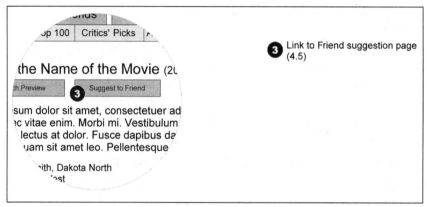

Figure 10.4 Annotations are useful for describing the behavior of interactive screen elements. They're usually marked by corresponding numbered circles—one in the wireframe pointing to the functional element and one next to the annotation itself.

Another approach is simply to treat all your annotations the same, whether they relate to function, content, or rationale. The annotations will have different numbers, but will be formatted the same way. This approach eliminates a data point—that is, the kind of annotation for a given screen element—but that level of detail may not be necessary for your purposes. This approach may also make sense when there's a lot to say about only a few elements on the page.

Objectives and rationale

While annotations refer to specific content areas of a screen, objectives and rationale generally describe the *entire* screen. Although the sidebar on a wireframe will be dominated by identifying information, administrative information, and various annotations, your situation may require some additional context, and the sidebar is a good place to put it. You may want to set the stage for a wireframe by indicating the screen's objectives—for example, its role in the system, the overall rationale for including it, or the philosophy behind its design. Figure 10.2 includes an example of integrating a purpose statement into a wireframe. Besides reminding team members about the context, this information can help contain the conversation, focusing it on relevant feedback for the situation.

Now that you've indicated what user scenarios the screen is meant to address and the design objectives for the screen, you may need to spell out the rationale. Rationale connects design decisions to objectives or scenarios, showing how the design was derived from the given direction or requirements. An absence of rationale can be telling, because it could suggest that design decisions are without basis. Some of the content descriptions in Figure 10.2 also include rationale, usually to explain the prioritization of certain elements over others.

Version history

A version history accounts for all the changes that have been made to a document, at varying levels of detail. Some version histories note every minute change while others describe changes at a broad level. Not all wireframes are created equal, however, even within the same deliverable. Some wireframes, for better or worse, will get more attention than others, simply because they represent more important screens or have more complex functionality. These screens are likely to be updated more often than the less-important screens. To address this inherent wireframe asymmetry, it may be useful to attach version histories to each screen, in addition to the document as a whole.

Another reason to provide a detailed, screen-specific version history on each page is that it may simplify matters in the final, frenzied stages of the process when it becomes necessary to track the evolution of each page. On these individual screen version histories you can note field label changes, content direction changes, link changes, behavioral changes, etc.

Version history can take up a lot of space, and you'll need to decide how important it is relative to the other information included in your wireframe documentation. If you're keeping each version in a different file, one way to avoid taking up valuable real estate is to note only the changes from the last version.

Document Version History			Page Version History		
2.1	6/11/06	• Incorporated client feedback	2.1	6/11/06	• Client requested changes to "company name" field and asked us to explore labels for "submit" button
2.0	6/10/06	• Incorporated comments from final review with team			
1.5	6/8/06	• Added introductory pages • Renamed "flag" label throughout	2.0	6/10/06	• Analyst recommended adding separate company name and individual name fields
1.4	6/7/06	• Major revisions based on requirements gathering	1.4	6/7/06	• Removed phone, fax, and mobile phone fields due to requirements changes
1.3	6/3/06	• Adjusted language after meeting with tech lead	1.3	6/3/06	• Language changes to main navigation categories
1.2	6/3/06	• Feedback from analyst			
1.1	6/1/06	• Added annotations	1.2	6/3/06	• This page added after feedback from analyst
1.0	5/28/06	• Document created			

Figure 10.5 Compare the document's version history with the screen's version history. The document's history points readers to pages that have undergone changes since the last version, saving the specifics for each screen. This keeps the document version history relatively lightweight. It also puts the change details where they matter most—on the screen itself.

Layer 3: Optional Details

The elements that appear on the third layer are not only optional, they're controversial. If you want to see a good flame war, pick your favorite user experience online community and ask whether any of these elements should be present in wireframes.

There are pros and cons to including these elements, but remember that nearly every project team and circumstance is different. What works in one project may not work in another. Although this book will explore the pros and cons for each of these elements, their inclusion should be guided by only one thing: the purpose of the document in the context of your project. Have a highly collaborative team? Perhaps you can all work together to define the layout of the screens in the wireframes. Have clients that will react negatively to any content out of place? Perhaps you should leave out sample content.

Layout and visual design

Layout and visual design are not crucial to the success of wireframes. This is true, however, only in the idealistic view of system design, where design decisions are made in a logical order, and where stakeholders understand that before committing to a particular layout, you first need to identify what appears on each screen and what's most important. When you find yourself in this situation, feel free to dance for joy, mark the date on your calendar, and do similar dances every year on that day.

In many cases, you will need to show layout and design in your wireframes, perhaps because any other representation of content priorities is too abstract for your stakeholders or because you're working under an accelerated project schedule where you need to make as many decisions as possible in the shortest period of time. Whatever the reason, you'll need to decide just how much to show, and this can depend on the situation, as I'll describe later.

In general, however, the key decision is accuracy: the extent to which you expect the layout of a wireframe to reflect the layout of the actual page. Visual treatment is not an either/or element: You can have more visual accuracy or less of it. Some wireframes are rendered to be as accurate as possible, down to the type treatment. Others are mere guidelines for the design.

TABLE 10.1

Translating Design Elements to Wireframes

Design element	What it is	How it appears in the wireframes
Color	Color is a powerful design element that causes specific and subtle responses, which can vary from person to person.	Few wireframes contain color. It's generally agreed that color is premature at this stage because it causes such a basic response that it easily distracts from the matter at hand: what's on the screen.
Layout	Layout represents information priorities by creating visual relationships between different types of content.	It's nearly impossible to create a wireframe without layout simply because any document has some kind of layout, planned or otherwise. The real issue is whether the layout in the wireframe is meant to simulate what users will see on the screen, or not.
Typography	The treatment of the type—the font, the size, the style—make up the design's typography.	Some wireframes use no typographical treatments whatsoever, employing the same font, size, and style throughout. Others will vary the size to represent different priorities. High-fidelity wireframes—those that seek to capture the screen design accurately—will include full type treatments.

Featured Member Reviews

Write A Review

Reviews Voted Most Helpful

★★★★★ *AB from Anytown, ST*
(See my other reviews...)
99 of 999 people found this review helpful

Lorem ipsum dolor sit amet, consectetuer adipiscing elit. Ut rutrum sem a urna. Phasellus venenatis. Sed in lectus. Praesent non urna. Proin scelerisque lacinia pede. Nullam accumsan, magna sed sollicitudin volutpat, neque nunc mollis diam, ut tincidunt ipsum elit a neque. Class aptent taciti sociosqu ad litora torquent per conubia nostra, per inceptos hymenaeos. Nam mattis mauris eget turpis.

I found this review   helpful   not helpful

Figure 10.6 Design impacts more than just the entire layout of the page. You'll have to make design decisions about the details of a content area if you're producing a high-fidelity wireframe. In this simple content area from the high-fidelity wireframe at the beginning of the chapter, there are a lot of decisions to make about formatting the individual data elements.

Context in the overall design

The experience context shows how one piece of the experience—in the case of wireframes, a single screen—relates to the whole. You can easily set the context of the wireframe by showing a miniature site map or flow chart with the appropriate rectangle—the one representing the current wireframe—highlighted. Using a miniature version of the site map or flow chart helps stakeholders position the wireframe in the system's entire experience. This technique is only worthwhile, however, if the site map or flow chart has become entrenched; otherwise the miniature version has no meaning.

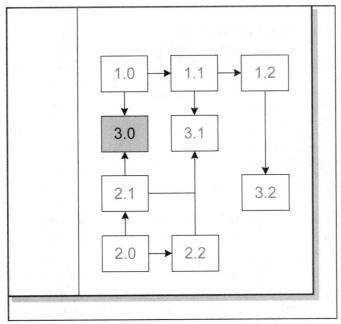

Figure 10.7 This corner of the wireframe document contains a miniature version of a flow chart. The highlighted rectangle indicates which wireframe is being described. If your team is already working with a site map or flow chart, including a miniature version of it with each wireframe can help show the screen's place in the whole system.

Sample content

Sample content is any representation of the content beyond its title, description, and relative priority to other content on the screen. Any time you try to show the content in some way, rather than simply describe it, you are using sample content.

Table 10.2 shows two approaches to the same content. The first approach is the actual content and the second approach is a description of the content. Since at this stage in the project you probably won't have final content—and you won't want to spend your wireframes meeting quibbling over prose—the description is preferable. Like content area priorities giving designers direction about the page layout, content descriptions can give copywriters direction about the subject and tone of particular text on the web page.

TABLE 10.2

Actual Content vs. Content Descriptions

Actual	Description
"By registering, you'll enjoy full membership benefits, including speedy service and 24-hour response to customer service inquiries. You'll have access to your entire order history and be able to set your preferences. Of course, we keep your registration totally private and won't share your information with anyone without your permission."	Explains benefits of registration while reassuring privacy.

Wireframes help establish the organization and relative priorities of content, not the actual wording or tone of it. For that reason, you only need to describe content, not quote it directly. Sample content is a layer 3 element because descriptions of content—a layer 1 element—should be sufficient for the kinds of decisions documented in wireframes. In order to prioritize a content area, in other words, you do not need to know what the actual content is, just what it could be. Like any element beyond layer 1, the decision to include sample content rests on the extent to which it needs to be discussed. In some instances, sample content, regardless of how it is presented, can distract stakeholders from the decisions at hand.

If you feel like sample content is essential for making decisions about priorities, then the wireframe can include it. With some audiences, it can be more difficult to explain why a wireframe doesn't include any content. Maybe putting sample content in your wireframes is worth the risk of having to curtail those conversations. At the same time, it might be just as easy to present a copy deck—a deliverable including all the site's content—at the same time you present wireframes.

There are several different kinds of sample content, from actual content that is prepared especially for the web site, to "greeked" text meant to look like prose. We'll discuss different sample content strategies later in the chapter.

Building Your Wireframes: The Basics

Of all the documents described in this book, wireframes may be the biggest. They have the potential to contain an enormous amount of detail and demand lots of attention from the rest of the project team. In this way, wireframes are a project in and of themselves, and require careful planning.

Prior to starting wireframes, you'll need to make several crucial decisions about the level of detail you'll show for each screen, the standards you'll use throughout the document, and the context you'll present alongside the wireframes. Only a situation analysis—an understanding of how the wireframes will be used—will help you make these decisions.

Timeline: When wireframes happen

As much as we like to think of ourselves as strict adherents to process, we have all fallen victim to the temptation to start designing screens when we have only a partial understanding of what needs designing or what users need. You may have the whole site planned out in your head, even on paper, but there is a time and place to show that work.

The first step in building your wireframes is assessing what you'll want to do with them—in other words, the situation where they'll be most useful. In assessing the situation, you are determining how much detail you want to put into the wireframes.

In some situations, you may be more concerned about the priority of content throughout the site, in which case you perhaps need only a handful of representative screens. If, on the other hand, you're ready to give the stakeholders an overview of the end-to-end user experience, your wireframes may have some detail, but not complete details. Another possible scenario is that your wireframes will serve as highly detailed documentation for the system engineers, which require substantial definition rules and functionality.

Audience: Who's reading your wireframes

If the situation defines the *amount* of detail, your audience will define the *kind* of detail. Engineers, for example, may want to know which database holds the content or field limits or what happens to certain areas of the screen in particular scenarios. Visual designers will be more focused on the details of the content itself, and how much text they need to accommodate in the screen layout.

Purpose: The role of wireframes

Knowing where you are in the project and whom the deliverable is for is not enough. You must also determine the need, answering the question, "What should this document accomplish?" For most deliverables, the need driving their creation is unique and obvious. For wireframes, this is not the case. Because wireframes can show so much, they are used for a variety of purposes. But remember: Wireframes fail when they try to do too much.

Like any other deliverable in this book, unless you can identify a real need for wireframes, you should not produce them. Still, if you find yourself in a situation where you are required to produce wireframes even though they are not the most appropriate, this document does permit a great deal of flexibility. Identify issues that need clarification—particular business rules or content priorities, for example—and build a deliverable that will drive toward addressing them.

We can boil wireframes down into two possible purposes: to describe a design that addresses a particular set of business needs and user goals, and to facilitate the understanding of business needs and user goals. Logically speaking, these are mutually exclusive: Describing a solution to a problem is different from describing the problem itself. This is a web development project, though, and who are we kidding? Logic need not apply.

When wireframes are used as a design tool they help determine how a site's design will solve a particular problem. Design begins when the designer has an understanding of that problem (for example, knowing what information people need in order to buy a pair of trousers from Gap.com or to manage their money at a banking site) and can devise a product that will successfully address it. Design tools express some aspect of the design and allow the project team and stakeholders to determine whether the approach addresses the problem, as it's been defined in the requirements.

Wireframes can also be used to help make sense of the problem at hand—a process called "requirements gathering." Unfortunately, sometimes you have no idea what the real problem is until you see a solution. By showing a potential solution, the design team can zero in on what, exactly, users need. It's a subtle but important difference. In the first way, you are trying to represent a solution to the problem. In the second way, you are trying to clarify the problem by showing potential (though perhaps inappropriate) solutions. In the second approach, you're not trying to get the solution right. Instead, you're trying to create a discussion piece that can help the project team refine its understanding of the problem.

This iterative approach to design—clarifying your understanding of the problem and revising the potential solution—can work well, and wireframes are suited to it. (One important risk to consider is how much time you put into developing these wireframes. It may be tempting to flesh out every aspect of the design, but without a thorough understanding of the problem, this may be wasted effort.)

Reality frequently dictates a mix of both situations, one of those not-so-rare occasions when we face a catch-22. Though requirements may be established, for example, they cannot be validated until stakeholders get their hands on initial designs. Some newer software development methods try to address this paradox (with faster design processes and shorter engineering phases, for example) but the jury is still out on whether these are effective tools for all types of projects and for creating user-centered products.

Wireframe contents: The nuts and bolts

Having established your situation, you are in a much better position for determining what goes in your wireframes. There are several parts to this decision, and you should try to answer all these questions before putting pen to paper.

How many screens will you show? Though it may be better to err on the high side—to show every permutation of every screen in the site—you need to make this decision based on what role the wireframes play. To simply sell an idea, a handful of essential screens may be all that is necessary. To prepare a complete set of documentation that describes the entire user experience, you may need dozens. For most teams, the wireframes constitute a substantial bulk of the design work—short of the design itself—and therefore require "decks" of between 50 and 100 pages, depending on the complexity of the site.

Answering this question is easiest if you've already prepared and presented a site map or flow chart because you've already discussed the pages with the stakeholders and project team. The decision about which pages to wireframe is a strategic one: You need to balance the need to document the pages with the time and effort it takes to create the wireframes, accounting for the level of detail you need to show.

How much detail will you show for each screen? You may decide to show more detail for screens that play a larger role in the overall user experience, and less on more minor screens.

Once you have a list of screens, identify the various views for each screen. Until you know the relationships between views, however, you may not be able to determine which views you'll need to document. For example, you may decide that two views that are practically identical and therefore do not need their own wireframes can be instead described with annotations on a single wireframe. For each view, determine what content you need to document. Only after listing the content displayed in each view can you distinguish between views that need their own wireframes and those that can be consolidated. This inventory of screens and views also permits you to establish a scheme for numbering and identifying each wireframe.

How will you represent content? To a greater or lesser extent, wireframes need to describe the content that users will see on the screen. Annotations allow you to include literal content descriptions (for example, "Use this space for a short product description with a link at the end to a longer product description.") But some wireframes include sample content. There are five kinds of sample content that can appear in a wireframe, and each is best suited for a different kind of content.

TABLE 10.3

Different Kinds of Sample Content

Sample Content	What it looks like	Use for	Don't use for	Address rendered
Actual content	This is whatever you have on hand that's as close to production content and data as possible.	Navigation labels, functional labels—in other words, those parts of the interface that the user interacts with.	Marketing copy, tabular data—Using actual copy or data in a wireframe risks changing the conversation to the content of the wireframe, and not the structure.	Peachpit Press, 1249 Eighth Street, Berkeley, CA 94710
Dummy content	Invented content that looks like actual content.	Content with obvious formats (like addresses or phone numbers) such that readers recognize the purpose of the content without getting sucked into the content itself.	Copy or tabular data—It's easy to mistake these for actual data and sidetrack the conversation. To fill a table, you may need to repeat dummy content, or invent lots of different dummy content—both of which are distracting and time-consuming to the reader.	John Doe, 123 Main Street, Anytown, ST 98765
Symbolic content	Strings of repeated letters or numbers to represent different fields. For example, 999-999-9999 for a phone number and MM/DD/CCYY for a date.	Tabular data, dates, information with recognizable formats (like phone numbers).	Prose, unless you want your entire wireframe to look like it's been redacted by the CIA.	XXXXXXXX XXXXXXX, XXXXXXX XXXXXXXXXXXXX, XXXXXXX, XX, 99999

TABLE 10.3 *Continued*

Different Kinds of Sample Content

Sample Content	What it looks like	Use for	Don't use for	Address rendered
Labels	Usually enclosed in brackets, a label provides a description for a field of content. Labels can include additional information about the field, like size and type. For example, [firstname—30] might represent a field that contains someone's first name and is limited to 30 characters.	Pretty much anything.	Labels are nice and flexible and should be able to cover most sample content needs. The downside is that they may be difficult for a nontechnical person to interpret.	[FirstName] [LastName], [StreetNumber] [StreetName], [City] [State] [ZIP]
Greek/Latin	Borrowed from graphic design, prose can be faked by using strings of pseudo-Latin text. (Some people call this "greeked" text and some people call it "latin," while others call it "lorem ipsum" or "lipsum" after the Latin words that typically come first.)	Anything that's typically rendered in more-or-less full sentences.	Lipsum in tabular data or to represent an address just looks silly.	Lorem Ipsum, dolorsit amet lorem, consectecur, st, 99999

What supporting information will you include for each screen? As described in the layer 1 elements above, there are several different kinds of supporting information you can show for each screen, describing its rationale and its position in the overall user experience. You can narrow down what to include by thinking about what's important to the main users of the document. For developers, bookkeeping is crucial and so you might emphasize the identifying numbers for each screen. Stakeholders may need the opposite view, where the supporting information reminds them how one particular screen meets their business goals, and those annotations that tie design decisions to business goals are emphasized. Designers may be more interested in rationale to help them understand why certain elements are present and more important than other elements

What contextual information will you include for the whole document? Most wireframe documents have at least one introductory page that sets the context, giving information like project information, milestones, and version history. Keep in mind that it's difficult for people to flip back and forth between the introductory pages and the interior pages, so don't put anything on the introductory pages that is essential to understanding what's inside. For example, developers may need to know what changed between versions of the wireframe, but version histories are typically included on the introductory pages. If your wireframes are geared toward developers, make sure each page includes its own version history. (Better yet, ask them what kind of information they want on each wireframe.)

Will you render wireframes on paper or in HTML? Here's another good way to get a group of designers worked up: Ask them whether it's better to do wireframes on paper or in HTML. Different teams do it differently, and though you may have a preference, you may find yourself in a situation where you have to go against your instincts.

Boxes and Arrows has several good articles on wireframing, and one in particular about using HTML for wireframes called "HTML Prototypes and Wireframes: All Gain and No Pain." Check this out for more information on using HTML for wireframes.

In the meantime, Table 10.4 a side-by-side comparison to get you started.

TABLE 10.4

Comparing HTML and Paper Wireframes

	HTML Wireframes	Paper Wireframes
Ease of creation	If you're handy with HTML, creating wireframes can be straightforward, but that depends on the complexity of the functionality you're trying to implement. More complex functions require more advanced programming—time perhaps best spent elsewhere.	Although you could go all out and render your wireframes nicely in an elaborate illustration program, this is hardly required. Presentation programs like Microsoft's PowerPoint or Apple's Keynote make putting together a deck of screen illustrations fairly easy.
Maintenance	Though small individual changes can be easy, alterations that affect many screens can be time-consuming.	Some drawing programs like Microsoft Visio and OmniGraffle make it easy to make changes throughout a document by adjusting a master shape or a background image.

TABLE 10.4 *Continued*

Comparing HTML and Paper Wireframes

	HTML Wireframes	Paper Wireframes
Versioning	HTML comments (enclosed in <!-- -->) make it easy to keep a version history inside the electronic version, but showing how the design evolved may require more HTML mojo than you have. For example, you might put each version in a separate layer and turn layers on and off to compare. HTML editors in general do not include track changes functionality like you might see in Microsoft Word. On the other hand, if your organization uses version-tracking software (like CVS), you can use that in conjunction with your HTML files to track versions.	With paper, the version history can appear adjacent to the wireframe itself.
Saving time and reuse	The jury is out on whether creating wireframes in HTML actually saves any time down the road. In some cases, the HTML needs to be dissected so much that it doesn't actually help the development team.	With paper, there's no time-saving in development, of course, though there may be an opportunity to reuse them for usability testing.
Documenting functionality	No one has yet found a simple way to incorporate annotations into HTML wireframes. Such documentation frequently appears at the bottom of the HTML page, or stuck in a tooltip that only appears with the correct positioning of the mouse.	Paper is ideal for capturing annotations.
Demonstrating functionality	No doubt HTML offers a more realistic demonstration of how the system will behave, allowing stakeholders to click through screen flows, forcing them to envision the system in more than just one dimension. The more realistic experience can support arguments against poorly conceived ideas offered by stakeholders (though even the best evidence may not shake someone from his or her bad notions).	Using paper to demonstrate functionality requires some imagination, a resource not always in abundance in wireframe review meetings. Because paper is so different from an online experience, you may find out too late that your stakeholders came away from the demonstration with a different set of expectations.

What program will you use to create wireframes? For paper wireframes, there are only a handful of dedicated "wireframing" tools on the market, and many people use other applications like OmniGraffle or Microsoft Visio or Microsoft PowerPoint. This decision should be driven by what level of fidelity you want to represent in your wireframes and your level of comfort with the application. Some designers use, for example, Adobe Illustrator, a very powerful, very complex illustration application with a very steep learning curve. There's no point in putting yourself through that ordeal unless you're either already familiar with the tool or are prepared to hike up that tough mountain trail. Even if you are willing, project timelines generally get the upper hand and you may be forced to work with whatever you can get to perform the fastest. For HTML wireframes, any available HTML editor—Macromedia Dreamweaver is popular—should do the trick.

To list the pros and cons of each tool would be futile—opinions about tools vary more than opinions about wireframes. Frankly, pencil and paper is perfectly good if it allows you to accomplish your goals.

Pain-Free[1] Wireframe Creation

OK, so every deliverable involves a little bit of pain, but design documentation—such as wireframes—helps alleviate the potential for much worse pain later in the process. Still, there are a few things you can do to facilitate creating this document.

Make a few lists before you start

Like most deliverables, wireframes require a bit of planning before sitting down to create them. There are a few lists you should make before you start wireframing. First, draw up a list of **scenarios** to identify all the different situations in which people will be using the site you're designing. You can take these scenarios right from the user profiles or use cases. These can be fairly high level, for example, "a user opens a new checking account." The wireframes may need to contrast the experience in two different contexts. On an intranet, for example, you may need to distinguish between administrative users and non-administrative users.

There are a handful of factors that vary across the scenarios, things like the kind of user or the date, or which products are being purchased. Planning out these

---

[1] Complete lack of pain is not guaranteed by the author or publisher of this book.

specifics is important because it allows you to be consistent in your wireframes. Imagine, for instance, that the wireframes illustrate a shopping process. A product is searched for, selected, customized, put in the cart, and purchased. This process encompasses several different screens. To make sure your stakeholders understand the experience, you should use the same product on all the screens.

This example may be self evident, but dig down a little deeper and you'll identify all kinds of variables that come together to reflect a story—dates, names, locations, search terms, currency amounts, quantities, product types, document types, contact information, identifying information, and so many other things. The more disparity between these variables in the wireframes, the more difficult it will be for readers to follow the experience. Once you identify the variables that are crucial to a user experience, write them down for each scenario so you can remain consistent.

Perhaps most importantly, create a list of **screens** to plan out which wireframes you're creating, for instance, your log-in screen, or your checkout screen, and every other significant screen a user will encounter as he or she clicks through the system. Doing this list in advance can help you decide what to call the screens, how to relate them to the site map or user flow, and will help you plan how much time it will take you to create each wireframe, and therefore the entire document.

There are several factors to consider when building these lists:

- **Importance:** Some screens or scenarios are more important than others because they are crucial milestones in the user experience. A product page on an e-commerce web site or a contact listing on an intranet, for example, are major landmarks in those systems.

- **Timeline:** If you only have a limited amount of time to create the wireframes document, be sure to prioritize the list of screens, estimate the amount of time it will take to create each screen (double that for good measure), and then only create those screens you can within the given timeframe.

- **Complexity:** Some screens will be inherently more complex than others because they have to support complex actions by the user, or they represent complex scenarios.

- **Politics:** Important people may have a lot of political capital invested in particular screens. Though some screens may not be difficult or essential to the user experience, they may be important to the people paying for the project.

Consider the complexity of the system

As applications grow more sophisticated, it will become necessary to distinguish between screens and views. A home page, for example, might appear differently depending on whether the user is logged in or not. A wireframe, especially if presented on paper, is static and will show one particular view, and therefore the scenario must be clear.

You can try to incorporate multiple views in a single wireframe, in order to document how the screen will respond to input from the user, or to highlight the differences between different views. But ultimately, trying to squeeze too much information onto a page could cause more confusion.

Use a simple numbering scheme

Individual wireframes may be identified by a numbering scheme, like the sections of a book.

You can use two numbers separated by a dot, such as X.Y, where X represents the major flow or navigation area and Y represents the page within that flow or area. The home page is always numbered 0.0. The first page of the first main navigation section would be 1.0. This approach works so long as the site can be easily divided into major flows or navigation areas.

You may find that your site is much more abstract—you're creating wireframes of templates, not specific pages in the hierarchy, for instance. In this case, your numbers could refer to template type or page type. So pages all derived from a particular template or matching a particular type of page (like a product details page vs. a product listing page) would be grouped under the same number.

The hardest part with numbering is deciding what to do when the architecture changes dramatically. You may have entire sections removed. Do you renumber? The answer varies depending on how well entrenched the numbering scheme is. On some projects, the screen numbering scheme is used in other documents, like a content inventory or a site map. To avoid having to redo those documents as well, you may continue to use the old numbers, even if they do lose some in the sequence. Regardless of your scheme, every wireframe should have a unique number, even if it represents only a slight variation from another screen.

Always include an introduction

Wireframes without an introduction are like medication without a warning label. Since there's always the risk that you won't be there to present your document, a one- or two-page introduction will spell out the context by indicating for the reader what's described (and what's *not* described) by the wireframes.

Risks: Don't Get Framed

There's a reason wireframes are controversial, and it's not just that they represent the crossroads of design and architecture. As a complex document that addresses a lot of different aspects of system design, wireframes present lots of risks. Don't get sucked in to the convenience of wireframes without considering these potential pitfalls.

Plan before you build

Once they're familiar with wireframes, project participants may want you to create them as soon as the project starts. At the beginning of the project, remind your stakeholders and team members what role wireframes will play, when they will be delivered, and what you need in order to create them. You may make wireframes look easy, but they don't grow on trees, so your stakeholders should not expect them to.

Establish priorities before doing layout

Making your wireframes look too realistic can convince stakeholders that they are looking at the final product, or an early draft of the final product. If this is what you're going for, great, but in your exuberance to produce a quality deliverable, you may find yourself needing to offer plenty of caveats.

TIP ▶ If you have to offer disclaimers about the look, layout, and design of your wireframes, you should make the wireframes less realistic.

Although it may be tempting to create high-fidelity wireframes, you may spend way too much time thinking about how the screen should look and not enough time thinking about how it should work. Before sitting down to do a wireframe, identify the objectives for the deliverable itself: What messages are you trying to communicate? What ideas are you trying to hammer out? If you start brainstorming in a direction that takes you away from these objectives, you need to be honest with yourself. Be ruthless about what appears in the wireframe and what does not. If you've scheduled your wireframing for the beginning of the design process, you still have many design decisions to make: Do not cheat those decisions by making them too early.

Start with simple labels

Names stick. It's an unfortunate reality. A placeholder hastily slapped on to fill a blank on a wireframe can last through the life of a project, if for no other reason than that everyone else is unwilling to decide on a real name. If these labels make it into the final design, it's either because they went through testing and users liked them, or because the project team is lazy and didn't come up with something beyond a placeholder. The words in the design are as much as part of the design as the color.

Wireframes could include caveats indicating that labels are temporary, but even caveats are not a surefire way to get labels under careful scrutiny. You can also format them to look temporary, using all-capital letters or enclosing them in some kind of brackets. At the very least, use the plainest language possible, in case the temporary labels become forever tattooed on the site. Your best bet is to include an activity in the project plan to review labels.

Design for maintenance

One major advantage to keeping wireframes low-fidelity is maintenance. It can be difficult to keep your wireframes up-to-date with the latest changes. Clients might ask you to update a wireframe with information that's not immediately relevant to it. For example, if the wireframe gives an overview of the content priorities on the screen, the client might ask you to fill in the specific content for the screen. You could probably squeeze the content in, but then the document would become much more complicated to maintain.

On the other hand, even relevant updates may seem like a waste of time depending on where you are in the process. For example, changes to the screen's contents identified during the final design phase—when the graphic designers are creating the actual screen designs—may be pointless to translate to wireframes, since the wireframes are no longer serving as a guide to the design team.

Here are some strategies for keeping wireframes up-to-date:

If the tools permit, tie deliverables together, so that updates to the copy deck, for example, are reflected in the wireframes. If your wireframes are based in HTML, this is theoretically a straightforward exercise. Microsoft Office applications like Excel, Word, and Visio have these capabilities but can be a little temperamental when trying to share them among many people.

If the tools permit, allow the wireframes to draw upon a library of shared elements—parts of the wireframe that are used repeatedly. This allows you to make changes to an element in one place and have it changed throughout the document. Microsoft Visio permits nested backgrounds, which means that any page in a Visio document can have several backgrounds that it shares with other pages in the document. By establishing a strategy for using these backgrounds early in the process, you can know how to leverage them effectively in your document.

Make changes on the fly. One advantage to showing wireframes on screen is that you can make changes in the document as the discussion progresses. One former colleague used to keep Visio open during requirements meetings, and used it to begin compiling wireframes even before the design phase. This allowed him to respond to changes in requirements quickly and to capture his ideas as they were occurring to him. On the other hand, it also ran the risk of committing to a design idea before fully understanding the scope of the site. A less risky approach is to make changes as they are being discussed in the feedback meeting. This eliminates losing any comments between the client's mouth to your ears to your notebook to your desk to your computer, and allows stakeholders to respond instantaneously.

Don't update wireframes. You may decide that keeping the wireframes up-to-date just isn't worth it. They serve a particular purpose in your process, and once they've outlived that purpose, there's no point in investing further time into them. It's a legitimate decision, to be sure, but one that needs to be weighed very carefully against the disadvantages.

The brute-force approach is simply to build time into the project schedule to keep wireframes up-to-date. Project teams rarely plan for enough time for documentation updates, thinking they won't take long to do. But initial rounds of feedback and the corresponding updates may require as much if not more time than it took to create the first draft. This is perhaps unique to wireframes because they involve such a substantial change in how we perceive the project: Wireframes take us from intangible requirements to somewhat tangible screen concepts.

Use sample content consistently

Wireframes for even the simplest sites represent screens meant to address particular scenarios and particular user goals. To put wireframes together effectively, you may need to identify a sample scenario, ensuring that the wireframes present a coherent experience. In a commerce-enabled web site, for example, the wireframes might show a product screen, a shopping cart screen, and a checkout screen. If you've included any kind of sample content, the reader of the wireframes will perceive the progression of screens as part of the same scenario. If the sample content on these screens is not consistent, the reader will be confused. The appearance of some other product in the cart, for example, can disrupt the flow of the wireframes. Though this is more of a presentation risk, it must be addressed in the creation of the wireframes. If you've anticipated the scenarios you're illustrating through the wireframes, you can identify the crucial variables in each scenario—dates, names, addresses, products, and other application-specific widgets—and make sure these variables stay the same throughout the wireframes.

TIP ▶ To ensure a consistent flow in the wireframes, plan the crucial variables — dates in a scheduling application, or products and shipping details in a commercial application—in advance.

Presenting Wireframes

If you thought creating wireframes was fraught with risk, wait until you present them to a new client for the first time. Some of the mitigation measures you took to avoid the risks in creating the wireframes will help in presenting them. Whatever you do, though, don't go into a meeting without prepping the meeting participants beforehand.

For new clients who have never seen a wireframe, hold a prep meeting to show them samples, setting their expectations of what they'll get.

For clients who have seen wireframes before, have a conversation with them about what they liked and didn't like about the wireframes they saw in the past. If they ask for greater detail, you have an opportunity to set their expectations about what you'll show them. Bring a sample wireframe from another project—one in a format that you'd like to use for this project—and get their feedback on it.

If you're new to a project team, ask them to show you wireframes they've used before and describe what worked and what didn't work. Ask them about how they incorporated wireframes into their process and if the level of detail was sufficient for subsequent activities.

With expectations set, you may be able to address many of the challenges described in this chapter.

The Meeting Purpose

As much as sitting in meetings may be the bane of your professional existence, the advantage to calling a meeting yourself is that you get to set the agenda. Run a good meeting and you'll become everyone's best friend (whether this is a good thing is your call). Wireframes meetings are difficult to run and may go on longer than planned because of the potential for distraction. But there's only one reason you'd call a meeting, right? There are some questions that need answering, right? That's why you're in the meeting: to answer your questions.

To keep a tight rein on the meeting, always set an agenda and always announce the purpose of the meeting by quickly running through the questions you need answered at the top of the meeting. With wireframes, there are three kinds of meetings.

The buy-in meeting: Selling an idea

Suppose you have a new concept for navigation. The best way to sell the idea is to show it in action. Wireframes can be a good way to do this, demonstrating how users will click from one screen to the next, how the content supports the navigation, and vice versa. In this case, a narrative approach—in which you narrate the user's path through the experience—helps meeting participants put themselves in the user's shoes.

On the other hand, you might need buy-in on the entire system—a deck of 80 or 100 screens that document every nuance of the proposed web site. In this case, the message is comprehensiveness: You want to show that the team has covered every scenario and addressed every requirement. You may be facing a marathon meeting to go through every screen, in which case a scenario-based structure for the meeting is best (see below). If, however, you've conducted a series of buy-in meetings on portions of the site, the final buy-in meeting can be more focused, reminding stakeholders of the process you've taken to get to this point, providing overviews of key scenarios.

For each kind of participant in the meeting, the hook will vary. That is, the thing that sells participants on the idea will depend on who they are.

For clients, the people sponsoring and paying for the project, there are—for better or worse—a couple motivations behind the approval of a concept:

- **Do they get it?** Understanding is crucial, especially for unusual requirements or interaction models that have little precedent. Wireframes can be useful for illustrating an idea, but it's difficult to measure understanding when much of the conversation is still in the abstract. If you have a comfortable rapport with your clients, you might ask them to walk you through the wireframes after you've explained it once to see whether they really got it.

- **Does the idea suit their ego?** Everyone wants to believe that their clients are ego-free. (And if you are on the client side, you are *clearly* an exception.) On the other hand, if a concept incorporates one of their ideas or somehow addresses something that they've previously raised, this will go a long way toward getting their buy-in.

- **Does the idea make sense to their understanding of their business?** The "their understanding" part is crucial to that question. You may have certain notions about how your clients' business should operate, but these are useless unless you've convinced them that such an approach is appropriate. Either way, the wireframes must show that you've addressed a crucial part of their business. For many stakeholders, the system you're building (especially public-facing web sites) is incidental to the business—an additional sales channel that doesn't compete with their more traditional channels, for example. In the government, making information available on the web is a legislated mandate, but there are lots of mandates with which agencies comply that aren't high priorities for them.

Though these questions are mostly about stakeholders, they are relevant to the other meeting participants, designers, and developers. To a certain extent, understanding, ego, and business perspective play a role in their reaction to a concept. There's one more question that you need to consider when presenting an initial idea to other members of the team:

- **Can they build it?** Designers and developers will be looking at wireframes imagining the effort it will take to translate the design into something "real." The best way to prepare for this is to first ask yourself all the questions you think they'll ask you, and then have an informal conversation with these project participants—running the ideas past them in an informal setting allows you to anticipate the most difficult question of all: Is this realistic?

Ultimately, the best way to get buy-in on an idea is to have everyone participate in coming up with it. Project team members who contribute to an idea will be supportive when selling it to stakeholders. Stakeholders who contribute to an idea will be more likely to (and let's be honest here) fund it.

The feedback meeting: Getting input

If a buy-in meeting is to sell a mostly complete idea, a feedback meeting is to flesh out a somewhat complete idea. Because the conversation will be much more elaborate—discussing the ins and outs of your proposed solution—the scope of the meeting must be shorter. You can't get feedback on a deck of 80 to 100 screens in one sitting (unless your team likes sitting for ten hours at a time).

For the feedback meeting, the agenda should focus on exactly what you need feedback on. Even if there are many other things to work out, prioritize your questions to keep up the momentum of your design process.

Feedback isn't quite brainstorming. Brainstorming starts with a clean slate and permits limitless ideas, more or less. The focus of a feedback meeting is less "how do we solve this problem?" and more "does this approach effectively solve the problem?"

When presenting wireframes in this context, therefore, you'll need to show enough of the concept to explain it, but not so much as to stifle the feedback. If a solution seems mostly complete, participants may wonder what they're doing there and realize that "feedback" was a euphemism for "buy-in." Use feedback meetings to answer questions you may have about the approach you're taking.

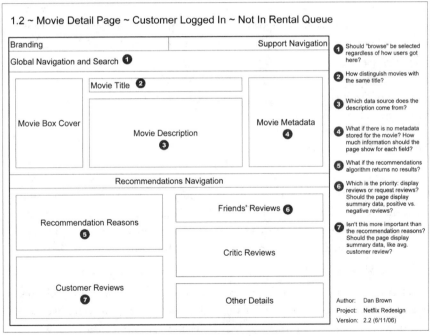

Figure 10.8 This wireframe is all ready for a feedback meeting. The space for annotations contains a list of questions for the meeting participants to consider. By putting the questions right on the wireframes, the meeting agenda is built into the document.

The brainstorm meeting: Developing wireframes together

When you brainstorm around wireframes, you need to keep the scope in check. Collaboratively designing every element on every screen will drive the project team crazy. To control the scope of brainstorming meetings, focus them around a particular scenario, a series of screens for supporting particular user behaviors, or even around a single type of user. For example, one meeting might trace a user's path as he or she tries to buy a particular product online, while another might trace a customer's attempt to find out when the package will arrive.

Once you have a focus for the meeting, don't try to dissect every aspect of the screen. Instead keep the agenda tight by addressing only the salient parts of the screen contents—the information users need in a particular scenario, the functionality that will move them toward their goal, or the messaging priorities for different entry points. Straightforward, tangible, and practical goals make for productive meetings.

How to Structure Your Wireframes Meeting

There are several different ways to structure any kind of meeting about wireframes. Often, the narrative approach is easiest because it follows the path of the user, but you may have a situation where that approach is inappropriate—if there are many different ways to walk through the site, for example, or if the screens are very abstract. Ultimately, the choice of structure is driven by the purpose of the meeting: Use the questions you need answered to define a way to present the wireframes.

The narrative approach

Wireframes can be very confusing to other people on the project team. Very abstract wireframes don't look like screens and participants may not understand what they're looking at. By contrast, very detailed screens may cause tangents in the presentation because they offer so much to respond to. A narrative-style meeting, based on a series of scenarios, can establish context and guide the conversation.

In selecting scenarios for wireframe presentations, start with the basic processes—with no errors, exceptions, or deviations. For example, on a banking web site, describe the process for setting up a basic checking account—a process where the user doesn't already have another account, or where they don't get a credit card to go along with their new checking account, just the basics. Depending on the purpose of your meeting, you may not be able to get through much beyond that, especially if the purpose of the meeting is to get feedback or brainstorm the details of the process.

Once you have run through the basic process and you're confident that the other meeting participants get it, you can show how the process changes in different scenarios.

There are two ways to structure meetings using a narrative approach: by flow and by user, and frequently a combination of both. Each "chapter" in your meeting could cover a different flow, a different discrete task performed by the users, for instance, finding a product, browsing the online store, committing a product to the shopping cart, checking out. This approach makes sense when every user is going to have pretty much the same experience.

On the other hand, the web site experience may be different for different users—a content management system where different users perform different tasks, for example, or a banking site where the experience varies depending on the kinds of accounts a customer has. In these cases, your meeting structure is a little more complex. Some "chapters" of the meeting are processes that all users have in common—getting help or logging in, for example. The rest of the meeting should then be structured based on different user types.

The "content type" approach

If your site contains various levels of information hierarchy and several different screen designs on each level, consider presenting each level in its entirety. For example, if a storefront has three different kinds of category pages and four different kinds of product pages, this approach suggests you present all three category pages followed by all four product pages. (In the narrative style, for comparison's sake, you would present a category page and then the product page that follows.)

Although the exact style of presentation will vary with the purpose of the meeting, the best way to use this approach is to present all the screens of a particular type and then analyze or critique them all together. The structure of each screen of a given type may vary, but the overall purpose of each screen is the same (otherwise they wouldn't be of the same type) and some feedback may apply across the board. Be sure to allow participants to see all the wireframes at the same time (presuming there are no more than five or six variations on a screen).

The "priority order" approach

During the design process, the team may identify the most important screens in the system. These screens generally represent the main reason why someone has come to the site. On a web-based storefront, it could be the product page, the screen that makes or breaks the customer's decision to buy something. These are the 20 percent of your screens that will take 80 percent of the traffic. It's the screen where most of the action happens (This used to be the home page, but these days, with the proliferation of search engines like Yahoo! and Google, many customers bypass the home page entirely, so its value is rapidly diminishing.)

One way to conduct these meetings is to start with that screen. This approach follows software engineering best practices by addressing the "highest risk" items first, from which follows the idea that by solving problems on that page, you address global problems throughout the system.

By dealing with these key screens first, you avoid the risk of saving them until later in the meeting when important people might have left, or the participants have started to tire. Missing someone's input on crucial screens can cause further delays down the line.

This is not to say that the paths users take to these important screens are insignificant. There's a hierarchy of pages below that most important screen, those that allow customers to take the next step and those that bring the customer to that screen. Rank these pages according to risk—which ones have the greatest impact on the project—and present them in that order. The screens can be introduced relative to the most important one, for example: "This is the page users see immediately following the project page once they've added the product to their cart." You may not be able get through more than two screens, but you've at least reviewed the two most important screens and gotten implicit feedback on the rest.

The risk with this approach is that the team sees screens out of context—not necessarily how the customer will see them—and it may be difficult to imagine the customer experience.

Risks: Don't Get Your Wires Crossed

Getting bogged down in content

Regardless of your meeting's purpose, the focus of the conversation must be on the relative priorities of the elements on the screen. Wireframes without any sample content—or with unrecognizable sample content—help keep the conversation focused by avoiding the issue entirely.

If you can't avoid putting sample content in your wireframes, there are a couple things you can do to prevent the meeting from running away from you. Most importantly, set the agenda and the expected outcome. With wireframes, it's easy to dive right in and start talking about screens. By establishing the purpose of the meeting up front, listing the wireframes you'll discuss and what you want to talk about for each one, you have a means of staying on topic. That being said, making your wireframes as accurate as possible can help mitigate this risk: If the content is accurate, they don't have a reason to talk about it.

When the conversation does get into label names, editorial issues, and factual errors, you need to reassure your stakeholders that you take their concerns seriously, but that you need to address other issues at the moment. Capture their issues publicly—on a whiteboard or flip chart—and include these issues in the meeting minutes or an informal follow-up email. This will make it clear that you've heard their concerns and give you a means for moving past extended conversations about content. The ball is now in your court to ensure these content errors do not make their way into the final product—or even the next version of the document.

Steer the meeting toward priorities

Like content, the design of a wireframe can distract stakeholders from the conversation at hand. Many of the mitigation strategies are the same: set an agenda, keep the wireframe as devoid of design as possible, and capture design issues to address later.

Discussions about design, however, can by symptomatic of deeper structural concerns. Try to turn design conversations into conversations about structure or priority.

TABLE 10.5

Redirecting Wireframe Conversations

They Say	You Say
I don't like the color of the button	The color makes the button stand out. Do you think that the button should not stand out so much?
I don't like having to scroll to see this information	The screen has important information escalated to the top and we've tried to avoid diluting the important information with information that's not as important. Is this information more important than the stuff above the fold?
This isn't our corporate typeface	The wireframe won't accurately reflect your corporate branding, but the final design will. Do you think this information needs to be more visually prominent than other things on the page?
There is too much going on; it's too busy	Of all the information on the screen, which is the most important? Let's rank the different pieces of information on this screen.

Unlike conversations about content, which usually have no bearing on the underlying structure, comments about design can reveal important requirements about the task at hand.

Keep an open mind

Requirements are the bread and butter of software engineering, and by extension, web development. A requirement is a statement describing what the system is supposed to do. They usually come in packs (read: enormous documents that no one ever reads more than once, or past the first few pages). Good requirements are stated in such a way that they don't dictate design. For example, "the system shall allow the user to remove an item from the list of items they would like to purchase." It is usually through requirements that you gain an understanding of what you're supposed to design.

The wireframes are a response to requirements: Through the requirements you learn what the system is supposed to do, and the wireframes show how the system does it. The dichotomy is rarely so clean, but this is the theory anyway.

The risk is that in running through the wireframes, some stakeholder will have a sudden epiphany. If she's nice, she'll admit that she's proposing a new feature. If she's not so nice, it'll sound something like this: "Why doesn't the page show product recommendations based on previous purchases like we talked about at the kickoff meeting? I distinctly remember describing it in great detail."

On rare occasions, wireframes are used specifically for this purpose—putting concepts in front of stakeholders or customers to get them to think through everything the system should do. Mostly, however, wireframes are used after the requirements have been defined and approved. Still, it's generally inevitable that a new requirement will appear over the course of reviewing the wireframes.

Part of this is human nature. Until you see something, it's hard to think through all of its implications. From a document preparation point of view, there is little to be done about that—this is a project management and methodology issue.

Still, there is at least one thing you can do to avoid being surprised by important requirements: Create quick-and-dirty wireframes before the requirements process is over. These wireframes are only for you and your most trusted compatriots, a tool to validate the requirements and help surface any that you might have missed. Focus not on meeting user needs but on addressing all the requirements. The aim here isn't to develop award-winning design, but to poke holes in the requirements document. If you do a quick version of the design process and find unanswered questions, you've found a hole.

Otherwise, the ways to mitigate this risk include better project planning, better expectation setting, and better presentation methods.

Manage team interactions

Perhaps this isn't a risk anymore, but in the early days of web design, wireframes were controversial because they crossed the line between information architecture, interaction design, and graphic design. (That's one of the reasons this chapter advocates leaving layout and design out of wireframes.) As a potential territory issue, wireframes can create a lot of stress on design teams.

Other than keeping wireframes focused on priorities, there is little you can do in the document itself to mitigate this risk—it's more of a project management and methodology issue. Developing wireframes collaboratively, however, offers a key advantage to mitigating the risk: By working on them together, the team creates joint ownership in the design. With joint ownership come fewer territory issues.

As described above, brainstorming is a tricky endeavor, requiring careful orchestration: It's very easy to go way out of scope or way off topic. The bottom line is that if problematic team dynamics are a real risk in your situation, brainstorm wireframes together, but do your situation analysis beforehand and take the role of facilitator.

Wireframes in Context

Wireframes can't exist by themselves. They grow out of work and documentation, and they're just one stepping-stone among many along the way to the final product. This section talks about the bigger picture: how wireframes relate to other documentation and to the project as a whole.

Relationship to Other Deliverables

As powerful as wireframes are in representing many aspects of the user experience, they are not self-contained documentation. They rely on an understanding of user needs and an overall strategy for the foundation. They cannot describe 100 percent of the user experience, and they must work with other design documents to provide a complete picture.

Wireframes and user-needs documentation

In the deliverables that describe users—personas and usability testing documentation—you have expressed, in essence, checklists. Your solution will work if it successfully addresses everything specified in these checklists. The wireframes represent one view of that solution, but they may not address everything expressed in the user-needs documentation.

Whether it happens in the document itself or in your presentation of the document, you must show how the wireframes address previously defined requirements.

At the same time, because wireframes represent only part of a solution, it would be impossible for them to address every requirement. To show that you aren't neglecting these requirements, but merely waiting for a more appropriate time to address them, you can explicitly call attention to them. For example, your usability report might show that users responded positively to content written in a casual tone and with lists rather than long paragraphs. Of course, if you're leaving content out of the wireframe, you cannot show that you are addressing the requirement; this needs to happen elsewhere. To make these distinctions clear in the wireframes document, you can include references to usability results or personas on individual screens to show what you've addressed. The document can also include a table at the beginning that compares the screens presented to high-level goals or requirements.

	Flow Chart	Wireframes	Tech Spec	Final Design
Requirement 1.1: The system shall allow users to view movie information and add a movie to their rental queue.	●	●	●	●
Requirement 1.1.1: The system shall display the movie title, a short description of the movie, and the movie's main actors and director.	○	●	◐	●
Requirement 1.1.2: The system shall allow users to add the movie to their rental queue.	●	●	◐	●
Requirement 1.1.3: The system shall indicate whether the movie is in their queue or not.	○	◐	○	●
Requirement 1.1.4: The system shall display reviews written by other users, showing the most popular reviews (determined by votes) and the most recent reviews.	○	◐	◐	●
Requirement 1.2: The system shall allow users to rate movies and write their own reviews.	○	◐	◐	◐
Requirement 1.2.1: The system shall allow users to easily assign a rating (between one and five stars) to a movie.	○	●	◐	●
Requirement 1.2.2: The system shall employ the user's movie ratings to determine recommended movies.	●	○	●	○

Figure 10.9 This table shows which requirements are addressed by the wireframes and the extent to which the wireframes address each requirement. The table compares wireframes in the context of requirements to other kinds of documents, anticipating that stakeholders might expect to see every detail specified in the wireframes.

Wireframes and strategy documentation

This book describes three kinds of strategy documents, all of which establish a foundation for building the overall user experience. One of these documents, the competitive analysis, compares your web site with others to identify best practices or differences in what's offered. Wireframes are a useful tool for summarizing how each site presents information and allows an apples-to-apples comparison of screen layouts.

Another strategy document, the concept model, describes an underlying structure for the system. Your wireframes' introductory pages can explain how the wireframes support the underlying structure or organize the wireframes in terms of the concept model. A concept model represents an overall organizing principle, and so may be concealed from the user in the final product. Your wireframe should acknowledge how it makes use of the model without burdening the users with knowing what the model is.

The last kind of strategy document, the content model, helps plan content migration and creation. Content models identify all the content contained on the site while wireframes describe how the content will be displayed. If the wireframes represent templates, the content model should reference the wireframes to show what kinds of content will be presented in what templates.

Ultimately, the goal is to show the stakeholders that these preliminary deliverables have built a foundation for later work. Although this may feel like a ploy to justify the work, the real purpose is more important: to keep the stakeholders focused. The strategy at the beginning identifies what's important to the project, and the design realizes those priorities.

Wireframes and other design documents

The key to successful design documentation is recognizing that no one document can capture every detail about the user experience. Therefore, there's no need to burden wireframes with information that other documents do better. It's easy enough to show how the different documents relate to each other: A screen in the flow chart is the same as a screen in the wireframes is the same as a final screen design. Use the same reference numbers throughout.

The Impact of Wireframes

Throughout this chapter, I've been very strict about the purpose of wireframes, and most situations call for being a stickler about that sort of thing. As a document, wireframes can be incredibly powerful in communicating many aspects of the user experience—how information is prioritized on the screen, how users interact with that information, how design is derived from requirements and business goals. To paraphrase a superhero, with great power comes great risk. Until your team and stakeholders find a comfortable working relationship and agree on the role of wireframes in the design process, these can be murky waters.

In some design methodologies, wireframes can both represent design ideas and help stakeholders zero in on what they need. Wireframes can be especially powerful for identifying these parameters—or "eliciting requirements"—because people tend to recognize what works only when they see it. Wireframes, therefore, are an ideal tool for a looser design process that permits developing a design and revisiting it throughout the life of the project. Developers call this an "iterative" approach. Moving right to wireframes after identifying high-level requirements can accelerate the entire process.

Many recent innovations in software development methodologies eliminate wireframes, moving straight from lightweight requirements to functional prototypes (working models). Although this approach offers clear advantages of speed, it requires a certain level of agility from both the project team and the stakeholders. Many organizations may not be able to muster the speed required.

You might wonder whether there's a better way to do wireframes, one that isn't fraught with such risk. But for all their risks, wireframes can be an incredibly useful tool for visualizing the behavior of the system in relatively short order. By seeing and almost touching the solution, team members can identify potential risks with the entire project early in the lifecycle. Removing wireframes from the process entirely burdens other documents with the responsibility to respond to the requirements.

Wireframes in a changing landscape

Rapid changes in technological capabilities and development methodologies won't render wireframes extinct, but will force them to evolve to meet the demands of a new landscape.

As mentioned earlier, there's a growing trend in software development methodologies to move faster, work on smaller chunks of a project at a time, and revise often. Wireframes, as a deliverable with many pages and only a handful of versions, won't survive long in that environment. New tools will emerge that render the original purpose of wireframes—to visualize the solution—obsolete. These tools will allow teams to create functional prototypes quickly. Wireframes will become a tool to provide guidance for the prototype, further compressing timeframes for creating the wireframes.

At the same time, interfaces are becoming more dynamic, especially on the web. It won't do to divide a system into discrete screens because users will be able to do so much on a single screen. Future visions of the Internet focus on a "participation economy," an environment where users contribute and manipulate content more than they consume it. Information priorities, the bread and butter of a wireframe, take on new meaning when systems are designed as containers of contributed (and therefore somewhat unpredictable) content, rather than portals to a centralized content source. The "old" web is one of back-and-forth communications: You send me your credit card information and I'll ship you some books. The online bookstore, in that model, was a central content source for books. In the participation economy, information about books is distributed—anyone who reads (or sometimes doesn't read) a book has something to say about it—information about customer needs is distributed, and even fulfillment is distributed. Navigation is difficult to plan when you're not exactly sure what's being navigated. And, of course, describing content becomes almost completely meaningless when your stakeholders' customers are writing it. The wireframe as a representation of information priorities and content structure may be no longer necessary.

But the wireframe itself won't go away. Humans will always gravitate toward pictures and toward simple representations of complex ideas, which are—in the end—the whole point of a wireframe.

CHAPTER ELEVEN

Screen Designs

skrēn' də-zīnz (n.)

Screen designs are a collection of images in some electronic format that show what the final web site will look like. Also known as screen comps (short for "composites"), mock-ups, page design, visual design, graphic design, interface design, design concepts, pretty pictures.

This is it. This is more or less what it comes down to: the final design. You've been through user research, through concept modeling and content inventories. You've developed initial design documentation, some preliminary prototypes, and you've done usability testing and refined the design. Now you have a set of screen designs!

Of course, it never really happens exactly that way, and if it does, there's a lot of detail we're leaving out. Screen designs don't magically pop out at the end of the design process. They work in cooperation with other design documents to capture the complete user experience, and may be developed in tandem with those documents. Like any other deliverable in this book, screen designs are a stepping-stone to something further up river.

This chapter doesn't deal with the actual process of doing a design—there are already countless books on the subject—but what to do with your screen designs once you have them. Screen designs, treated as a deliverable, entail the same kinds of preparation and presentation challenges as any other document.

Screen Designs at a Glance

At first glance, a screen design is almost indistinguishable from the final product. Hopefully, it looks just like how the final site will look. Unless you've made it in HTML or some other interactive prototype, the screen design won't do anything when you click on it, and nothing will be functional. It's just a facade, meant to show you what the site looks like without actually being the site.

Besides functionality, there are a few other ways in which screen designs are not like the final product. Screen designs won't necessarily show every page of the web site, and they won't necessarily show how the screen layout accommodates different amounts and different types of content.

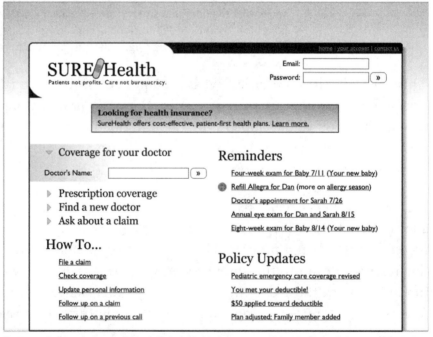

Figure 11.1 A screen design should be indistinguishable from a screenshot—that is, until the user clicks on it. This is a design for a fake health insurance company. Like a wireframe, it contains enough sample content to give stakeholders and the rest of the project team a sense of how the screen is supposed to behave. (A quick web search indicates that SureHealth is the name of several real sites and products out there. This site is a figment of the author's imagination and is in no way related to or derived from any existing works.)

Screen Design Overview

Purpose—What are screen designs for?

Screen designs show stakeholders and other team members what the site will look like.

Audience—Who uses them?

Stakeholders should approve screen designs before the team moves forward with development. The project team should already have a good idea of how the site will operate from wireframes and other design documentation, but the screen designs are the final piece of the puzzle.

Scale—How much work are they?

Coming up with the design can take a couple of days or a couple of months, depending on the size and scope of the project. The number of screens you decide to mock up can also affect the level of effort you'll expend. If you want to show multiple design concepts and allow stakeholders to select the one they like best, you'll have to factor that into your resource planning. Generally speaking, a different designer does each concept. Putting the supporting materials together and preparing for the presentation can take anywhere from a couple of hours to a couple of days.

Context—Where do they fall in the process?

On paper, creating the screen designs is the last step before development starts. Traditional methods suggest a strong dependency on wireframes, brand strategy, a set of design objectives, and other documentation. In reality, the positioning of this activity varies depending on your methodology. Rapid design methods (discussed in detail in the "Screen Designs in Context" section later in this chapter) might require starting the visual design shortly after nailing down your requirements.

Format—What do they look like?

Screen designs look like screens. Unlike wireframes, screen designs are almost always presented in electronic form, projected or viewed on a monitor. Most design teams create the presentation so that the design takes up the entire screen. You should also prepare a separate document containing supporting information.

Challenges

As with any document, the preparation and presentation of screen designs come with their own set of challenges. One of them might have nothing to do with the document itself, however. Lots of people don't think of screen designs as a document, as something with context and structure that should be carefully planned. The greatest challenge with this document, then, is changing how you think about it. You may need to shift your mind-set entirely. Instead of planning on sending along a set of graphic or HTML files, think about how you want to package the designs. If someone outside the project were to look at these, what would they need to know in order to understand them? This kind of information can transform a set of seemingly arbitrary screens into client-ready documentation.

The other challenge comes with preparing the screens: You need to set boundaries around what you'll show to the client. Are the screen mock-ups meant to be accurate representations of the web page, or just a general impression of the overall design? Going in one direction, you can set yourself up for serious criticism if the final rendition deviates from the mock-up. In the other direction, your stakeholders may want reassurance that they're getting an accurate picture of the final design—or worse, they may question your approach if you can't show them a final design.

Many of the challenges designers face in preparing screen designs are the same as those they face when preparing wireframes. How to represent content, which screens to show, and the degree of fidelity to the final product are all problematic issues for both wireframes and screen designs. Unless a challenge is unique to screen designs, this chapter will leave those common issues alone. Refer to Chapter 10 for more information about wireframes and their challenges.

Screen designs are, in many ways, the most difficult documents to package and present because even modern web design methodologies put a lot of emphasis on this step in the process. You can try to adjust your methodology, building the design iteratively, or presenting the designs in conjunction with wireframes. But there's no need to see the challenges of screen designs as a problem. Spending a little time working with your project team and stakeholders to set expectations is usually all you need to do to overcome the challenges facing designers and screen designs.

Creating Screen Designs

First, let's distinguish between "Screen Designs: The Designs" and "Screen Designs: The Whole Story." The whole story includes a variety of contextual information, rationale for the designs, and—in the case of offering the client multiple design directions—a framework for deciding upon a direction.

There's more to any given piece of a screen than is shown in the visual design: Content areas are fed by databases, functional elements control data or display, and the system responds when the user clicks on different areas of the page. All this information is hidden from view in the screen design. At the same time, in creating the document, we can include these so-called "related decisions"— other functional and behavioral details related to a piece of the screen.

At the same time, more than just about any other document, screen designs depend on explanations—justification for particular decisions about the layout, type, color, or any other design element. Explanations can range from the simple to the complex. A simple explanation might be "We positioned this content area high up on the page and near the center because the wireframes indicated it was the most important content on the screen." A more elaborate rationale may dig into the client's brand strategy and marketing plan, described in layer 3, later in this chapter.

You don't have to be very explicit in distinguishing these different kinds of information in the document, but you should think carefully about them, because they form the basis of your whole story. The greater challenge is capturing the supporting information in a document without crowding the screen itself. You may need to prepare a document that captures all the supporting information described in the following sections, but when you present the screens, show them in their entirety.

Layer 1: The Story Outline

In its simplest incarnation, visual designs are a collection of screens with identifying information. Even though you should add more information later—rationale and related decisions—start with the basic structure. In this first layer, you need to think about what order in which to present the screens (a topic covered a little later in the chapter) and how you'll line up the screens if you're presenting more than one approach.

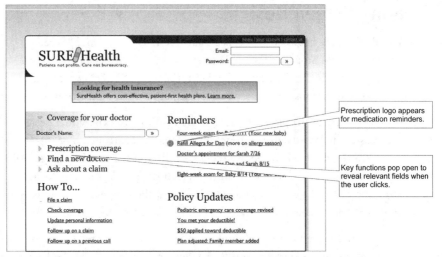

Figure 11.2 This excerpt shows how a screen design can be obscured by supporting information. Projecting something like this during a presentation won't give participants a good idea of what the screen actually looks like.

The basic design(s)

Of course the document needs to include the screens themselves, and you have a couple options here. For years, design teams showed a static image of the screen design. Designers would prepare a design in Adobe Photoshop or some other application, without any of its moving parts, frozen in a stasis of 800 x 600 pixels. They'd throw these static images up on the screen and ask team members, clients, and stakeholders to imagine it as a dynamic web page, and we all happily played along. This approach is completely legitimate, even if it feels artificial.

Alternately, as web sites grow into more complex applications, designers may jump right to HTML. This approach is becoming more tempting with the advent of CSS (Cascading Style Sheets), which allow designers to control every aspect of the look with code.

Identifying information

Besides the design itself, the most essential piece of information is its identifier. The name of the screen should relate to any previous references to the screen. For example, if the site map and wireframes refer to the home page as, well, "Home Page," you don't want to call it "First Page" or "Level Zero" when presenting the screen designs. Duh, with a capital D.

The other piece of identifying information is the name of the overall concept. This is especially necessary if you're presenting more than one concept. Meaningful names, like "Three-Column Approach" or "Minimalist," help stakeholders keep the different designs straight, and allow you to emphasize the most essential aspect of the concept. There's more on this in "Give Design Directions Meaningful Names," a bit later.

Layer 2: Experience Context and Rationale

Although the basic screen designs document consists of the mock-ups themselves and little more, capturing the rationale and other contextual information can help clarify your design decisions. In an effort to lead into the next set of activities in the project, you can also include some technical considerations for building out the design.

Design and content documentation references

By referencing earlier design documents, you create continuity in the project, showing how one set of decisions leads to another. This kind of continuity can reassure stakeholders and avoid unnecessary back and forth because people may be unwilling to go back on earlier decisions if they understand the impact that doing so would have on current work.

Site maps, user flows, and wireframes are all obvious candidates for reference material. Each of these documents describes pages and screens on the site from a different angle, and the screen designs are no different.

As a final deliverable, you might combine screen designs with wireframes, showing them side by side to capture both the look of the final product and its behavior.

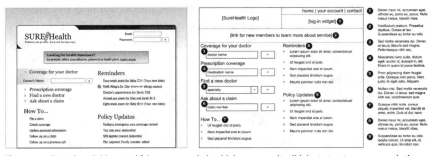

Figure 11.3 Even though it's a total fake, our sample health insurance site didn't start out as a screen design. Presented here adjacent to the original wireframe, the document provides a complete picture of the user experience—what users will see and how the screen behaves.

You might also reference the concept model. References to the concept model (Chapter 6) show how the screen is the "manifestation" of one of the abstract concepts in the model. For example, imagine a concept model for a health insurance web site that describes several underlying concepts, including claims, covered services, and visits to a doctor. Each of these concepts is a complex collection of information that must appear on a screen. A set of screen designs might refer to the model to show how the concepts are realized in different ways throughout the user experience.

Technical and production issues

As a nod to what comes next, your document might include technical considerations—that is, any issues related to translating the design into HTML. You might include a smaller version of the screen with lines drawn to show how the screen will be broken up into different regions appropriate for coding. (In the old days, you would cut up a design to make it fit into an HTML table, but these days all the cool kids are using Cascading Style Sheets. The regions of a design rendered in CSS are known affectionately as DIVs, after the HTML tag for defining them.) In the CSS, each of these regions gets a name, called either an ID or a class name. You may be tempted to supply these to the developer, but in the end, the person doing the HTML and working with the programmers should come up with the region identifiers. They will have a more intimate understanding of the technical issues in developing the front end, and may have specific needs for the HTML that you are not aware of.

If the page is long and requires the user to scroll, you might show how much the user sees when the page first loads—the content "above the fold." Of course, this varies depending on the screen resolution, so you might need to show several if you're concerned about different people having different settings.

On the production side, your design might imply acquiring a number of images. If you're lucky, your client has a vast library of digital imagery, indexed and ready for the picking. More likely, you'll need to buy or create the images yourself. (Of course, when I worked for the Transportation Security Administration we realized that the security regulations we put in place were the same ones that made it difficult for us to take pictures of transportation scenes. Oh, the irony.)

Regardless of how you'll acquire the imagery, you can include an inventory of everything you need to help the team and the client get a sense of cost or level of effort. When people are looking at designs, sometimes they forget the amount of time, resources, and work it takes to (a) make them in the first place, and (b) turn them from concept to reality.

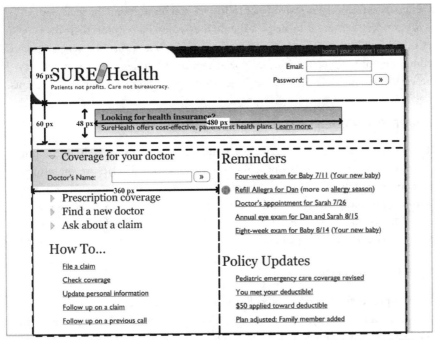

Figure 11.4 The design team prepared a version of this screen with defined areas to show how it might be divided up in HTML. This diagram also specifies pixel measurements to help the development team translate the design into HTML and CSS more effectively.

Some design teams split the graphic designers from the HTML developers. Though this is a somewhat old-school practice, some teams still divide the labor this way because front-end development is becoming more complex. One way to supplement screen designs to facilitate the transition from graphic design to front-end development is to create a style sheet that catalogs the various typefaces and colors employed by the design. The style sheet would include a reference to every use of type (headlines, navigation, body text, links, etc.) and the appropriate type treatment. For colors, you can provide a palette that provides the appropriate color values.

Creative brief references

Your team may prepare a creative brief, a document for establishing an overall direction for the design. It's usually short (one or two pages) and contains sections on the look, the audience, and any requirements imposed by the brand.

Creative briefs are useful to designers because they establish boundaries, and boundaries give designers valuable starting points for the creative process.

Designers can use the creative brief to inspire a central theme for their design work, or they can use it to shape a theme they come up with on their own. A lot of this depends on the kind of creative brief you create. It may be very abstract, containing only thoughts or feelings that capture the tone of the site, or it may be very concrete, documenting specific color, type, and messaging requirements.

Layer 3: Business Context and Rationale

The elements described in layer 2 place the screen designs squarely in the middle of the user experience—showing how this document relates to the project tasks immediately preceding and immediately after it. In some cases, you may also want to show how design decisions can be traced back to earlier stages of the process—back when the client and project team were making decisions about the overall business strategy.

Brand strategy references

For our purposes, a brand is the collection of experiences a person has with a particular organization. By the same token, it's the thoughts and feelings evoked by interacting with a company through those experiences. A company like Microsoft injects its brand into its products by using certain design conventions, but its brand is also created when people use its products. This give and take between a brand and a user experience is what makes it difficult to nail a brand down.

Attempts to nail down a brand are captured in a "brand strategy," a document for establishing what kinds of thoughts, feelings, and actions a person should have or do when experiencing an organization. It's touchy-feely like that. Different brand strategists and marketers have different ways of capturing a brand strategy, so there are any number of ways you can reference it in your design. Generally speaking, brand strategies are more general than creative briefs (described earlier) because creative briefs are usually specific to a particular medium or channel (like the web site, or an advertising campaign) while the brand strategy addresses the entire experience of the organization.

In referencing the brand strategy, a screen design shows how it fits into the overall brand and how it complements the organization's other channels for communicating and interacting with its customers.

Business strategy references

Any good web site needs to rest on a solid business strategy—vision, goals, metrics, and processes. A business strategy defines how the web site makes sense from an economic point of view, or how it will provide some value based on its cost. It gives the web project shape by keeping it focused on a particular set of desired outcomes and it establishes criteria for success. No modern web development project should start without some document defining its objectives and criteria for success. After all, how will you know whether the project is successful if you haven't committed to a definition of success?

There are a lot of steps between a business objective and a design decision. An objective like "reduce customer service calls for people seeking claim status" does not imply a particular set of design decisions, but it can provide a rationale for it. This objective, for example, may be the basis for escalating claim status links to the home page of the insurance site.

Even if you decide not to capture them explicitly in a document, you may want to prepare some thoughts on how the design supports the overall business objectives. You may not hand this document in with the rest of the deliverable, but it can help with the presentation of the designs.

Compiling Screen Designs: The Basics

Before you decide which of these elements you need to include in your deliverable, you must do a situation analysis to determine what information will be most meaningful to your project.

The impact of who, when and why

In typical web design methods, showing a screen design is one of the last steps before turning it over to development, but variations abound. You might run a usability test or two against a screen design, pushing it more toward the middle of the overall design process. You might also pump out a design with only a cursory understanding of the requirements, using it as a straw man in refining the requirements through brainstorming or user research.

These circumstances will no doubt affect the design—you can only design with what you have to work with—but they will also affect how you present the design. Compare the presentations of two designs, one prepared after weeks of work and another after an initial brainstorming session. The first one makes reference to other documents, especially requirements and other design documents like wireframes. It represents templates and content that have been discussed at length in the abstract. Much of it may already be in the design team's heads, having gestated there over the course of the project. The main message in this collection of screen designs is, "Here's how we met the project requirements."

The other set of designs—the one prepared as a straw man at the beginning of the process—does not have as much information to draw from; the starting point for this design is much different. This document has a different message: "We responded to what we heard in our initial meeting and made some assumptions about the rest." The design serves as a tool for uncovering requirements.

TABLE 11.1

How Circumstances Affect Emphasis in Screen Design Documentation

Screen Design	Emphasis
Straw man designs	The contextual information you provide can emphasize which design decisions were driven by your initial requirements meetings and which were driven by assumptions.
Final designs	You want to emphasize the traceability of your design decisions. The work in your earlier design documentation—site maps and wireframes—should trace back to your strategic endeavors and your research into users.

Of course, your methodology may call for the designs to play some other role altogether, in which case your best bet is to think about how they facilitate the transition from one stage of the process to the next. Whatever that "glue" might be, it should form the basis of your screen design documentation.

Embellishing the Story

Treating screen designs like deliverables means thinking carefully about how the document is composed and how supporting data is displayed along with the basic designs. Here are some suggestions to help plan the screen designs document.

Never create anything you don't like...but don't be emotionally attached to any one design. If you can detach yourself, you'll see the design document as a tool for gathering information, refining your understanding of the design problem. This isn't to say that you shouldn't defend your design, especially if the criticisms of it are insubstantial. If you have a rationale for particular design decisions, stick to them. At the same time, keep in mind that there are bigger things at stake than the integrity of your design, such as the working relationship between you and the client. Ultimately, your responsibility as a designer is to provide the best design possible, and if the people with the money want to launch something you don't agree with, your responsibility is to make sure the client understands the risks you perceive.

Use a separate document for supporting information

Since a screen design should come as close to the final product as possible, showing screens with all kinds of callouts and other notations will distract from the main purpose. Instead, prepare two separate documents—one containing all the screens untouched by notations, and the other using smaller versions of the screens alongside notations that fill in the whole story. You can print out this second document to distribute at the presentation meeting, while projecting the untouched screens for everyone to look at.

Consider intermediate steps

The gap between initial design documentation and screen designs can feel interminable. It can take designers a couple of weeks to process all the information, brainstorm, come up with some ideas, revise and refine those ideas, let alone prepare a final deliverable. If you need the client to provide a sense of overall design direction, consider using a mood board.

Borrowed from "traditional" marketing and advertising, the mood board takes all structure and explicit message out of the web page, leaving only color, type, and innuendo. The mood board shows an assortment of imagery and textures meant to capture a feeling without committing to anything specific with respect to the screen design. This approach helps nail stakeholders down on what they like and what they don't like. As an intermediate step between, say, wireframes and visual design, mood boards show that the team is making progress while also gathering valuable information.

Give design directions meaningful names

Sure, you can walk into a presentation and refer to each of the designs by the name of the designer or some arbitrary identifier, like A, B, and C. But you may be wary of attaching a design to a particular designer because it can bias the stakeholders and, frankly, it can be difficult to distinguish design A from design B long after the meeting is finished.

Instead, give the designs meaningful names, like "Three Column Layout" or "Blue and Green Palette." The more you avoid value judgments—like "Professional Approach" and "Fun Approach"—the less you'll bias the stakeholders. Giving the design directions meaningful names makes them much easier to refer to in later conversations, and prevents the client from assigning their own names, which could be inaccurate or—worse—insulting.

What to Watch For

Screen designs are definitely the kind of deliverable where the risky stuff happens in the presentation. Still, there a couple of potholes to watch for on the road to preparing this document as well. Though they have less to do with the document itself and more to do with your process of getting there, they can have a profound impact on how you put it together.

Think through design implications

Quality control is a methodological issue, to be sure. Like the editorial process for writing an essay (or a book), creating a screen design requires a mechanism to check whether 1), it meets all the requirements, and 2), it doesn't paint you into a corner.

These two requirements are tall orders. Done correctly, the requirements process yields a document that can act as a checklist. Still, it's easy enough to overlook requirements, especially in large projects. Even more likely, some requirements may not be clear, and so the designer may have to make assumptions about how the site works. Even the most thorough requirements processes can leave stones unturned, revealing questions and concerns only when the site becomes more of a reality.

The best way to mitigate this risk is to give yourself plenty of time to revise the design, and to have a good business or requirements analyst who can ensure that you've met all the requirements. You can also play with your methodology, doing design and requirements in tandem to allow the one to inform the other, and vice versa. The best way to control for complex requirements is to limit the scope of the project. If you only need to design a handful of screens, it's easy to make sure you get them right.

The other risk is not much easier. A major concern in web design is whether a screen design can accommodate all the page's variations. The screen design shows only one example of the kinds of content that can appear on the page, but any modern web site worth its salt will have content dynamically fed. Even static sites go through changes over time, and a site design will not evolve as rapidly as the content on the site. Therefore, the design needs to be able to accommodate all kinds of change, variation, and growth.

One way to do this is to look at each content area and think about its worst-case scenario. For a block of content like an article or headline, you might think about this in terms of the longest and shortest blocks of text that will appear, or the amount of variation in word length. As the web browser attempts to justify the text, longer words may be difficult to accommodate.

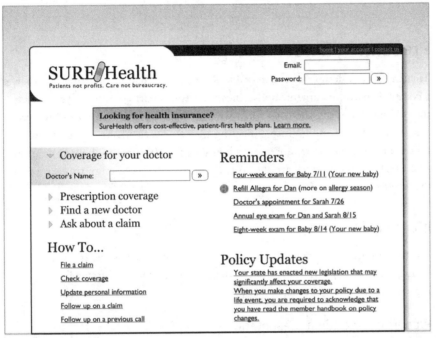

Figure 11.5 In this mock-up, the designer has used especially long content in the Policy Updates section to show how the design accommodates it.

Focus on key pages

This may seem like an easy risk to avoid, but you should be sure to show pages that provide a comprehensive view of the user experience and demonstrate that you've met user needs, while at the same time, avoid creating every page on the site. It's a delicate balance. On the one hand, you want to be able to illustrate how the user will experience the site, but on the other, you want to be efficient, creating only those pages that are useful for development. From a production perspective, your screen designs need to show how to handle every unique design element. For example, unless the header varies wildly from page to page, you really need only one, maybe two examples of it. Creating a mock-up of every page on the site gets redundant fast.

Enter wireframes. If they're done correctly, the wireframes will be an inventory of every functional element and content container on the site. If you create a list of all these elements and then select pages that have a mix of all these elements, you can address all the design needs. In order to illustrate a comprehensive user experience, however, you may need to mock up a few extra pages.

Presenting Screen Designs

Treating screen designs as a deliverable means more than just putting together a comprehensive document. It also means getting smart about how you present the designs. Gone are the days when we could paste paper printouts of screen designs to a board and go into a meeting like we're ace advertising creative types. That kind of show doesn't cut it anymore. Web sites are becoming more sophisticated, and so, too, are the working sessions where design teams present the fruits of their labor.

Meeting Purpose

Most meetings about screen designs fall into one of three types. If you're not asking for final approval on a design, then you're either seeking feedback or asking stakeholders to choose a direction.

Preparing for a client presentation

Before presenting designs to stakeholders and clients, you can hold an internal meeting to prepare for the discussion. Sounds like a lot of meetings, I know. But think about it this way: A little preparation before showing designs to stakeholders can avoid longer client meetings later down the road. By refining the designs and getting your stories straight, you prevent unnecessary back and forth in client meetings.

Soliciting feedback on design

Once you've gotten your stories straight, thought through the designs, and refined them within an inch of their lives, it's time to get feedback from the people footing the bill. Your stakeholders play a strange role in this process, especially since nine times out of ten, they're not the site's target audience, but they still need to approve the design. Even in this day when user-centered design is so prevalent, it's a rare client who asks, "How did the design perform in testing?" Mostly, if they don't like the background pattern, it doesn't matter a lick how well it tested.

There are two kinds of feedback, good and bad, and I'm not talking about positive and negative. Good feedback is meaningful, constructive, and actionable. It clarifies the design problem or offers direction without compromising the integrity of the overall vision. Bad feedback—well, that's the kind we dread to hear—entails stakeholders offering criticism based on personal taste, without rationale or a nod to the system's target audience.

As facilitator of this meeting, your job is to get all the feedback into that first group, even if it means taking meaningless critiques and reframing them into something designers can sink their teeth into.

Table 11.2 offers examples of comments stakeholders might make about the health insurance site from Figure 11.1.

TABLE 11.2

Turning Meaningless Critiques into Meaningful Feedback

They say	You respond
That color blue is ugly.	What don't you like about it? Have you seen a blue that you preferred?
I don't know what I'm looking at here.	Well, what was the first thing you saw on the page?
The page title is too big.	We were responding to user research that said users need to know where they are in the process. Is there something else on the page that deserves more prominence?
I don't think our users will like this.	What three things will cause a negative reaction in users? What do you think users will do when they encounter those things?
I don't like the curves.	They were meant to take the edge off, remaining professional but emphasizing friendly. Do the curves evoke something else to you? What feeling should the design evoke?

Have someone at the meeting capture the feedback. If you can record the audio, that's even better. By having a good record of the meeting, you protect yourself from scope creep—attempts to make the project bigger than its original parameters. Of course, such a careful record of the meeting requires you be clear about how you will respond to their suggestions, because they will hold you to your suggestions as much as you'll hold them to their comments. In responding to their requests, you basically have one of three choices:

- **Push back**: You might flat out refuse to take a suggestion and present a good reason for your refusal. The client may offer a counter argument, at which point you can continue to make your case, or offer one of the other two responses.

- **We'll look into it**: This statement is another powerful weapon in the Internet consultant's arsenal. If you're not sure about a suggestion but can't hash it out right then and there in the meeting, the next best thing is to add it to a list of action items. Of course, at the next meeting, the client will want to know the outcome.

- **Agreement**: Sometimes the client has a point or makes a good suggestion. If you take their suggestion, make sure you understand exactly what they have in mind so you don't surprise them later down the road. Occasionally, clients forget exactly what they wanted, and may get indignant when you point out that it was something they asked for. You can bring out the original meeting record to remind them, but don't gloat. That never ends well.

You might be wondering about feedback from the target audience. You could put the designs in front of users and get their feedback, but if you have an opportunity to talk to users, you should be doing usability testing, where you solicit feedback in the context of use, not just in watching users hurl rotten fruit at a screen.

Selecting a design direction

Your team may be commissioned to create a selection of designs for the client to choose from, and you'll need to hold a meeting to allow the client to do just that. In the agenda for that meeting you should be clear that the goal is to select a single direction to refine further. Clients may be tempted to request revisions to more than one design, or—worse—to see a new design composed from elements of the others.

If the purpose of your meeting is to ensure a single selection at the end, there are a couple things you can do at the beginning to make that happen. Besides stating your purpose, you might provide an overview of all the designs—nothing elaborate, just a few quick sentences about each design direction. This is easier if you've given each design direction a specific name. An introduction to a design for a medical insurance site might read like this:

```
First we'll look at the three-column approach, which packs in
a lot of information above the fold. This addresses a user
need we heard during research and testing. Your main audience
indicated that there was a lot of essential information they
needed before they could begin the application process.
```

The purpose of these introductions is not only to give an overview of the design directions, but also to establish that that you'll be going through three (or two or four) distinct directions. In addition to this technique, you can outline your next steps for the client, explaining how the selected design will be refined and expanded. (If you're not sure what your next steps are, now would be a good time to figure that out.) Again, by establishing that the input for the next stage of the process is one and only one design direction, you make it clear what kind of decision you need from the stakeholders.

Despite your best efforts, you might not get what you want. In this case, do not use the car sales approach: "What do I need to do to get you to walk out of here with one design direction?" This is discouraging and startling for your clients and reinforces the stereotype that consultants are nothing more than used car salesmen in nicer suits. Instead, you should conclude the meeting by summarizing the potential impact that this change will have on the project schedule. In other words, the client should know that asking you to mix and match from multiple designs or to refine more than one direction will add time and/or resources to the project schedule.

Seeking sign-off on design

The sign-off meeting, where the client approves the design, is a necessary milestone for moving forward in most methodologies.

You may be tempted to add this to the agenda of a feedback meeting, using one meeting to both get feedback and seek approval, but of course this can't work. A client won't want to approve a design until he or she sees it in its final version. And though the efficiency of combining meetings is appealing, it is in your best interest to have the client sign off on the actual final product. This is because changes in the design made after sign-off take place in a sort of no-man's land of approval.

Since the client has probably seen the design previously, the content of a sign-off meeting is fairly straightforward. It doesn't hurt to recap the original story, but the main purpose of the meeting should be to show how the final version addresses concerns previously raised by the client. (You did take meeting notes, right? See the section on "Soliciting Feedback on Design" earlier for details.) Go through each suggestion raised at the feedback meeting and show how you addressed it in the revision. If you considered it but didn't take the suggestion, you need a good reason why not. Showing "failed" designs—ones that incorporate a poor suggestion—usually backfires because inevitably the lack of quality is lost on the client. Instead, describe in detail what steps you took to explore the suggestion and why you discarded the ideas.

Meeting Structure

There's no great trick to presenting designs, but there are a few decisions you need to make. In many ways, dealing with screen designs is like dealing with wireframes because you're presenting only a representation of the site, not the site itself. The main distinction in presentation approaches is whether to show the screens in a way that approximates the final user experience, or in some other order.

Setting up the designs

Introductions before screen designs are the hardest because everyone in the meeting wants you to cut to the chase. You want to save the punchline and control every nuance of the presentation, but you can feel the tension in the room as your audience patiently waits for you to build the context, and so the introduction becomes rushed and awkward. The flourish of pulling the metaphoric sheet off the concept car never happens quite as smoothly as you imagined it the night before, when you couldn't sleep.

So, here's an idea: Send the designs around beforehand. The day before your presentation, preferably an hour or two before close-of-business, send an email with a link or a handful of attachments. Sound crazy? Hear me out. This trick buys you a couple things:

- First, you ease the tension. Everyone has seen the designs. If you need ten minutes at the beginning of the meeting to establish context, you can do it without people being antsy. Here's the magic phrase: "I'm sure you've all had a chance to look at the designs by now, but before we discuss them, there are a few things I need to cover."

- Second, you know that your worst-case scenario is that everyone shows up at the meeting with tons of questions and lots of feedback. They know you know this, and so you've bought yourself a ticket for another magic phrase: "I'm sure you have tons of questions for us. We'd like to go through our designs and discuss the thought process and rationale for each one. This might answer some of your questions. Then, if you still have questions for us, we'll discuss them after the presentation."

The point here is not to delay the inevitable. Instead, it's to prevent the meeting from descending into utter chaos and to gather feedback in a structured way.

The order of the screens

Like wireframes, screen designs illustrate many aspects of the user experience, and the order in which you present them will highlight different aspects. Select the order carefully to make sure your meeting focuses on what's important. Chapter 10 goes into this issue in greater detail, but there is a nuance with screen designs.

With screen designs, you might be asking stakeholders to select one design direction from among two or three. Some design teams present several options for design direction, in other words, several overall approaches to the screen design. Even a singular vision can yield different implementations and the stakeholders might want to see several different approaches to "realizing the brand"—that is, turning the concept of their organization into a visual reality.

Imagine your design team has prepared three different design directions. For each design direction, the team has developed three pages—the home page, a gallery page, and an interior page. The question is whether to show each type of page or each design direction. As usual, there's no right answer to this question, just pros and cons, as shown in Table 11.3.

TABLE 11.3

Pros and Cons

Approach	Pros	Cons
Presenting each direction	• Stakeholders can get a sense of the entire design direction • Matches user experience • Allows you to tell complete design story	• May focus on functionality, rather than design • Difficult for stakeholders to compare how similar design problems were addressed in each direction
Presenting each type of page	• Stakeholders can compare apples to apples, seeing how each design direction solves the same design problems	• Stakeholders don't see a fluid user experience

Experience shows that most people present each design direction, showing three or four screens from each approach before moving onto the next one.

Avoid Pointing Out the Bad Things

You'd be surprised how often I've sat in meetings with designers who launch into the story behind their design and before barely 30 seconds pass, they start talking about the design's weaknesses. I've seen many an insecure designer apologize for his design even before he has sold its strengths. A design will have its fair share of critics, so the person who created it should focus on being the design's champion and advocate.

Besides, if even the designer isn't convinced that his or her designs solve the problem, you might ask why you're presenting the design in the first place.

Using an overview

Whether you're presenting multiple design directions or not, you may want to provide an overview, a quick look at everything on the agenda. Perhaps you show a single slide with thumbnails of all the comps for each of the design directions. Or maybe you just flip through the designs quickly.

In many ways, this serves the same purpose as sending the designs around to the stakeholders before the meeting. The benefit is that if you don't get through every screen in your presentation, you've at least provided an overview.

During the overview, keep remarks short and to the point—you're just trying to give them an overall sense of the design direction and plant important ideas in their heads.

Using designers to present designs

Unfortunately, superior design skill does not imply superior presentation and speaking skills. Lots of designers can do presentations well, but you should find out if this among their skill set before throwing them in front of a roomful of clients. (And if you're the designer, be honest with yourself about your comfort level for presentations and public speaking. If this isn't on your list of "things to improve for the year" then consider one of the strategies that follow.)

One risk to the presentation is the bias that comes when specific people are associated with particular designs. If your stakeholders have had a negative experience with one of the designers, they may be biased against the design, even if it is superior. If the design team is inconsistent in their presentations, then some of the designs may have an unfair advantage because their story got told better.

If people on the design team are eager to present their work to the stakeholders, and you've collectively decided that the risks are acceptable, have them practice on other team members first. Public speaking, while benefiting from some spontaneity, is always done better when practiced. You can have the designer prepare a list of talking points beforehand. Additionally, you can give the designers an outline of general concepts that they should follow for their designs.

Some design teams may decide that it's more appropriate to have a single person present all the designs, in which case a creative director or project manager can tell each design's story. There are three things to do to prepare the storyteller. First, each designer should capture the high points of his or her design in five or six bullet points, and send them to the storyteller. Next, hold a meeting where each designer can walk through his or her design. This gives the storyteller a rundown of what inspired each design, the rationale behind the design decisions, and what makes each one unique. Finally, the storyteller should do a dry run with the designers, retelling the stories and confirming that he or she hasn't lost any of the major points.

Presenting Designs: The Emotional Roller Coaster

Most of the things that derail a wireframes meeting could also derail a meeting in which you're presenting screen designs. Meeting participants may be distracted by sample content or some other nuance that's irrelevant to the conversation. But screen designs come with their own risks as well.

Manage stakeholder expecations

It's rare that someone will take a look at a wireframe and say, "I just don't like this." A wireframe is, in many ways, purposely detached from any emotion. The stark monochromatic, monotypographic display leaves little to react to, other than the structure and contents. But that's what you want in a wireframe discussion. Screen designs, however, are ripe for evoking an emotional response.

You may never know what triggered the negative reaction, a particular color or typeface, something reminiscent of a former spouse. You can attempt to defend your design, which should be a relatively straightforward process if you've thought through your rationale for the critical design decisions. To do this, look at each of your talking points: consider each of the main ideas you want to highlight in the design and think about why they are included in the design. Perhaps you've adopted a particular layout or color scheme, or perhaps you're employing color and contrast to emphasize certain elements on the screen. None of these decisions is arbitrary; there's a reason the designer did it that way. By putting the rationale in front of the critic, you might deflate their argument.

Still, when it comes to emotional responses to design, the rational approach may not work. There may be little you can say to sway troublemakers from their opinions. If you've gone back and forth a couple times and the critic is sticking to his guns, there's no point in pursuing the argument. There's also nothing to be gained by ending the discussion with "Well, we can agree to disagree," because such a statement sets you up on opposite sides from your stakeholders. If you make your stakeholders feel like you're all on the same side, they're more likely to trust your judgment further down the line. At this point, it's time to switch gears and use the opportunity to learn more about what your stakeholders like and dislike, so you can prepare a more compatible design in the next round. You might ask questions like "If you could change one thing about this design, what would it be?" to help you zero in on what makes them tick. You can also try to steer clear of the negative; after they've had an opportunity to list what they don't like, say to them: "You've given us a good list of things we should look at, but now give me three things that you like about the design." Suddenly, it's not one list, but two.

Avoid Frankenstein design

In good, old-fashioned web design, the design of a screen is viewed holistically. That's why design teams tend to squirm when their clients ask them to "take the header from this design and the sidebar from this other design, and slap it next to the main content are from that design there." A designer composes a design as a singular unit. The design may be made up of discrete components, but they're not meant to be dismantled and rebuilt like Legos. They play a role in the larger design, to balance and complement the other components. To some designers, this is tantamount to asking Shakespeare to replace Romeo with Hamlet because the whole oedipal/tragic romance thing is really in these days.

As with the previous risk, the strategy here is to zero in on what the stakeholder likes about each of the components. Then, the aim will be to re-create what the stakeholder likes without compromising the integrity of the design. Designers can take what they learned and incorporate it into their own design, rather than cutting and pasting from one design to another.

Perhaps this approach will change in the future, as web sites become more "componentized," with individual blocks of content used and reused. New technologies allow for the distribution of content and functionality independently of an entire web site, so the "integrity of design" argument may not hold up for much longer. In the future, designers may focus on designing individual components and how they stitch together, but they may also need to address the scenario in which components are used outside the main design.

Screen Designs in Context

The discussion in this chapter assumes a somewhat traditional method for your design process, where screen designs are the culmination of several weeks of work building on a series of incremental documents like site maps and wireframes. Screen designs incorporate some of the information contained in other documents, but supplement it with additional information—a series of complex decisions involving layout, color, type, and brand strategy.

Those of you using "rapid design" methodologies may find some of this discussion, well, antiquated. Rapid design methods (also known as agile methods) advocate refining a whole design as you go, whereas more traditional methods operate more like a series of lenses, each one bringing the final product more into focus. With rapid design methods, the team usually breaks a web site down into smaller pieces, defined by individual functions or user scenarios, and attacks that whole piece at once.

So screen designs may not be the punch line to your weeks of work. Instead, you may build a complete design right out of the gate, and refine it over time.

Relative to other software development methods—many of which serve as the basis for web development processes—rapid design methods are very young, emerging only in the last decade or so. Not coincidentally, these methods emerged at the same time as the Web, a medium that moves much faster than traditional software, and created demand for faster development. Being so new, these methods still need some ironing out—for instance, in their intersections with visual design. Many teams don't formally solve this problem, but instead mash up the methods and fly by the seat of their pants.

Whatever method you use, you need to determine how the screen designs fit into the project and how they'll cooperate with other user experience documentation. Here are a few ideas.

Screen Designs and User Needs Documents

Screen designs have a mutually beneficial relationship with user research and usability efforts. Initial screen designs can serve as research tools, providing something for users to react to. Screen designs can play a major role in usability testing if you're not ready to test a functional prototype—they provide the next best thing to the end product.

Of course, it works the other way, too. What you learn in user research can affect the design of a screen. This relationship can be made explicit in the screen design documentation, using the outcome of research or testing to provide a rationale for design decisions.

Screen Designs and Strategy Documents

In doing strategic work, you're laying a foundation for building a design. The strategy documents provide information that will impact the design, if not directly contribute to it. Designers must understand, for example, a site's underlying concept before they develop a screen design. A content inventory gives designers an overview of the scope of information available on the site, and understanding this range helps them accommodate all the content.

The competitive analysis can play a crucial role in the design process. Besides capturing the range of features available on competitive sites, the team can identify design issues and challenges. They can also have a design conversation with the client, establishing what they like and don't like about each competitive site's design.

Screen Designs and Other Design Documents

Viewed in the framework of traditional methodologies, a screen design is the last layer of documentation that describes the overall user experience. A site map defines the overall structure, a user flow the mechanisms for completing tasks, wireframes the relative priorities of content, and a screen design ties it all together.

Inevitably, screen designs alter earlier depictions of the site. Because they come closest to reality, a screen design depicts the user experience in a way we haven't seen in any of the other documents, and can shed light on a particular approach or nuance that earlier documents could not. As much as screen designs are conceptually the last layer of design, in reality the relationships between the visual designs and other design documents are much more complex.

Imagine a health insurance web site that allows people to check on claims. The wireframes and user flow called for a series of screens to allow people to zero in on a claim, using patient name, date of service, and claim number. Once rendered as a screen design, however, the design team sees—even before any user testing—that the mess of dates and numbers does not make for good navigation. In light of their user research, they realize that most people either have very few claims a year or many claims, and that in either case, dates of service aren't a sufficient means for categorizing them. They need to step back to an earlier design stage and rethink how people accomplish this task, focusing perhaps on the name of the physician or the type of service rendered.

So, although there are explicit relationships between these documents—a screen represented as a little rectangle in a flow or site map is the same as a wireframe is the same as a final design—there are also some less explicit ones as well. As the team develops a solution, they are also developing a clearer understanding of the design problem. Design methodologies that take this layered approach need to accommodate this give and take between documents.

Page Design in a Pageless World—Are Screens Next?

Looking back on early web design, there was some comfort to the fact that the culmination of our work fit into a rectangle 640 pixels wide and 480 pixels high. Over the intervening decade, a lot more changed than standard screen resolutions. Web sites grew from being collections of static files into being windows into vast storehouses of data.

The last few years have seen another stage of growth, where databases can be pulled together—for example, geographical information from this mapping web site can be mashed with housing listings from this other web site to make data for a new web site. With this new stage of growth, some web sites hold no data at all; they just draw it from other sources. They behave differently, too—more like desktop applications—and because of this, the notion of a web "page" recedes. It is no longer a useful unit of measure for our work, just like the 640 x 480 rectangle has also receded into obsolescence.

Technological advances lead to more sophisticated relationships between people and information. Data becomes more manipulable, more filter-able, and more portable. So, while designers lose the safety and comfort of the page's formal structure, their challenge does not diminish. Giving users unprecedented access to data in a variety of forms makes the designer's role more important. What changes is what we ask them to design. Today, we deal with screens of all shapes and sizes—low-res cell phones, full-color PDAs, flat-panel monitors, wall projectors—but there's no telling how we will access and receive information in the future.

What won't go away is the need to engage in some process to identify a solution to these ever-increasing design problems. This isn't confined to screen designs alone. All forms of documentation will continue to play some role in this process, even as methodologies seek to compress the time between thinking of an idea and turning it into a reality. Documents serve as waypoints in the design process. They summarize the team's understanding of the design issues at any given moment and describe a vision for the solution. They provide a means for everyone to align their understanding and serve as a springboard for discussion.

Striving for a document-free process is a good endeavor. It forces us to think about minimum requirements for documenting our work and better ways to communicate ideas during the creative process. Striving for and achieving, however, are two different things. Achieving a document-free process means finding a way for team members to communicate that doesn't require committing ideas to a shareable format. That is difficult to imagine. Even an email message or a chat constitutes some kind of documentation. More effective documentation does not necessarily mean better designs, but it can mean more efficient processes and better communication among members of the team. As technologies grow more complex and design teams expand to include people who specialize in different forms of information management, the need for better communication will only increase.

Index

A

access privileges, 175
accountability, 2
actual content, 286
administrative information, 273
Adobe Illustrator, 290
Adobe Photoshop, 316
affinity diagrams. *See* concept
  models
agile methods, 336
Anderson, Stephen, 226
annotations, 275–276
audience
  for competitive analyses, 109,
    122
  for concept models, 141
  for content inventories, 169,
    180
  for flow charts, 232, 243–244
  for personas, 18, 25–26
  for screen designs, 313
  for site maps, 202, 212
  for usability reports, 75
  for usability test plans, 51,
    61–62
  for wireframes, 267, 269, 283
audience profiles. *See* personas
audits, content, 167
author information, 179

B

backdrops, 147
background information, 59
behaviors
  expected, 60
  persona, 22–23
best-practice improvements, 84
beta web sites, 104
binary decision points, 236
blueprints. *See* wireframes
Boxes & Arrows online
  magazine, 267, 288
brainstorming meetings
  concept models and, 157,
    159–160
  flow charts and, 251
  personas and, 38–39
  wireframes and, 300
brainstorming process, 9, 80, 160
brand strategy, 320
bullet points, 62
business objectives, 254
business process flow charts, 231
business strategy
  flow charts and, 254
  screen designs and, 320–321
  site maps and, 211–212
buy-in meetings
  flow charts and, 252

personas and, 37–38
site maps and, 221
usability test plans and, 65
wireframes and, 297–298

C

callouts, 88–90
Cascading Style Sheets (CSS),
  316
chunks, content, 176–177
classifying content, 183–184
clients, 5
color elements, 8
  content inventory, 181–182
  screen design, 334
  wireframe, 279
communicatingdesign.com web
  site, 4, 215, 246
competitive analyses, 107–135
  audience for, 109, 122
  balancing information in, 126,
    127
  challenges of, 111–112
  competitive framework in,
    112–115
  conclusions in, 117–118, 124,
    127, 129, 132
  context for, 109, 132–134
  creation of, 112–126

greeked text, 287

groups

    of pages on site maps, 209

    of steps on flow charts, 239

H

Handbook for Usability Testing, The (Rubin), 91

Harvey balls, 29, 30

hierarchies, 206, 224

    See also site maps

history, version, 277–278

HTML

    screen designs and, 316, 318

    site maps and, 208

    wireframes and, 288–289

I

Illustrator program, 290

imagery, screen design, 334

improvements

    best-practice, 84

    user-recommended, 84

incomplete scripts, 64

information

    administrative, 273

    author, 179

    background, 59

    contextual, 288

    pieces of, 8

    supporting, 9, 323

    version, 179, 277–278

    See also layers of information

input, soliciting, 65

interactive pages, 208

interface designs. *See* screen designs

Internet technology, 309–310

    See also web sites

intranets, 194

introduction meeting, 219–220

introductory pages

    content inventories and, 178–179

    screen designs and, 328–329

    wireframes and, 292–293

inventories. *See* content inventories

inventory approach, 255

iterative approach, 309

K

key pages, 325–326

key take-aways, 125

L

labeling

    competitive analyses and, 120

    site maps and, 223–224

    wireframes and, 287, 294

language, visual, 8, 214–216, 246

latin text, 287

layers of information, 3–4

    in competitive analyses, 112–120

    in concept models, 142–147

    in content inventories, 170–179

    in flow charts, 234–241

    in personas, 19–25

    in screen designs, 315–321

    in site maps, 204–212

    in usability reports, 77–84

    in usability test plans, 52–60

    in wireframes, 271–282

    See also information

layouts

    concept model, 150

    persona, 30

    screen design, 334

    site map, 214

    wireframe, 278–280

links in site maps, 205–206

    descriptions of, 216

    details about, 209–210

links in wireframes, 274–275

location of web content, 171

logistics, usability test, 54

M

Macromedia Dreamweaver, 290

maintenance

    of flow charts, 249–250

    of wireframes, 288, 294–295

management

    of projects, 208

    of team interactions, 305–306

Maurer, Donna, 184

meaningful feedback, 327

meeting structure

    competitive analyses and, 129–130

    concept models and, 158–160

    content inventories and, 189–190

    flow charts and, 252–255

    personas and, 39–41

    screen designs and, 330–333

    site maps and, 221–223

    usability reports and, 97–98

behavior descriptions in, 22–23

brainstorming, 38–39

bridging to other documents, 43–46

buy-in meeting for, 37–38

challenges of, 18–19

competitive analyses and, 45

concept models and, 45, 162–163

content inventories and, 45

contents of, 29–30

context for, 18, 43–46

creation of, 19–36

definition of, 15

demographic information in, 23–24

design documents and, 46

ensuring value of, 34

examples of, 16–17

feedback meeting on, 38

flow charts and, 46, 258

layers of information in, 19–25

layouts used for, 30

meeting structure for, 39–41

motivations expressed through, 20

names for, 19–20

overview of, 18

personal background information in, 24

photographs in, 24–25

presentation of, 36–43

priority order meetings for, 39–40

problems related to, 34–36

purposes of, 18, 26, 47–48

quotes in, 23

scale of, 18

scenarios in, 21

screen designs and, 46

showing relationships between, 33

site maps and, 46

situations related to, 27–28

strategy documents and, 44–45

subtypes of, 35–36

summarizing users in, 31–32

system features and, 22

technology comfort level and, 24

third-party research and, 34

timeline for, 25

usability reports and, 44, 101

usability test plans and, 44, 68–69

user needs documents and, 43–46

wireframes and, 46

perspective, maintaining, 131

photographs, persona, 24–25

Photoshop program, 316

planning process

  content inventories and, 189

  screen designs and, 322–324

  wireframes and, 290–291

post-test questions, 56–57

PowerPoint program, 290

preference data, 92, 93–94

preparatory meeting, 157

presentations

  of competitive analyses, 127–132

  of concept models, 156–161

  of content inventories, 187–191

  of flow charts, 250–257

  of personas, 36–43

  of screen designs, 326–336

of site maps, 218–224

of usability reports, 96–100

of usability test plans, 64–68

of wireframes, 296–306

See also meetings

pre-test questions, 56–57

priority order meetings

  personas and, 39–40

  wireframes and, 302

problem clarification, 254

problem statements, 124

problems solved approach, 158

process charts. *See* flow charts

process identifiers, 237

project culture, 7

project management, 208

project manager, 5

project plan, 191

project team, 5

prose, 62–63

prototypes. *See* wireframes

purposes

  of competitive analyses, 109, 119, 120

  of concept models, 141, 148

  of content inventories, 169, 179–180

  of flow charts, 232, 242–243

  of personas, 18, 26, 47–48

  of screen designs, 313

  of site maps, 202, 212

  of usability reports, 75

  of usability test plans, 51, 67

  of wireframes, 266, 269, 283–285

Q

quality control, 324–325
quantitative data, 82, 83, 91–94
questions
  open-ended, 57
  pre- and post-test, 56–57
  predefined responses to, 57
quotes
  in personas, 23
  in usability reports, 81–82

R

rapid design methods, 336
rationale, wireframe, 277
recommendations, usability, 81, 84
relationships, persona, 33
requirements
  documentation of, 6
  flow charts and, 254
  gathering of, 284
  screen designs and, 324
  wireframes and, 304–305, 307
research
  competitive, 128
  persona, 34
Rice, Sarah, 192
risks
  competitive analyses, 125–127, 131–132
  concept model, 160–161
  content inventory, 186, 190–191
  flow chart, 247–250, 255–257
  screen design, 324–326
  site map, 216–218, 223–224
  usability report, 94–96, 98–100

usability test plan, 64, 66–68
  wireframe, 293–296, 303–306
role-playing, 248–249
Rosenfeld, Lou, 186
Rubin, Jeffrey, 91

S

sample content, 281–282, 286–287, 295–296
scale
  of competitive analyses, 109
  of concept models, 141
  of content inventories, 169
  of flow charts, 232
  of personas, 18
  of screen designs, 313
  of site maps, 202
  of usability reports, 75
  of usability test plans, 51, 66–67
  of wireframes, 269
scenarios
  error, 240
  flow chart, 241
  persona, 21
  usability test, 54
  wireframe, 274, 290–291
schematics. *See* wireframes
scope
  of content inventories, 178
  of wireframes, 266
scope creep, 66–67, 257
scores, competitive, 116
screen designs, 311–339
  audience for, 313
  basics of compiling, 321–322
  brand strategy and, 320
  business strategy and, 320–321

challenges of, 314
competitive analyses and, 337
concept models and, 318
content inventories and, 337
context for, 313, 336–338
creation of, 315–325
creative briefs for, 319–320
CSS used for, 316, 318
definition of, 311
design documents and, 317, 337–338
development process for, 322–324
direction meeting on, 328–329
emotional responses to, 334–335
example of, 312
feedback meeting on, 326–328
formatting of, 313
HTML used for, 316, 318
identifying information in, 316–317
introductions to, 328–329, 330
key pages in, 325–326
layers of information in, 315–321
meeting structure for, 330–333
mood boards and, 323
names given to, 323–324
order for presenting, 331–332
overview of, 313
personas and, 46
presentation of, 326–336
production issues related to, 318–319
purpose of, 313
quality control for, 324–325
risks related to, 324–326
scale of, 313

methodological questions about, 67–68

objectives of tests in, 52–53

overview of, 51

personas and, 44, 68–69

pre- and post-test questions in, 56–57

preparation of, 60–63

presentation of, 64–68

purpose of, 51, 67

risks related to, 64, 66–68

scale of, 51, 66–67

scenarios in, 54

screeners in, 55–56

scripts used in, 57–58, 63, 64, 66

strategy documents and, 69

test results and, 69

user needs documents and, 68–69

user profiles in, 55

usability testing

explanation of, 49

formative vs. summative, 61, 85–86

future of, 70–71

methodological issues, 67–68, 103–104

reasons for conducting, 60–61

screen designs and, 337

user experience flow charts, 231

user groups, 87

user needs documents, 2–3, 13–104

competitive analyses and, 133–134

concept models and, 162–163

content inventories and, 193

flow charts and, 257–258

personas as, 15–48

screen designs and, 337

site maps and, 225

usability reports as, 73–104

usability test plans as, 49–71

wireframes and, 306–307

user profiles

usability reports and, 82–83

usability test plans and, 55

See also personas

user role definitions. *See* personas

user-recommended improvements, 84

V

version history, 277–278, 289

version information

content inventories, 179

wireframes, 277–278, 289

Visio program, 215, 218, 290, 295

vision, consistency of, 1

visual designs. *See* screen designs

Visual Display of Quantitative Information (Tufte), 114

visual language, 8

on flow charts, 246

on site maps, 214–216

Visual Vocabulary, 204

W

web sites

beta versions of, 104

communicatingdesign.com, 4, 215, 246

componentization of, 336

technological advances in, 309–310, 338–339

traffic information for, 173–174

whiteboard approach, 159–160

wireframes, 265–310

administrative information in, 273

annotations in, 275–276

audience for, 267, 269, 283

brainstorming, 300

buy-in meeting for, 297–298

challenges of, 270–271

competitive analyses and, 307

concept models and, 307–308

content areas in, 271–272

content inventories and, 308

context for, 269, 280–281, 288, 306–308

creation of, 271–296

definition of, 265

descriptions of content in, 272

design documents and, 308

design elements in, 278–280

display of screens in, 285–286, 291

examples of, 266–268

feedback meeting on, 298–299

flow charts and, 260–262

form elements in, 275

formatting of, 269

HTML vs. paper, 288–289

identifying information in, 273

impact of, 308–310

introductions with, 292–293

labels used in, 287, 294

layers of information in, 271–282

layout indicated in, 278–280

links displayed in, 274–275

maintenance of, 288, 294–295

meeting structure for, 300–302

wireframes *(continued)*

   narrative descriptions of, 300–301

   numbering scheme for, 292

   objectives described in, 276–277

   overview of, 269

   personas and, 46

   planning process for, 290–291

   presentation of, 296–306

   priority of content in, 272–273, 302

   purposes of, 266, 269, 283–285

   questions about building, 285–290

   rationale explained in, 277

   redirecting conversations about, 304

   requirements and, 304–305, 307

   risks related to, 293–296, 303–306

   sample content in, 281–282, 286–287, 295–296

   scale of, 269

   scenarios related to, 274, 290–291

   scope of, 266

   screen designs and, 317, 326

   site maps and, 226

   strategy documents and, 307–308

   system complexity and, 292

   technological change and, 309–310

   timeline for, 283, 291

   tools for creating, 290

   usability reports and, 101–102, 307

   user needs documents and, 306–307

   version history in, 277–278

worksheets, 178, 182–183

World Wide Web. *See* web sites

writing copy, 8

Y

yes-no values, 115

About the Author

Dan Brown started writing about deliverables and documentation after presenting a poster on wireframes at the IA Summit. His work on the web started in 1994 and he discovered information architecture in 1997. Since then, Dan has consulted on projects for both federal and Fortune 500 clients, including the Federal Communications Commission, the U.S. Postal Service, the Transportation Security Administration, US Airways, Fannie Mae, First USA, British Telecom, Special Olympics, AOL, and the World Bank.

Dan speaks and writes extensively on user experience design, information architecture, usability, and content management. His writing has appeared in Boxes and Arrows, UX Matters, CHI Bulletin, and Interactive Television Today. He has taught at American University, Georgetown, and Duke. He is very active in the local Washington, D.C., information architecture community, organizing regular workshops and bimonthly reading groups. Dan is well respected in the user experience community for his ability to communicate complex ideas and create compelling deliverables. His Visio "skillz" are feared and admired worldwide.

In 2002, Dan collaborated with information architects around the world to establish the Information Architecture Institute, the first professional organization dedicated to the craft. He was nominated to the Institute's board of directors in 2005 and served on its advisory board.

When not thinking about information architecture, design, or content management, Dan likes cooking for his family, making lattes, picking mandolin, reading comics, playing video games, and adding to his extensive Lego collection. Dan lives in Bethesda, Maryland, in a newly renovated 1922 bungalow with his wife and many, many pets. He is eagerly awaiting the arrival of their first child.